D1526468

THREE CRISES IN EARLY ENGLISH HISTORY

Personalities and Politics during the Norman Conquest, the Reign of King John, and the Wars of the Roses

---

Michael V. C. Alexander

University Press of America,® Inc.
Lanham • New York • Oxford

4720 Boston Way
Lanham, Maryland 20706

12 Hid's Copse Rd.
Cummor Hill, Oxford OX2 9JJ

Printed in the United States of America
British Library Cataloging in Publication Information Available

Library of Congress Cataloging-in-Publication Data

Alexander, Michael Van Cleave.
Three crises in early English history : personalities and politics during the Norman conquest, the reign of King John, and the Wars of the Roses / by Michael Van Cleave Alexander.
p. cm.
Includes index.
1. Great Britain—History—Medieval period, 1066-1485. 2. Great Britain—History—Wars of the Roses, 1455-1485. 3. Great Britain—Politics and government—1066-1485. 4. Great Britain—History—William I. 1066-1087. 5. Great Britain—History—John, 1199-1216. 6. Great Britain—History—Invasions. 7. Crises—Great Britain—History. 8. Normans—Great Britain. I. Title.
DA175.A44 1998 944'.02—dc21 98-8367 CIP

ISBN 0-7618-1187-7 (cloth: alk. ppr.)
ISBN 0-7618-1188-5 (pbk: alk. ppr.)

™ The paper used in this publication meets the minimum requirements of American National Standard for Information Sciences—Permanence of Paper for Printed Library Materials, ANSI Z39.48—1984

Contents

Preface

In this almost frenzied age, books pour off university and commercial presses while important articles appear in academic journals in a seemingly endless stream, forcing scholars to limit their reading to subfields of their chosen disciplines. Because of the steady accumulation of knowledge, the problem is even greater for college students, who find it almost impossible to stay abreast of all the new developments, let alone master the lasting achievements of past generations. As a consequence the average person's knowledge is increasingly fragmented, and most of us know more and more about less and less.

This book's goal is not to add new details to the existing body of knowledge about early English history. Rather, its goal is to meet the needs of students and general readers who might profit from a clear, concise, and up-to-date account of the causes and consequences of three long crises that affected English government and society in fundamental ways: the Norman Conquest, the baronial uprising that led to Magna Carta, and the Wars of the Roses.

After teaching English history at the college level for some years, I realized that students cannot be expected to read a monograph on each of those crises as well as a textbook, several biographies, and a collection of documents during a single semester. They need a shorter treatment of each crisis, although a more detailed and analytical one, with some discussion of the recent literature, than the average textbook provides. Textbooks can be exciting, but they usually move so fast and cover so many topics that they generally ignore historiography and fail to convey the dramatic interplay between personalities and politics, simmering domestic and foreign-policy problems on the one hand and individual decisions of great consequence on the other. Moreover, because of the vast outpouring of scholarly work on all periods of English history since World War II, most textbooks, except those written by collaborators, tend to be a generation or two behind the times in terms of current research. No one can read everything that is published on the full range of English history in any given year, and as a consequence whole decades elapse before important research findings become known to students and non-specialists. If this book can speed up the process a bit and provide students and general readers with a quick but thorough understanding of the three crises I have chosen to discuss, I will be well satisfied.

Finally, a word or two about the significance of genealogy and family relationships during the late middle ages. Family relationships were more important at that time than they are today, and no one can fully understand English history during that era without some understanding of genealogy. Unfortunately, blood was often thinner than water, and on numerous occasions first cousins and even brothers were bitter enemies, especially at times when wealth and power hung in the balance. For those reasons, there will be occasional references to genealogy in the pages that follow as well as seven geneaological tables at the beginning of the book.

Christiansburg, Virginia
March 12, 1998

Note on Money

Until 1971, when English money went over to a decimal system, the pound sterling (£1) contained 240 pennies (240d.) and not just 100 as today. Those 240 pennies were grouped in twenty shillings (20s.) of twelve each. Hence, £1 = 20s. = 240d. Although pounds, shillings, and pennies were the most important coins and monetary units during the centuries covered by this book, there were many others, of which the most frequently used was the mark, which was equal to two-thirds of a pound (i.e., 13s. 4d.).

How to determine the value of money during those distant centuries is an almost impossible problem. Suffice it to say that anyone with a yearly income of £30 could live in some degree of comfort, whereas those with over £500 a year were truly affluent. The incomes of the country's Earls varied from as little as £700 a year to as much as £6,000 annually in the case of Warwick the Kingmaker during his heyday in the 1460s. Undoubtedly the richest magnate during the whole period was John of Gaunt, Duke of Lancaster (d. 1399), who owned estates in thirty-three of England's forty counties as well as in

Ireland and Calais. All in all, his annual income was probably in the neighborhood of £13,000, a prodigious sum for that era. By comparison, one of the largest and strongest castles of that age, Château Gaillard, was constructed by Richard I in 1197-1198 at an estimated cost of £11,000. However, there was some inflation between the 1190s and the 1390s, especially during the years 1185-1225.

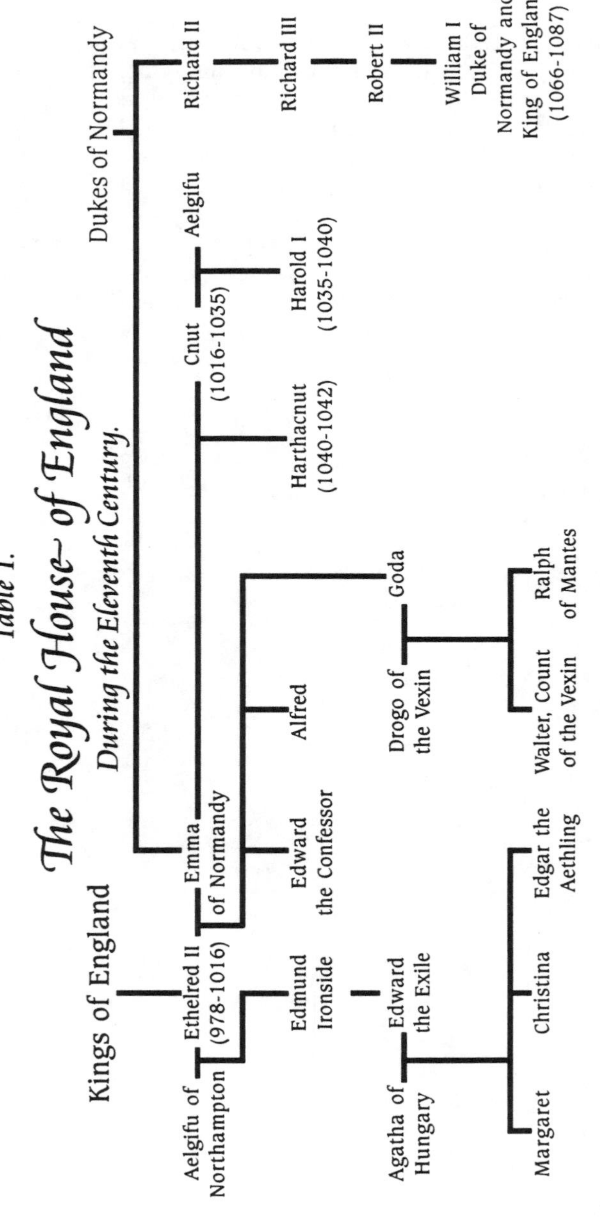

<u>Note</u>: The dates signify the regnal years of England's rulers during the Eleventh Century.

Table II.

The House of Godwine

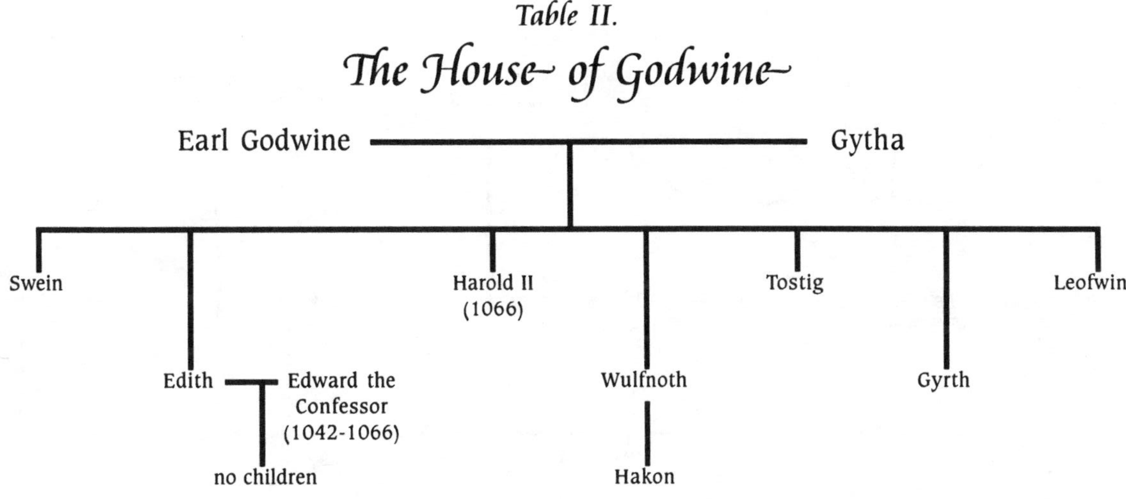

Note: The dates signify the regnal years of Edward the Confessor and Harold II.

Table III.

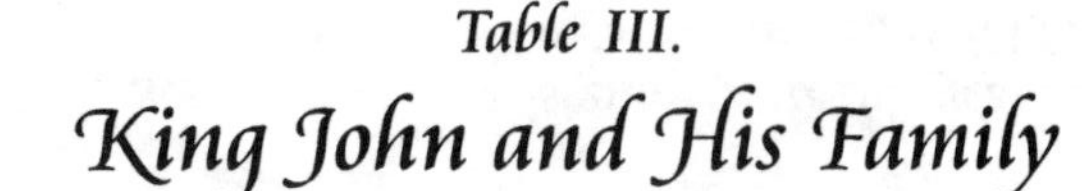

Henry II (d. 1189) — Eleanor of Aquitaine (d. 1204)

- Prince Henry (d. about 1173)
- Geoffrey (d. 1186) — Constance of Brittany
  - Arthur of Brittany (d. 1203)
- Matilda — Henry the Lion, Duke of Saxony
  - Otto IV, Holy Roman Emperor (d. 1218)
- Richard I (1189-1199)
  - no children
- Isabelle of Gloucester — John (1199-1216)
  - no children
- John (1199-1216) — Isabel of Angoulême
  - Henry III (1216-1272)

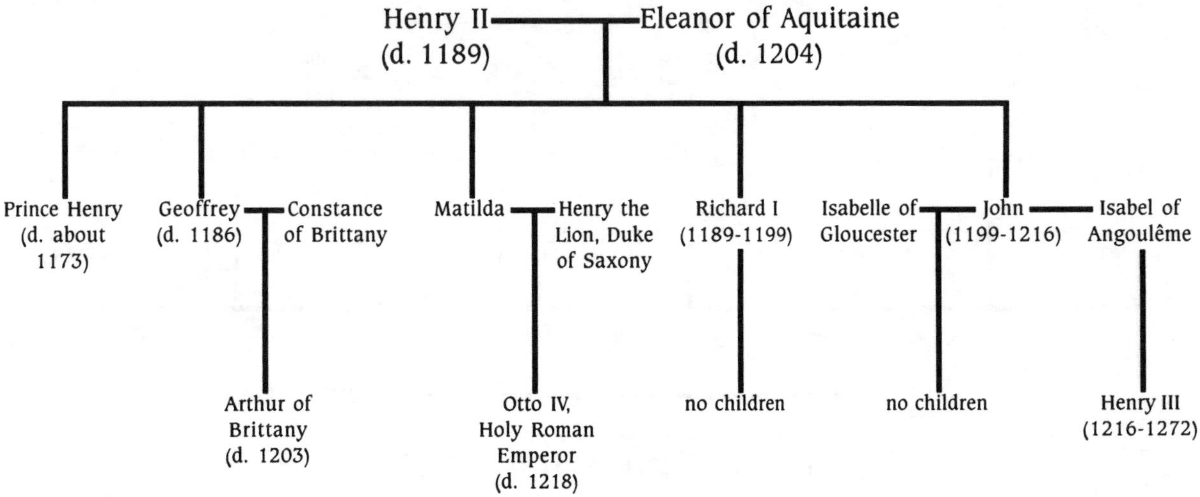

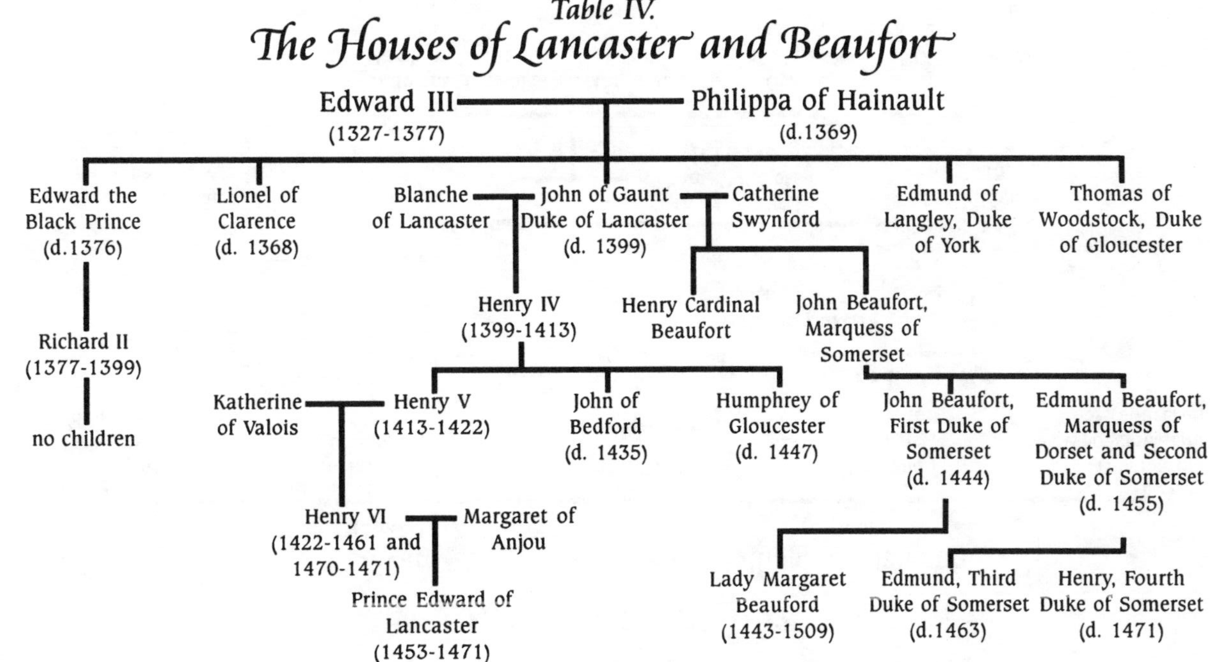
Table IV.
The Houses of Lancaster and Beaufort
Edward III (1327-1377)
Philippa of Hainault (d.1369)
Edward the Black Prince (d.1376)
Lionel of Clarence (d. 1368)
Blanche of Lancaster
John of Gaunt Duke of Lancaster (d. 1399)
Catherine Swynford
Edmund of Langley, Duke of York
Thomas of Woodstock, Duke of Gloucester
Richard II (1377-1399)
Henry IV (1399-1413)
Henry Cardinal Beaufort
John Beaufort, Marquess of Somerset
no children
Katherine of Valois
Henry V (1413-1422)
John of Bedford (d. 1435)
Humphrey of Gloucester (d. 1447)
John Beaufort, First Duke of Somerset (d. 1444)
Edmund Beaufort, Marquess of Dorset and Second Duke of Somerset (d. 1455)
Henry VI (1422-1461 and 1470-1471)
Margaret of Anjou
Prince Edward of Lancaster (1453-1471)
Lady Margaret Beauford (1443-1509)
Edmund, Third Duke of Somerset (d.1463)
Henry, Fourth Duke of Somerset (d. 1471)

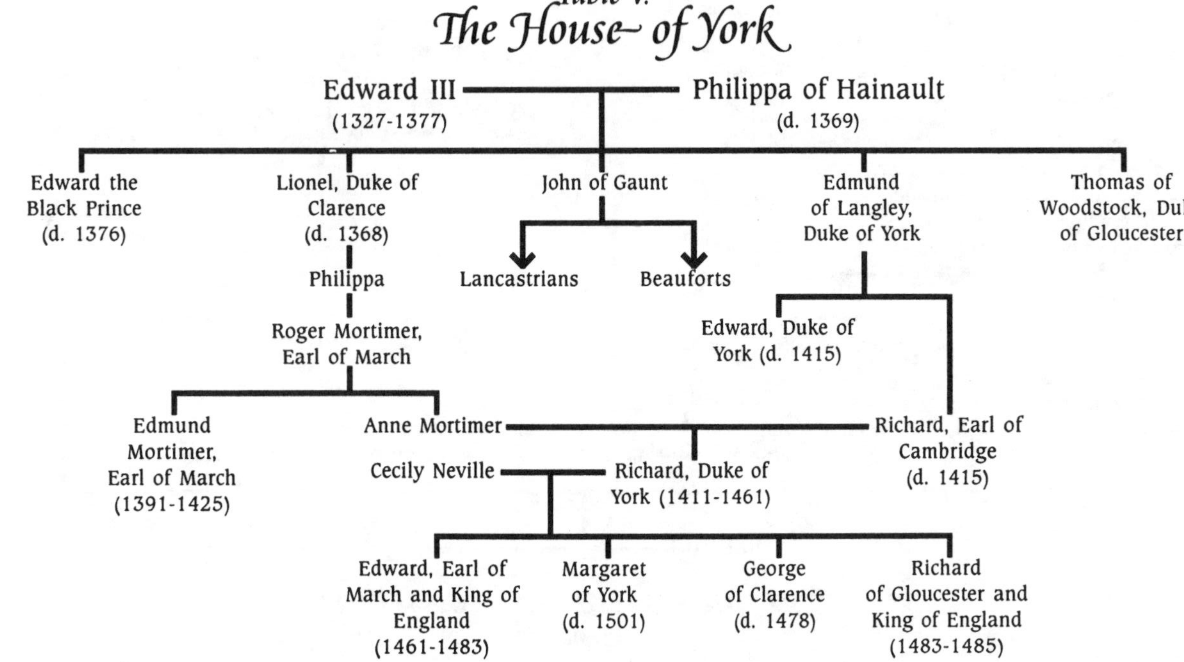
Table V.
The House of York
Edward III (1327-1377)
Philippa of Hainault (d. 1369)
Edward the Black Prince (d. 1376)
Lionel, Duke of Clarence (d. 1368)
John of Gaunt
Edmund of Langley, Duke of York
Thomas of Woodstock, Duke of Gloucester
Philippa
Lancastrians
Beauforts
Roger Mortimer, Earl of March
Edward, Duke of York (d. 1415)
Edmund Mortimer, Earl of March (1391-1425)
Anne Mortimer
Richard, Earl of Cambridge (d. 1415)
Cecily Neville
Richard, Duke of York (1411-1461)
Edward, Earl of March and King of England (1461-1483)
Margaret of York (d. 1501)
George of Clarence (d. 1478)
Richard of Gloucester and King of England (1483-1485)

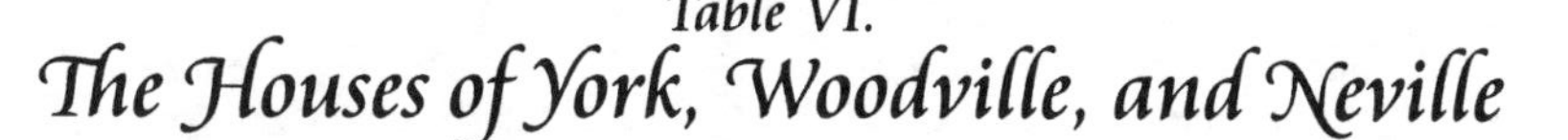

Table VI.
The Houses of York, Woodville, and Neville

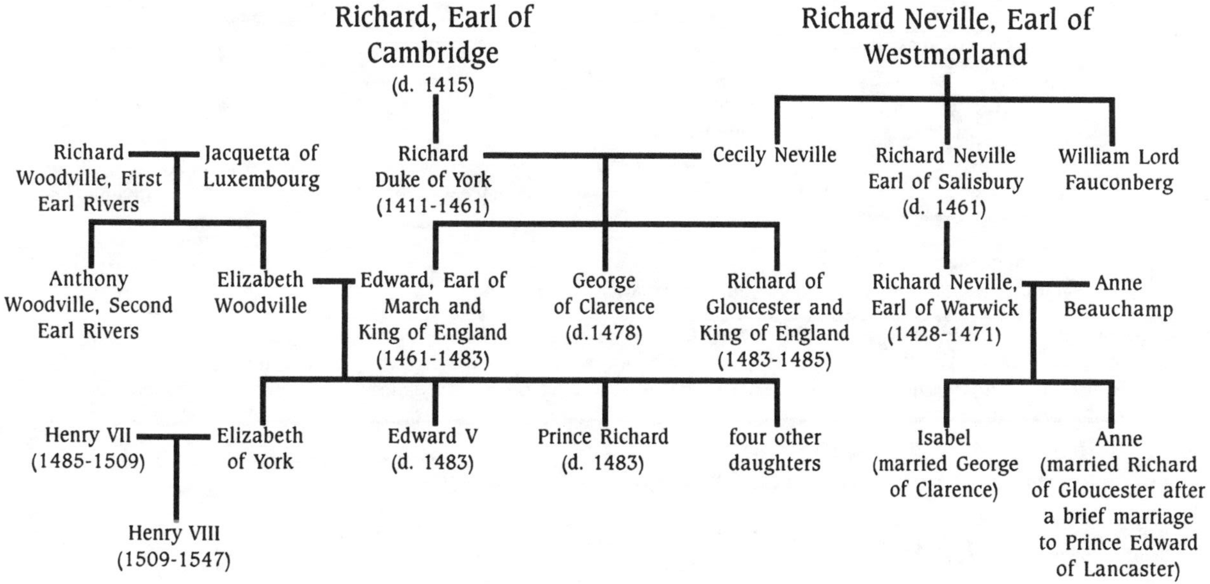

Richard, Earl of Cambridge (d. 1415)

Richard Neville, Earl of Westmorland

Richard Woodville, First Earl Rivers — Jacquetta of Luxembourg

Richard Duke of York (1411-1461) — Cecily Neville

Richard Neville Earl of Salisbury (d. 1461)

William Lord Fauconberg

Anthony Woodville, Second Earl Rivers

Elizabeth Woodville — Edward, Earl of March and King of England (1461-1483)

George of Clarence (d.1478)

Richard of Gloucester and King of England (1483-1485)

Richard Neville, Earl of Warwick (1428-1471) — Anne Beauchamp

Henry VII (1485-1509) — Elizabeth of York

Edward V (d. 1483)

Prince Richard (d. 1483)

four other daughters

Isabel (married George of Clarence)

Anne (married Richard of Gloucester after a brief marriage to Prince Edward of Lancaster)

Henry VIII (1509-1547)

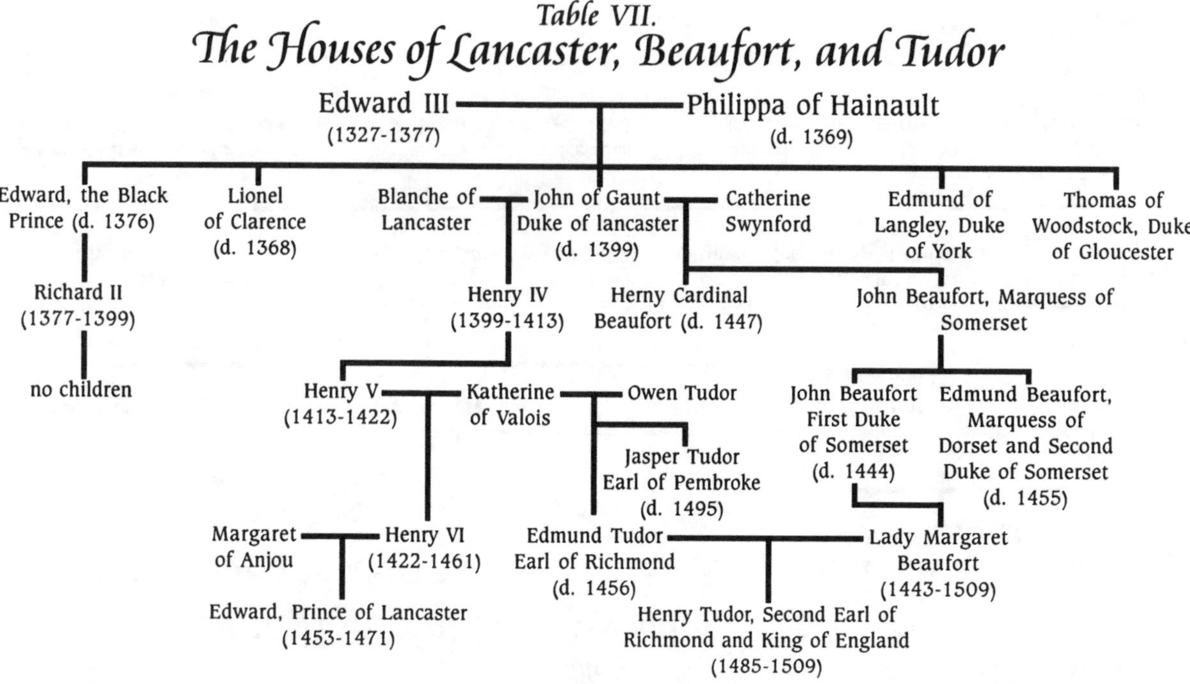

Table VII.
The Houses of Lancaster, Beaufort, and Tudor
Edward III (1327-1377)
Philippa of Hainault (d. 1369)
Edward, the Black Prince (d. 1376)
Lionel of Clarence (d. 1368)
Blanche of Lancaster
John of Gaunt Duke of lancaster (d. 1399)
Catherine Swynford
Edmund of Langley, Duke of York
Thomas of Woodstock, Duke of Gloucester
Richard II (1377-1399)
Henry IV (1399-1413)
Herny Cardinal Beaufort (d. 1447)
John Beaufort, Marquess of Somerset
no children
Henry V (1413-1422)
Katherine of Valois
Owen Tudor
John Beaufort First Duke of Somerset (d. 1444)
Edmund Beaufort, Marquess of Dorset and Second Duke of Somerset (d. 1455)
Jasper Tudor Earl of Pembroke (d. 1495)
Margaret of Anjou
Henry VI (1422-1461)
Edmund Tudor Earl of Richmond (d. 1456)
Lady Margaret Beaufort (1443-1509)
Edward, Prince of Lancaster (1453-1471)
Henry Tudor, Second Earl of Richmond and King of England (1485-1509)

The Norman Conquest*

Some years ago a distinguished authority on medieval England, R. Allen Brown, described the impact of the Norman Conquest in these words:

> In the broadest sense, to set down the results of the Norman Conquest is to write the rest of English history down to the present day, and to add the histories of all those countries who were to feel the impact or the influence of Post-Conquest England.[1]

Despite the great importance of Professor Brown's contributions to the study of the eleventh and twelfth centuries, few scholars today would support such an extreme statement about the significance of the Norman Conquest. Yet almost all would agree that it was a turning point in English history, comparable in importance to the Reformation, the Glorious Revolution, or the Industrial Revolution. Indeed, Sir Frank Stenton held for many years that "sooner or later every aspect of English life was changed by the Norman Conquest";[2] while Professor David Douglas described William the Conqueror as one of the "principal makers of medieval Europe."[3]

Because of the Conquest's profound impact on English life and society, which will be discussed in the last section of this essay, the origins of that famous event are a matter of great importance. Some historians are inclined to seek its underlying causes as far back as the reign of King Ethelred II (978-1016), while others hold that the complicated chain of events that led to the Conquest began during the early years of Ethelred's son and eventual successor, Edward the Confessor (1042-1066). Regardless of the approach adopted, it is essential to know the main events in English history for several generations before 1066 if one is to understand why the Conquest occurred and what its main effects on English government and society were.

Ethelred II, who ascended the English throne in 978, was a weak ruler who failed to meet the challenges of his day. Except for Archbishop Dunstan, who died in 988, his advisers were equally weak, and during the last years of the tenth century the country's eastern sections

---

* The notes for this chapter begin on page 53.

suffered devastating raids from Viking warriors who thought England's wealth was theirs for the taking. In 1002 King Ethelred banished his common-law wife, Aelgifu, from his presence and married Emma of Normandy, whose powerful brother Richard might help him withstand his enemies.[4]

Emma's brother was Duke Richard II of Normandy; and from the moment she became Ethelred's wife, the fates of England and that vigorous province in northwestern France became intertwined, with each taking an abiding interest in the affairs of the other. As a consequence, when additional Viking raids caused the royal family to leave the realm in 1012, it took refuge at the Norman court at Rouen, where Ethelred's children by Emma--Edward, Alfred, and Goda--remained for many years, although the King himself returned to London in 1014 and resumed the throne.

With King Ethelred's death in 1016, England fell under the rule of a Viking dynasty that held power for twenty-six years. Its greatest member, King Cnut, ruled the country from late in 1016 until his death in 1035; and despite his purge of the Old English aristocracy during his first months on the throne, he restored order and prosperity to the countryside. Moreover, he married the widowed Emma of Normandy in 1017 as a way of neutralizing her brother Richard, who might otherwise have helped Ethelred II's sons recover the throne one day. But indirectly that marriage led to the very result Cnut hoped to avoid.

In 1040, after the death of Cnut's older son, Harold I, his heir by an earlier wife, the English throne passed to Harthacnut, his younger son by Emma of Normandy. Harthacnut was his mother's favorite and she entertained great hopes for him, despite his weak and sickly nature. Because his health took a turn for the worse shortly after his coronation, Emma wondered if he would live long enough to make a proper marriage and father a son of his own. For that reason she convinced him to invite his much older half-brother, Edward the Confessor, who had lived at the Norman court since 1012, to return to England and be groomed as heir-apparent.

In his late thirties on his return to England in 1041, Edward the Confessor had spent his formative years in Normandy.[5] Not surprisingly he knew almost nothing about England and spoke English poorly, if at all. His friends and all his closest companions were Normans; and once Harthacnut died in 1042 and Edward took the throne, the English people considered him a stranger in their midst. Edward did nothing to dispel that impression because he saw no need to court popularity. A true son of Ethelred II, he was indolent and easy-going and spent much of his time in amusements like hunting and hawking. Although chiefly interested in the trappings of power, he was nevertheless extremely protective of his rights and authority, resenting all suggestions that he was a puppet ruler. Thus his advisers were compelled to manage him carefully, dissembling and telling him half-truths most of the time. Otherwise they would find themselves replaced by other men, which bred suspicion and jealousy among the country's magnates. Worst of all, Edward's difficult personality strengthened the tendency toward regional separatism that was already evident in England.

Since King Cnut's earliest years, England had been divided into three great earldoms, each of which enjoyed considerable autonomy. Like most medieval rulers Cnut relied on several great followers to help him govern the realm, and within years those great nobles became sub-Kings in all but name. Cnut's followers were still in office when Edward the Confessor took the throne in 1042, and they had no desire to see power gravitate to London and be wielded by a ruler with so many foreign friends and mannerisms. In the far north, Earl Siward of Northumbria dominated the scene, while in the earldom of Mercia in the midlands the powerful Leofric exercised his customary power. Yet the most influential of all the Earls was Godwine of Wessex, the richest and most capable nobleman of the era.

Godwine's name does not appear on any English document before 1017, although he probably arrived in the country about 1010 as a youthful subordinate of the Viking marauder Wulfnoth. Once Cnut seized the throne in 1016 from Edmund Ironside, Ethelred II's son by his first wife, Godwine gave unwavering support to Cnut and performed valuable services for him. For that reason Cnut bestowed dozens of estates on Godwine and ultimately granted him the earldom of Wessex, the wealthiest in the land. By the time Edward the Confessor mounted the throne in 1042, Earl Godwine held scores of manors scattered across southern England from Dover in the east to Exeter in the west. His yearly income of £4,000 was only twenty per cent less than the annual revenues of the crown itself. In contrast the yearly revenues of the Earls of Mercia and Northumbria were only about £1,300 each.[6]

Because of Earl Godwine's enormous wealth and comparable political skills, he wielded great power during the early years of Edward the Confessor. After all it was an easy matter for him to travel from his principal residence at Bosham, Sussex to the capital for an audience with the King, which Siward and Leofric could not do without considerable trouble. Yet Godwine always had to contend with several of Edward's Norman favorites.

The first of those Norman favorites was Edward's nephew Ralph of Mantes, the younger son of his sister Goda, who had been married for some years to Drogo, Count of the Vexin along the border of eastern Normandy and France. Shortly after 1042 Ralph appeared in England and was named Earl of Herefordshire with responsibility for the defense of the Anglo-Welsh border. Before his death in 1057, Earl Ralph built the castle of Ewyas Harold in western Herefordshire, the first true castle to be constructed anywhere in the British Isles.[7]

Godwine's second and more dangerous Norman competitor was Robert of Jumièges, who became Bishop of London in 1044. An ambitious and politically-minded cleric, Robert of Jumièges developed a burning hatred of Earl Godwine and his six sons, whom he sought to destroy during the political crisis of 1050-1052, a precursor of the turbulent events of 1066, as we shall soon see.

However, in the mid 1040s Robert was too weak to prevent Godwine from enjoying great influence. Indeed, in 1043 Godwine persuaded the King to grant his eldest son, Swein, a violent and unruly man,[8] the new earldom of Cornwall in southwestern England. The establishment of that earldom, which consisted of the western sections of Wessex along with the Mercian counties of Oxfordshire, Gloucestershire and Herefordshire, increased the tension between the Godwines on the one hand and the elderly Leofric of Mercia, on the other.

Despite his weakened relationship with Leofric, Earl Godwine was soon making energetic efforts on behalf of his second son, Harold, a worthier and more reputable person than Swein. Early in 1045, Godwine persuaded the King to create the earldom of East Anglia for Harold. That earldom consisted of extensive lands in Suffolk, Essex, and adjacent counties in eastern England.

By 1045 the King had reached his forty-second year, and most Englishmen felt it was high time for him to marry and father an heir to the throne. Godwine himself felt that way; and during the autumn of that year he convinced Edward to marry his daughter Edith. Thus, should any children be born of the match, Godwine's grandchildren would inherit the throne one day.

Unfortunately for Godwine's hopes, his daughter Edith, who was some twenty years younger than the King, never became pregnant. Why their marriage produced no offspring is unclear. Perhaps Edith was unable to conceive, although it is possible that Edward the Confessor was sterile or impotent or possibly without any interest in women. Recently a distinguished historian has advanced an intriguing theory to explain why Edward fathered no children by his wife of many years. According to Eric John, just before summoning his half-brother back from Normandy and recognizing him as heir-apparent to the throne, Harthacnut made Edward swear to forego all sexual relations for the remainder of his life. Despite his poor health in 1041, Harthacnut was still a young man who might marry and have a child of his own one day; and should he actually have a son, Harthacnut wanted that son to face no opposition from any children fathered by his older half-brother. Anxious to return to the land of his birth, Edward swore the oath Harthacnut demanded of him, whereupon he appeared at Westminster and was hailed as heir-apparent. Thereafter Edward took his oath to Harthacnut with great seriousness and, as a consequence, never sought to have children by Edith or any other woman for that matter.[9]

Whatever the truth of Mr. John's theory, Earl Godwine was the King's father-in-law from the autumn of 1045, and during the next five years he continued to press his family's interests, despite the deep resentment their enormous power provoked. Bitter hatred of the House of Godwine developed, and that hatred triggered a political crisis that began during the autumn of 1050 and led to the Godwines' temporary banishment from the kingdom.

The crisis of 1050-1052 began shortly after the death of Archbishop Eadsige of Canterbury on 29 October 1050. Almost immediately a bitter contest for the most important clerical position in the realm began. At first it appeared that Aelfric, a monk of Canterbury and a relative of the Godwines, would receive the vacant position. There are indications that the cathedral chapter actually elected Aelfric and submitted his name for royal approval. But before Aelfric's election could be certified, Robert of Jumièges convinced the King that it would be dangerous for a Godwine protégé to hold such an important office. In that event the Godwine family would have Edward at their mercy and he would become their puppet in all but name. Alarmed, the King refused to accept the outcome of the Canterbury election, as was his legal right, and gave directions for a second election. He even instructed the monks of Canterbury to choose as the next primate the Bishop of London himself, Robert of Jumièges, which they did without protest. That move was applauded by the northern Earls, Siward and Leofric, causing the Godwines to accept it with a heavy heart.

Before the Archbishop-elect left for Rome to secure papal recognition and a pallium,[10] a Witan, or council of the country's leading magnates, met at Westminster. For several days the Witan debated what to do about the royal succession because the King had still fathered no children by Edith, his wife of over five years. Moreover, Edward was almost fifty, an advanced age by the standards of that period. Should he die without fathering a son or designating an heir, a struggle for the throne would probably result, thereby triggering new Viking attacks on

England.

As the Witan continued to meet and debate, a consensus developed that Edward the Confessor's heir should be his first cousin once removed, William II of Normandy.[11] The new Archbishop was especially vocal in promoting Duke William's candidacy, and he seems to have received strong support from Earls Siward, Leofric, and Ralph and their many followers. Only the Godwines favored a different candidate, but they were easily outvoted. However, because of the Godwines' outspoken opposition, King Edward required Earl Godwine to surrender his son Wulfnoth and Wulfnoth's son Hakon, who were sent as hostages to Normandy to ensure that the Godwines would abide by the Witan's decision.

In theory the choice of Duke William to be heir-apparent made political sense in 1051. It would strengthen the Anglo-Norman connection that dated back to 1002, and in that way it might end the threat of a new Viking attack. Even more important in the Confessor's eyes, the selection of Duke William would weaken the Godwines and keep them from seizing the throne for their leader on his death. Moreover, with Duke William's help, the King should be strong enough to withstand the Godwines' power during the remainder of his reign, in which case he would never have to submit to their domination again. All those arguments appealed strongly to Edward, and in 1051 he welcomed the Witan's decision that the throne should pass to William of Normandy, although his cousin was not descended from the ancient House of Cerdic and had no English blood in his veins.

As for William himself, there were good reasons to believe that he would welcome the chance to become England's ruler one day. Although thinly populated by modern standards, England was already one of Europe's leading countries with rich farmland, good harbors, prosperous iron and tin mines, and flourishing cities and towns. Its fine coinage and abundant wealth, if somewhat exaggerated in European minds, should help him maintain tighter control over the turbulent barons of the western sections of his large duchy.

Since ascending the Norman throne at the tender age of seven, William had faced repeated plots and rebellions. Several of his guardians were murdered, and an especially dangerous uprising in 1047 prompted his feudal overlord, Henry I of France, to send him military aid as a way of repaying political favors rendered some years earlier by William's father, Robert the Devil (d. 1035). Shortly after the French troops enabled William to win the great battle of Val-ès-Dunes in 1047, they returned to Paris, leaving the young Duke to fight on alone against his older and more experienced enemies. During the next decade William waged campaign after campaign and gradually subdued those who had hoped to overthrow him, acquiring political and military skills of a high order in the process.

As early as 1050 William enjoyed an enviable reputation although he was still only twenty-two. Because of his obvious courage and ability, the other rulers of western Europe regarded him as a "comer" who was likely to exercise great power in the future. This was especially true after the Count of Flanders, Baldwin V, an ambitious regional figure as well as the brother-in-law of Henry I of France, offered him his daughter Matilda's hand in marriage. The exact date of their marriage has never been established--indeed, it could have occurred at any point in 1050, 1051, or 1052.[12] But by the time the English Witan met in 1051 to consider the succession issue, William was betrothed or already married to Matilda, either of which would have been known by the magnates at Westminster. Such considerations strengthened the hand of those who favored William's candidacy to the throne as a way of preventing future Viking attacks on England and holding the Godwines at bay.

Once the Witan made its decision with Edward the Confessor's warm approval, Archbishop-elect Robert departed for Rome in order to obtain a pallium. However, on his way to the Eternal City, the new Archbishop stopped over at Rouen and conveyed the offer of the English throne to William. All this took place during the middle of Lent, and by the first week of April if not sooner William knew that a great future lay in store for him, provided of course that he outlived the Confessor and nothing happened to deprive him of his promised inheritance.

While Robert of Jumièges was absent from England, the Godwines were far from idle. Although dismayed by Robert's election to the archbishopric and William of Normandy's nomination to be the Confessor's heir-apparent, the Godwines were still a powerful family with great resources. They therefore pressed the King to fill the vacant bishopric of London with their long-time supporter, Spearhavoc, the current Abbot of Abingdon and the King's leading goldsmith. Edward agreed to his father-in-law's request, and Spearhavoc was named to the bishopric vacated by Robert of Jumièges.

However, on Robert's return to England at the end of June, the primate was furious about those developments. Indeed, he refused to consecrate Spearhavoc on the grounds that he had bought the bishopric and was thus guilty of simony, for which there is no proof at all; and the Archbishop also insisted that his former diocese be granted to another Norman cleric, a monk named William, who was his most trusted associate at Canterbury as well as a priest of the Chapel Royal. Robert also launched a campaign to vilify Earl Godwine in the King's eyes.

Fifteen years earlier, in 1036, the King's younger brother Alfred had returned to England during the reign of King Harold I (1035-1040). Captured in Sussex by Earl Godwine's troops, Alfred and several companions were briefly imprisoned there before being taken in chains to London. Several weeks later they were transferred to Ely Abbey, where they were blinded before being killed a month later.[13] During the summer of 1051 Archbishop Robert brought this matter before the King, who quickly agreed that Earl Godwine had been responsible for his brother's death fifteen years before. The Archbishop also insinuated that Godwine was not only plotting to murder the Confessor even now but was also in possession of several manors seized from the archiepiscopal see. From that time Edward shared the Archbishop's burning hatred of Godwine, whom he was determined to humiliate if a suitable pretext could be found.[14]

An opportunity to strike directly at the Earl arose shortly after a visit to Westminster by Count Eustace II of Boulogne, the second husband of Edward's sister Goda.[15] Why Eustace chose to visit the English court during August of 1051 is not entirely clear. Perhaps he was sent by Duke William, Eustace's overlord, to tender thanks for the Witan's promise of the throne, but it seems more likely that Eustace's visit was personal in nature. At any rate, after several days at Westminster, Eustace and his attendants returned to Dover, where they arrived about nightfall, too late to embark for the continent. They demanded overnight lodgings in such an arrogant and condescending way that the townspeople were infuriated and a fight broke out. During that altercation some twenty of Eustace's men were killed along with a comparable number of townspeople while many other people were badly injured. In a fury Eustace rode back to Westminster and demanded that the Dover "rabble" be brutally punished for their temerity. Because Dover lay within the earldom of Wessex, the King instructed Godwine to sack the town and ravage the surrounding countryside as a way of appeasing Eustace.

At that point Earl Godwine was confronted with a difficult choice. If he carried out the royal command and sacked the town, he would lose the support of his own people. But if he ignored the King's order, he would be guilty of willful disobedience and could be severely punished. Because of all the tension of recent months and his need to retain the support of his own followers, Godwine chose to ignore the King's command. Moreover, given the obvious hostility of the King and his rancorous Archbishop, the time seemed to have come for the Godwines to make a stand, even if the odds against them were extremely great.

The Earl and his sons raised an army quickly and set out for Gloucestershire, where the Witan was scheduled to meet on 7 September. On his arrival in the West Country, Godwine demanded that Count Eustace and his attendants be handed over to him for punishment. He also called for the surrender of the Norman garrison in the Herefordshire castle of Ewyas Harold. During recent years those troops had terrorized the local people, and the Godwines hoped to rally nationalistic support by punishing them severely.

Unfortunately for the Godwines, their demands fell on deaf ears in the Witan. Earls Siward and Leofric, who were present with hundreds of their armed retainers nearby, paid no attention to them, as did Ralph of Mantes, the influential Earl of Herefordshire. Moreover, Archbishop Robert seized the moment to denounce Godwine for murdering Prince Alfred in 1036 and plotting to assassinate the Confessor during recent weeks. After the Archbishop's verbal assault, Godwine took the floor and sought to defend himself. But Edward dismissed his father-in-law's arguments out of hand and made it clear that nothing he could do would heal the bitterness that now existed between them.

Confronted by such great enmity, the Godwines left the hall and rode back to their camp at Beverstone, fifteen miles away. Thereupon Edward adjourned the Witan for seventeen days, after which it was to reassemble in London and weigh the evidence against Earl Godwine, who now stood formally accused of high treason. Although Edward ordered him to appear and answer all the charges against himself, Godwine ignored the Confessor's summons on the grounds that he had no chance of receiving a fair trial.

By that point England was on the verge of civil war. The Godwines were determined to avoid another political humiliation, while the Norman faction was anxious to prevent a compromise settlement. Luckily, an effort to mediate the dispute was made by Bishop Stigand of Winchester, who won the Godwines' everlasting friendship thereby. After the peace-minded Stigand failed to heal the breach, he relayed a royal offer to withdraw all charges against Godwine and his sons, provided they abjured the realm for five years. Hurriedly Godwine and his family considered the King's offer and reluctantly accepted it. With Archbishop Robert and a band of horsemen at their heels, Godwine and his son Tostig rode with many other members of their family to Thorney Island, where they set sail for Flanders. Because Tostig had recently married Judith, the half-sister of Count Baldwin V, they received a warm reception at Bruges, where they spent the next year in relative comfort. As for Harold Godwine and his brother Leofwine, they made their way to Bristol and boarded a ship bound for southern Ireland.

Once the the House of Godwine scattered in opposite directions, Edward was in a position to deal with his wife Edith. The Archbishop urged him to divorce her at once, which the Confessor refused to do. If he did as Robert suggested, Edward's subjects would expect him to remarry and father an heir to the throne, an unwelcome prospect for him. Therefore, Edward merely banished Edith to a nunnery, although he confiscated all her estates and movable goods.

Shortly after sending Edith away, the Confessor took punitive steps against her family. In gratitude for Earl Leofric's help, the King stripped Harold Godwine of the earldom of East Anglia and assigned it to Leofric's eldest son, Aelfgar. About the same time he conveyed dozens of manors that had formerly belonged to Swein Godwine to his own nephew, Ralph of Mantes; while he granted almost all of western Wessex to another relative, Odda. As for Earl Godwine's extensive estates in southern England, Edward added them directly to the royal demesne.

During the winter of 1051-1052, while making all those territorial changes, Edward may have received a visit from Duke William of Normandy, as the "D" version of the Anglo-Saxon Chronicle holds and many prominent scholars maintain. However, William's leading biographer, Professor David Douglas, contends that the Duke was still confronted by so much opposition within his turbulent province that he was unable to leave Normandy at that time. Moreover, the "D" version of the Anglo-Saxon Chronicle, which was alternately kept at York and Worcester, was often mistaken about events in southern England. Furthermore, no other contemporary source, not even the writings of William of Jumièges or William of Poitiers during the next generation, made any mention of such a visit when it was clearly in their and the Duke's self-interest to do so.[16] Because of Professor Douglas's unrivaled knowledge of William's movements as well as the skimpy nature of the surviving evidence, which consists of only a few lines that seem to have been added to the "D" version of the Chronicle at a later time, it appears that the Duke did not set foot in England before September of 1066 at the earliest.

Whatever the truth of the matter, it was obvious to most politically-minded Englishmen that King Edward was in league with the Norman faction at his court. That faction was led by Robert of Jumièges, whose main associates were his successor in the see of London, William of Normandy, and Bishop Ulf of Dorchester, who had been named to his post in 1049.[17] Other men who belonged to the Norman faction included Ralph of Mantes, Earl of Herefordshire, and Osbern

Pentecost, Ralph's most trusted associate in western England.

The great power wielded by the Norman faction caused resentment in many quarters and triggered a nationalistic backlash that played into the Godwines' hands. By the summer of 1052 the Godwines saw how they could form a "patriot party" that would enable them to return to their homeland and rid it of most of the despised foreigners. Paradoxically, the Godwines' cause was also strengthened by the harsh steps the Confessor had taken against them during his hour of triumph.

When Edward deprived the Godwines of their estates and all their movable goods, thereby breaking the country's richest family at a stroke, the other English magnates shuddered and wondered who would be next. If the King could destroy his wife's kinsmen that easily, what was to prevent him from adopting similar courses against other nobles who displeased him? Siward and Leofric had opposed the Godwines in the past, but now they viewed the situation in a different light. If the property of the most powerful family in the land was not sacrosanct, neither was their own; and if the Godwines ever returned and recovered their power, banishing Edward's Norman favorites in the process, it would probably be in their self-interest to remain neutral and leave the King to his fate. That dramatic shift of opinion paved the way for the Godwines' triumphant return during the summer of 1052.

On 22 June 1052 Earl Godwine sailed across the Channel to Kent. Once he went ashore at Dungeness, he was welcomed by the local people; but royal troops arrived within a week and compelled him to withdraw to Pevensey, in Sussex. Ultimately he returned to Flanders and mobilized a considerably larger army with which to defeat his son-in-law and the Norman faction at court. In addition, Earl Godwine sent a messenger to Ireland to inform his sons Harold and Leofwine of his plans. They were directed to merge whatever troops they could raise with the other Godwine forces on the southern coast, a few miles west of the Isle of Wight, during the last days of August.

By the 30th of August all the Godwine troops had gathered on England's southern coast before sailing eastward. Calling at such ports as Pevensey, Romney, Hythe, and Sandwich, they recruited hundreds of additional men. On rounding the eastern tip of Kent, they sailed north and entered the Thames before setting fire to the royal manor of Milton. Deeply alarmed, the King consulted his advisers, who assured him that London would not fall. But on Monday the 14th of September, the Godwines' ships reached Southwark, where the citizens did nothing to halt their progress and royal troops ignored the King's call to arms. The next morning a royal emissary suggested a peaceful meeting between the two sides. Before Godwine would appear, he insisted on the unconditional return of his family's estates, although he promised to recognize William of Normandy as the Confessor's heir-apparent. With a heavy heart Edward accepted those terms and agreed to a formal reconciliation with his father-in-law, which caused most of the Normans to flee the capital in haste. These included Archbishop Robert, Bishop Ulf of Dorchester, and Osbern Pentecost and his retainers, who soon sailed across the Channel, never to return.

On Tuesday the 15th of September, the King and the Godwines met at Westminster. After kneeling and swearing homage to his son-in-law, Earl Godwine gave convincing answers to all the absent Archbishop's charges. Thereupon the primate was formally outlawed for provoking an unnecessary quarrel between the Confessor and his greatest subject. Finally, Edward received Godwine back into favor and agreed to accept Edith's return to court from the abbey where she had been sequestered.

Within a week Harold Godwine recovered the earldom of East Anglia, and by the end of September all the other Godwine titles and estates had been restored to them. Wisely, Earl Godwine did not call for the expulsion of any other Normans from the realm. Bishop William of London, a rather taciturn man without political ambitions, was allowed to remain in office, and laymen like Ralph of Mantes and Richard the son of Scrob, who had just built "Richard's Castle" in Herefordshire, were left in peace. But the many Normans who had fled across the Channel were forbidden to return at any future point. The see of Dorchester was declared vacant as a result of Bishop Ulf's flight, and it was soon granted to a Saxon cleric, Wulfwig; while the great archiepiscopal see of Canterbury was assigned, doubtless at Godwine's urging, to Stigand, the peace-minded Bishop of Winchester.

The appointment of Stigand to be Archbishop without informing the Papacy in advance was Godwine's only mistake in 1052. Pope Leo IX could not be expected to countenance the unilateral deposition of an Archbishop less than fifteen months after granting recognition and a pallium to him. This was soon realized in England, and Stigand never seems to have considered a journey to Rome in quest of official recognition.[18] As a consequence, during his many years in office--he was finally deprived by the Conqueror in 1070--Stigand consecrated no Bishops at all because of the equivocal nature of his position. Furthermore, Stigand was not invited to officiate at important ceremonies the Archbishop usually conducted. For example, although Stigand was always treated with great deference by the House of Godwine, when Harold Godwine's new religious foundation at Waltham, Essex was dedicated in 1062, Archbishop Ealdred of York came south to officiate.

Stigand's appointment to the archbishopric created several other problems as well. During the eleventh century there was mounting criticism of abuses like pluralism and clerical marriage, which the Papacy and most great noblemen wished to see eradicated. But Stigand refused to cast his wife aside, and he also clung tenaciously to the bishopric of Winchester after his translation to Canterbury. In addition he was Abbot of Gloucester for many years and administrator of Ely Abbey for a time. Stigand was thus one of the greatest pluralists of the age; and by linking their fortunes so closely to his, the Godwines inadvertently turned their back on the cause of religious reform, which proved a serious liability during the political crisis of 1066.

All that lay in the future, however, and for the moment the choice of Stigand to be Primate of All England seemed to be a wise move. A tactful and conciliatory man, Stigand sought to resolve past problems between Earl Godwine and the King, who always preferred quieter times than the previous eighteen months had been. Godwine became a fixture at court once again, and he and the Confessor treated each other with exaggerated politeness, as if there had never been any discord between them. Indeed, it was while they were dining together on 12 April 1053 that Godwine suffered the stroke that ended his life several days later.

Because Swein Godwine had died in 1052, the earldom of Wessex devolved on Godwine's second son, Harold. Crafty and intelligent as well as courageous and charismatic, Harold Godwine possessed political skills of a high order. Endowed with unusual patience, he was England's most capable military leader since the death of Edmund Ironside in 1016.[19] Shortly after Harold's own death fifty years later, an otherwise hostile Norman chronicler described him as "extremely bold, very handsome in all his person, agreeable in his manner of expressing himself, and affable with everybody."[20] As a result of those qualities and his largely secular and somewhat sardonic outlook, he was a popular individual who inspired trust in others, just the sort of man the English people were happy to accept as their leader.

Edward never allowed Harold to wield unlimited power, however. The King himself supervised religious affairs, and during the 1050s he welcomed Norman clerics to England and granted valuable estates to their abbeys, especially Jumièges and Fécamp. The picturesque monastery of St. Michael's Mount on an island off the Cornish coast became a possession of Mont Saint-Michel at this time; and about 1059 Edward granted the church and rectory of Deerhurst to the Parisian abbey of Saint-Denis, probably because a monk of Saint-Denis was currently residing at Westminster and serving as physician to the royal family.[21] But in other matters, especially Harold's desire to promote national unity, the Confessor seems to have allowed his chief minister considerable latitude.

A more approachable and conciliatory leader than his father had been, Harold hoped to promote greater cooperation between the three great earldoms of Wessex, Mercia, and Northumbria. As a consequence, shortly after inheriting his father's title and estates, Harold resigned the earldom of East Anglia and proposed the appointment of Aelfgar to that position. That naturally pleased Aelfgar and his elderly father, Leofric of Mercia, who concluded that Harold was sincere in wanting better relations with them.

Three years later Harold took additional steps to cultivate genuine cooperation with Leofric and his family. During the spring of 1056 a border war broke out when the greatest chieftain of North Wales, Gruffydd ap Llwelyn, invaded Herefordshire and burned scores of farms and villages. Harold's former chaplain Leofgar, who was now Bishop of Hereford, raised an army with assistance from Elfnoth the sheriff, and together they sought to defeat Gruffydd's forces. But on 16 June Leofgar and Elfnoth were both killed, which compelled Leofric to rush to the scene. Away in the southeast, Harold was soon informed of these developments. He summoned his retainers at once, and within a week he and his men arrived to assist the beleaguered Earl, who then drove the Welsh marauders back into their own country.

Despite his efforts to secure better relations with the most powerful family of central England, Harold was soon confronted by the hostility of Aelfgar, who succeeded his father as Earl of Mercia in 1057. Aelfgar resented the steady gains made by the Godwines during recent years, suspecting their wealth and power were now so great that they could eliminate him at a moment's notice. Aelfgar's fears were not groundless. In 1055, after the elderly Siward of Northumbria died without a direct heir, the Confessor appointed Harold's brother Tostig, for whom he had deep affection, to take his place. In addition Edward granted valuable lands to Harold himself shortly after Ralph of Mantes' death in 1057. Indeed, Ralph's earldom of Herefordshire was dissolved at that juncture and all his lands conveyed to Harold, who was already the Confessor's richest subject. To make matters worse, Edward had recently established a new earldom, consisting of Essex and Kent, for Harold's youngest brother, Leofwine; and when Aelfgar himself surrendered the earldom of East Anglia on inheriting the older and richer earldom of Mercia, East Anglia was granted to yet another Godwine brother, Gyrth. Because of all those gains, total Godwine wealth increased by the beginning of 1058 to almost £5,800 a year, or more than four times that of Aelfgar's new earldom, which was worth only £1,300 per year.[22]

Hoping to rally help against the Godwines, who now had him surrounded, Aelfgar launched a verbal war again them in 1058. Harold responded in kind and urged King Edward to exile him that same year. This caused Aelfgar to negotiate an alliance with Gruffydd of North Wales, which was strengthened when the latter married Aelfgar's daughter Ealdgyth in 1059 or 1060. A short time later, in 1062, Harold led a brilliant campaign against Aelfgar and Gruffydd, whose combined forces he easily routed. Gruffydd died that same year and Aelfgar the next. The earldom of Mercia then passed to Aelfgar's sixteen-year-old son Edwin, from whom Harold had nothing to fear at the moment. Hoping to win Edwin's support, Harold cultivated him assiduously and exchanged professions of friendship with him within several weeks.

The increasing power of the Godwines, along with Harold's eventual destruction of the troublesome Aelfgar, is convincing proof of Harold's political and military skills. At the same time Harold was equally successful in his handling of the succession question, which came to the fore once again during the years after Earl Godwine's death.

In 1053 King Edward still feared that the Godwines would try to seize the throne one day. As long as the King clung to that fear and was determined to save the throne for a blood relation, he was likely to uphold the Witan's decision of 1051 that William of Normandy should be his eventual heir. Once Earl Godwine died and Harold inherited his mantle, the new Earl of Wessex hoped to convince Edward that he and his brothers had no designs on the throne, even if they wanted to keep it from passing to an unacceptable foreigner like William. Harold also sensed that Edward was deeply annoyed with William, who had done nothing to assist him in 1052 when the Godwines returned in triumph from their year of exile.[23] Thus, Harold hoped that Edward would be willing to ignore the Witan's earlier promise to William, who was currently opposed by Count Geoffrey of Anjou and his new ally, Henry I of France.[24] In effect, Harold needed only to find another blood relation of the King who could precede William in the succession and be groomed for the English throne one day.

There were two distinct possibilities. One was Walter, the elder son of King Edward's sister Goda (now the wife of Eustace of Boulogne) and her first husband Drogo, who had died in 1035. Walter was a first cousin of the English monarch as well as the current lord of the Vexin, a district on the eastern border of Normandy. But in the latter capacity Walter was an important vassal of Duke William, who would never allow him to cross the Channel and be groomed as Edward's heir-apparent. So Walter's candidacy had to be ruled out on purely practical grounds.

The second possibility was the man who is remembered to history as Edward the Exile, a nephew of Edward the Confessor. Edward the Exile was the son of Edmund Ironside and thus a grandson of King Ethelred II (d. 1016). Once Edmund Ironside himself died in battle in 1016 and the English throne passed to King Cnut, Edmund Ironside's son Edward, who was a teenager at the time, was sent to the continent, in the expectation he would die there at an early age. After spending several years in Denmark, Edward the Exile drifted down into central Europe and ultimately wound up in Hungary, where he was treated with great kindness by the Holy Roman Emperor Conrad II (d. 1039) and his successor, Henry III (d. 1056). Indeed, Henry III recognized the Exile as a foreign-born prince, granted him a substantial pension, and even arranged for him to marry a cousin of his own, a woman named Agatha. Clearly Edward the Exile had a strong claim to the English throne, a stronger hereditary claim in fact than William of Normandy, who had not a drop of English blood in his veins. But unfortunately for the Exile, he had been away from his native land for several decades by the early 1050s and may have forgotten how to speak his native language. In addition he had made a comfortable life for himself in Hungary, which he was reluctant to give up for the questionable prospect of the English throne. As a consequence, he showed no interest when two English clerics travelled to Hungary in 1054 and urged him to return to his native land.[25]

Harold Godwine refused to admit defeat, however, and two years later he himself went to the continent, ostensibly for the same reason although the evidence is inconclusive. According to Philip Grierson, Harold is known to have been at St. Omer in the Low Countries on 13 November 1056, when he met with Count Baldwin V of Flanders. Several days later Baldwin departed for Cologne, where on 6 December he had an audience with Pope Victor II, who had promised to mediate a dispute between Baldwin and the new Holy Roman Emperor, Henry IV (1056-1106). Mr. Grierson maintains that Harold went with Baldwin to Cologne, whence he seems to have accompanied the papal train into Bavaria. Before his election to the Papacy two years before, Victor II had been Bishop of Eichstatt, and for a time he had also served as Henry III's governor of Bavaria. It is possible that, during the Christmas season of 1056, the Pope introduced Harold to Henry IV, who had great influence over Edward the Exile, a pensioner of his father's for many years. If in fact, as Mr. Grierson maintains, Harold travelled into Bavaria that December, he would have been within a short distance of Hungary and the principal residence of Edward the Exile. Thus Harold may well have travelled to Budapest and reported the new Emperor's belief that he should return to England at long last.[26] Although Mr. Grierson's argument cannot be proved, it is safe to assume that only a man of great influence, such as the Emperor or Harold Godwine, the power behind the English throne, could have convinced the Exile to return to his native land, which he had refused to do only two years before.

Whatever the case, Harold himself returned to England during the spring of 1057, and several months later the Exile himself arrived with his wife Agatha and their children, Margaret, Christina, and Edgar. As Professor Douglas has written, Edward the Exile's return after so many years away "... was an important occasion, for he came in state, with the support of the Emperor, a great noble with much treasure."[27] Unfortunately, the Exile died several days after reaching southern England, before he could meet with his uncle, Edward the Confessor. At the time of his death, the Exile was probably in his late forties or early fifties, although his son Edgar was less than six years of age. To Harold Godwine, the Exile's death was an unfortunate but not an insurmountable problem because Edgar would serve his purposes equally well, perhaps even better. Harold himself was less than forty at the time, and he could easily serve as the boy's guardian and even his surrogate father, rearing him with his own children, which he apparently did. Then, whenever the Confessor died, Edgar's claim to the throne would be confirmed by the Witan, and Harold would undoubtedly remain in office as chief minister to the young man he had taken under his wing at a critical time.

Although little is known about Edgar's life between 1057 and the Norman invasion of 1066, it is clear that Harold considered Edgar the Aetheling the most suitable candidate for the throne.* Most politically-minded Englishmen felt the same way, and there are clear indications that the succession question was believed to have been settled once and for all. King Edward himself, who reached his fifty-fifth year in 1058, apparently felt that way and retired from politics altogether, which he delegated to Harold while devoting his own time and energy to the rebuilding of Westminster Abbey, his intended burial place. Furthermore, in 1061 Harold's brother Tostig, who had a deep interest in politics, left the realm with a group of pilgrims bound for Rome. They included Tostig's wife Judith, his brother Gyrth, Archbishop

---

* "Aetheling" was the Anglo-Saxon word for Prince, so most historians refer to him as "Edgar the Aetheling."

Ealdred of York, and several important thegns and clerks.* It seems unlikely that Tostig, Gyrth, and the Archbishop would have left the country at that juncture, given King Edward's advanced years and declining health, had they believed the succession still to be in doubt.

Yet Professor Douglas contends that Harold Godwine was already plotting to seize the throne for himself one day. Indeed, Professor Douglas maintains that from the time of the Exile's death in 1057, Harold "... seems to have begun to think of the succession for himself."[28] Because Harold was recognized as King by the Witan in January 1066, a few hours after the Confessor's death, the question of whether he had a long-standing plan to usurp the throne is one that cannot be ignored. Yet there is no evidence to support Professor Douglas's assertion that he was thinking of seizing the throne for himself as early as 1057.

The question of Harold's intentions is unlikely to be answered to general agreement because of inadequate sources. Historians who admire William of Normandy and sympathize with his cause will continue to believe that Harold Godwine, the Duke's greatest rival, was completely insincere about his support for Edgar the Aetheling's cause, which was little more than a hypocritical ploy to mask his own ambitions. By the same token, historians who regard the Norman Conquest as a setback for the English people are likely to remain sympathetic to Harold, who always questioned the wisdom of accepting a foreigner as King. Most scholars in the latter group contend that Harold had no long-standing plan to usurp the throne and contend that the Witan conferred it on him out of political necessity (i.e., because Edgar the Aetheling was still a minor at the time and could play no part in defending the realm from a Norman assault).

In the opinion of this writer, it seems unlikely that Harold had a conscious design on the throne before the end of December 1065, when the monarch was clearly on the verge of death. Had the Confessor lived long enough for Edgar the Aetheling to attain his majority, Harold would probably have remained on the sidelines and allowed him to enter his rightful inheritance. But because of Harold's pragmatic and somewhat cynical nature, it also seems likely that he often reflected on the pleasures that would come from being King one day, perhaps as early as 1059 or 1060. However, if Harold entertained such thoughts from time

* Thegns were landowners of moderate wealth, the precursors of lesser gentlemen in later times. They were expected to serve in the fyrd, or unpaid militia, whenever that institution was mobilized to meet an emergency.

to time, they were probably little more than drunken musings before 1062. During that year his prestige rose to great new heights because of his brilliant campaign against Gruffydd of North Wales and the troublesome Earl Aelfgar of Mercia, both of whom were dead by the end of 1063. Once Aelfgar's earldom passed to his young and inexperienced son Edwin, Harold had nothing to fear from any quarter in England. Moreover, in that same year Edward the Confessor celebrated his fifty-ninth birthday and, in view of his steadily declining health, it seemed increasingly probable that he would die before Edgar the Aetheling reached his majority. Yet to accuse Harold of scheming to usurp the throne even at that juncture seems unfair. Hypothetically at least, Duke William might die at any moment from natural causes or battle wounds, and in that event it would not have been dangerous to allow a boy of thirteen or fourteen to ascend the throne, especially if he had a prudent and experienced minister like Harold to guide him.

However, if Harold occasionally reflected on the pleasures of being King, his hopes suffered a grievous setback in 1064 when King Edward roused himself from his lethargy and ordered him to make a ceremonial visit to Duke William's court at Rouen. Despite his indolence during recent years, the Confessor was not totally unaware of the political currents swirling around him. Perhaps one of Harold's servants gossiped with a royal groom one day and mentioned the fact that Harold occasionally envisaged himself on the throne. For that reason as well as his own approaching death, Edward became suspicious of his brother-in-law's motives and concluded that he could not be trusted to respect the Aetheling's claims after his death. As a consequence, the King decided that the only viable option, if the throne was to be preserved for one of his own relations, was to revive the promise made to Duke William back in 1051. Accordingly, the Confessor summoned his chief minister to a meeting and commanded him to go to Rouen, where he was to renew the promise of the throne that the Witan had made back in 1051 to the Duke.

Doubtless Harold was dismayed by that development and hoped to avoid such a distasteful mission. But because of Edward's frail health and growing reputation for saintliness, it would be risky to disobey a direct command from the King. Moreover, Harold hoped to avoid any impression that a major difference of opinion had arisen between himself and his royal master. As a result Harold felt compelled to make a pretence of carrying out his instructions.

With a heavy heart Harold set sail from Bosham, Sussex and went ashore at Beaurain in the dominions of Guy, Count of Ponthieu and a leading vassal of the Duke of Normandy. Because there is no evidence that Harold's ship was blown off course by a storm, certainly not on the famous Bayeux Tapestry, it is difficult to avoid the conclusion that Harold deliberately avoided the Norman coast and planned to reappear in England after several weeks, claiming that he had failed to reach Rouen for reasons beyond his control. If that was his actual intention, it was wrecked by the fact that William was soon aware that Guy had Harold in his custody. Thereupon William sent instructions for Guy to turn the Englishman over to his agents, although Guy chose to escort Harold to Rouen in person. Thus, for complicated reasons, Harold became a prisoner of the very man he had worked to bar from the English throne for years.

Although William may have regarded Harold as his greatest enemy, he was in no position to put him to death or hold him in captivity for the remainder of his days. Harold's brothers back in England were powerful men with strong influence over the King and the Witan; and if any harm came to the acknowledged leader of the House of Godwine, English fears about William would be confirmed, strengthening the existing dislike of him and the resolve of the Aetheling's backers. In a sense, therefore, William had no choice but to treat Harold as an honored guest. He needed to win his trust and confidence before seeking his endorsement as the Confessor's rightful heir. If he could ingratiate himself with Harold, the latter might return to Westminster with a "favorable report" and convince the other magnates that their fears of the Duke were exaggerated. In that event his chances of being accepted by the Witan after the Confessor's death would be far greater.

By the same token, Harold knew it would be risky to offend William in any way. The Duke had a well-deserved reputation for cruelty. During the previous fifteen years he had often blinded, castrated, or otherwise mutilated his opponents; and on one occasion, after capturing a castle that held out against him for several weeks, he had the hands and feet of every man in the garrison cut off in full view of the local population. Clearly Harold wanted to avoid a similar fate, and he knew he must keep William from thinking he feared or distrusted him in any way.

For different reasons, therefore, William and Harold behaved as if they enjoyed one another's company when they would have preferred to slit each other's throats. William wined and dined the English leader, who responded with toasts and harmless pleasantries. And when William set out on a military campaign against the troublesome Duke Conan II of Brittany, he took Harold along so the latter could observe his ability to command. On his part, Harold seized the occasion to demonstrate his own military prowess; and because he fought with such valor and determination, the Norman ruler dubbed him a knight, a ceremonial distinction that had not yet appeared on English soil.

After Duke Conan's surrender to the the Norman army at Dinan, William and his men recrossed the border into western Normandy, where Harold swore homage to William, knowing that was the unspoken price of his release. In addition, according to a somewhat later account, Harold promised

> "... firstly that he would be the representative of Duke William at the court of his lord, King Edward, as long as the King lived; secondly that he would employ all his influence and wealth to ensure that after the death of King Edward the kingdom of England should be confirmed in the possession of the Duke; thirdly that he would place a garrison of the Duke's knights in the castle of Dover and maintain these at his own care and cost;[29] [and] fourthly that in other parts of England at the pleasure of the Duke he would maintain garrisons in other castles and make complete provision for their sustenance."[30]

After Harold made those promises, which he could always renounce later on grounds of duress, William accepted Harold as his vassal and confirmed him in all his offices and estates in England. In addition he gave him several handsome presents and released his nephew Hakon into his custody while continuing to hold Hakon's father Wulfnoth in Normandy, where he died some twenty years later. Shortly after that ceremony of pretended friendship, Harold departed with his nephew for the coast and boarded a ship bound for England.

Back in his own country, Harold looked for ways to strengthen England's coastal defenses because of the strong likelihood of a Norman invasion in several years. William's behavior in 1064 had convinced Harold of the Duke's firm resolve to obtain the English throne one day, by military force if that was the only way. Therefore, the southern coast, directly across the Channel from the Norman ports, should be prepared for the invasion that now seemed all but inevitable. As a consequence Harold soon found money to build two castles in Kent, one at Dover and the other at Clavering, with help from Normans who had already settled in England. Impervious to arrows and stones launched by the huge catapults of the period, those castles could be defended easily and would be good places to station garrisons with which to repulse a Norman attack. Unfortunately for the English people, Harold's attempt to safeguard the coast came too late. On the eve of the Norman landings in 1066, there were fewer than six castles in the realm; and except for the two in Kent, the others were all situated in the West Country, along the Welsh border. Undoubtedly the twelfth-century historian Ordericus Vitalis, who had been born in Shropshire in 1075, was correct in maintaining that the Anglo-Saxons' lack of castles was a major reason for their defeat by the Normans.

Although the evidence is skimpy, Harold seems to have adopted other policies, modelled on those of France, for the defense of his realm. On the continent the estates of the episcopal hierarchy and richer monasteries had long borne heavy obligations to the national government; and just before the Norman Conquest a similar system began to be established in England. Large monasteries like Peterborough Abbey in the east and Abingdon Abbey in the west were informed that in the event of a crisis, they would be expected to provide a certain number of armed men from their estates to assist the crown. Abingdon Abbey, for example, was required to send sixty men from its Berkshire estates alone.[31] This imposition of military quotas on monastic lands was the first step toward the feudalization of the English Church, which gathered speed after 1065 and was completed within a decade of Duke William's capture of the throne in 1066.[32]

Harold was also responsible for another innovation that was adopted during the last year before the Conquest. At that time the naval forces of eastern Wessex were organized in a system that would make it easier to repulse foreign landings. The five leading ports of the southeast--Dover, Hastings, Hythe, Romney and Sandwich, which eventually became known as the Cinque Ports--were required to provide the crown with up to fifty-seven ships for at least fifteen days of unpaid service each year. Each of those ships was to carry a crew of twenty-three men or more, including a steersman and a steersman's assistant. This system of coastal defense, which appeared shortly before 1066, was accompanied by the imposition of a new tax known as "ship-scot." Falling on such inland towns as Warwick and Leicester, "ship-scot" provided special funds for the central government to use for the construction and maintenance of a small fleet of warships.[33]

Although England's defenses were stronger than ever by the autumn of 1065, a serious rebellion in the north caused Harold to feel that all his efforts had been in vain. During the past ten years his brother Tostig had been Earl of Northumbria and ruled that part of the realm with an iron hand. Although a generous patron of Durham Cathedral, Tostig had seized property from the smaller churches of the region, often for his personal use. Worse, he had imposed heavy taxes on many of the richer inhabitants of the area, partly to finance a more effective defense against Scottish raids but mainly to enrich himself. And in 1063, after luring two popular landowners, Ulf and Gamel, to his residence in York under safe-conducts, his house servants executed them without any pretense of a trial. By the summer of 1065 the area was seething with discontent, and shortly after Tostig journeyed south to visit the King at Britford, near Salisbury, a plot to overthrow him gathered strength quickly. Some 200 thegns met in small groups before converging with their retinues on York, which they occupied during the last week of September. During the next few days they plundered Tostig's treasury while beheading several of his servants and household officials. Then, after declaring their determination not to submit to his rule ever again, they proclaimed him an outlaw.

Next the rebels elected Morcar, the younger brother of Earl Edwin of Mercia, to be their new leader, although he was only seventeen at the time. The rebel leaders had probably been in contact with the two brothers all along because Morcar appeared on the scene at once and proclaimed his willingness to assume the reins of government.

Because Tostig was a great favorite of the King as well a younger brother of Harold Godwine, the northern rebels knew they would have to compel the national government to accede to their demands. With Morcar at their head they set out for the south, attracting hundreds of reinforcements along the way and killing several of Tostig's followers at Lincoln, which they plundered without restraint. On crossing the border into Mercia they were joined by Edwin and a small army, who included several hundred Welsh auxiliaries. Within another week they arrived in Northampton and harried the local people before taking the road to Oxford.

Meanwhile at Britford, the government had learned of these troublesome developments. Harold, Tostig, Archbishop Stigand, and several other councillors met with the King on 28 October and debated what to do to resolve the crisis. Harsh words were spoken, and Tostig was criticized for provoking the uprising. He defended himself energetically and blamed Harold for his plight, claiming his older brother secretly planned his overthrow. After Harold's heated rejoinder Edward the Confessor insisted that there were more pressing matters to consider than the apportionment of blame. Then he suggested that the fyrd of Wessex be called out to confront the rebels. But it soon became apparent that the thegns of southern England had no interest in restoring Tostig to his position in the north, so the government had no option but to negotiate with the rebels. On 1 November the Confessor reluctantly agreed to the northerners' demands and recognized Morcar as the rightful Earl of Northumbria. He also directed Tostig and his wife to abjure the realm and spend the remainder of their lives abroad.

Furious at this turn of affairs, Tostig was determined to recover his earldom and gain vengeance on those who had plotted his overthrow. Unwilling to admit his own mistakes, he concentrated his fury on Harold, who had refused to lift a finger to help him. Tostig concluded that Harold was a Judas who must be overthrown and severely punished.[34] During the next year Tostig went to extreme lengths to achieve his goal but wound up destroying himself, as we shall see.

On leaving England Tostig travelled to Scotland, hoping its King, Malcolm Canmore, would assist him. Although the Scottish ruler was friendly and considered Tostig a useful pawn in future quarrels with the English crown, he gave Tostig no assurances of support. Tostig therefore decided to test his luck elsewhere and sailed across the North Sea to Flanders, where he spent the winter of 1065-1066 at the court of his brother-in-law, Baldwin V. Clever and cautious, Count Baldwin was unimpressed by Tostig's windy schemes. Yet Tostig was now a bitter enemy of his brother, Harold, the greatest foe of Baldwin's son-law, the Duke of Normandy. Because Tostig might prove a useful instrument against Harold at a critical moment, Baldwin made no move to expel him from his dominions. Rather he allowed Tostig to remain in Flanders as long as he liked and did nothing to keep him from seeking help from other rulers.

During the early months of 1066, Tostig sent emissaries to the courts of Sweyn Estrithson of Denmark and Harold Hardraada of Norway. Both Kings were distantly related to the Viking dynasty that had ruled England between 1016 and 1042; and because England's current ruler, Edward the Confessor, was a half-brother of King Hathacnut (1040-1042), both Scandinavian monarchs were indirectly related to him also. As a consequence Tostig hoped one of them would conclude a pact with him. On his part, Tostig was prepared to help either monarch seize the English throne after the Confessor's death in return for his restoration to the earldom of Northumbria and possible employment as an adviser to the crown. Sweyn Estrithson dismissed Tostig's quixotic proposal out of hand, but Harold Hardraada was a bolder and more impulsive man and accepted it without hesitation.

The greatest Viking general of the age, Harold Hardraada stood 6' 6" tall, some 8" taller than either Harold Godwine or William of Normandy, and he possessed exceptional strength even at the advanced age of fifty. Before inheriting the Norwegian throne in 1047, he had travelled to the east and served for a time as captain of the Varangian

Guards at Constantinople. Back in Norway, life probably seemed dull after the sophisticated pleasures of the Byzantine capital, and by the winter of 1065-1066 he was ready for another foreign adventure. Moreover, his father, Magnus the Good, had signed a treaty in 1038 with Harthacnut, two years before the latter's accession to the English throne. By that treaty, Magnus and Harthacnut had promised to support one another during future crises; and if the signer who died first had no direct heir, the one who survived would be the legal and political heir of the deceased. Thus, on Harthacnut's death in 1042, King Magnus could easily have opposed the Confessor's claim to the English throne, albeit with little chance of success because of his total lack of English blood. Although he did not do so, Magnus never renounced the treaty of 1038; and twenty-seven years later his energetic son, Harold Hardraada, was in a good position to contend that the Edward the Confessor had been a usurper all along. At the very least, Harold Hardraada was well placed to claim that he should be regarded as the Confessor's rightful heir, as Tostig urged him to do. In that way the basis was laid for a pact that led to a Viking assault on England during the summer of 1066, shortly before Duke William sailed across the Channel with an army and made his bid for power.

While Tostig was concluding his agreement with Harold Hardraada, the death that had been anticipated for so many years finally occurred. It is sometimes held that the Confessor's death was hastened by the overthrow of Tostig, for whom the King felt genuine affection, and the Witan's refusal to restore Tostig to his earldom by military force. There seems to be some truth to that view because, shortly after commanding Tostig to leave the realm, the Confessor's health declined steadily. In fact he was so ill during the next seven weeks that he kept to his bedchamber until Christmas Day, which he and his courtiers celebrated at Westminster and not as usual at Gloucester. Three days later Edward was too ill to attend the dedication of the recently rebuilt church of Westminster Abbey, his most cherished project since 1058. By that juncture the King may have lapsed into the coma that preceded his death on 5 January 1066.

During his last few hours Edward was attended by his wife Edith, his brother-in-law Harold, Archbishop Stigand, and several other members of the Godwine faction. Once Edward breathed his last, they declared that he had spoken several words shortly before dying. After consoling his wife the Confessor allegedly took Harold's hand in his and said, "I commend this woman and all the kingdom to your protection." He also gave detailed instructions for his funeral and asked Harold to find offices for any Normans who wished to remain in England.

Within minutes of the King's death, the Godwine faction proclaimed that Edward's last words meant that Harold was his intended successor on the throne. Of course it is far from clear that Edward actually spoke the words attributed to him by individuals with such a strong interest in promoting that particular point of view. It is also possible that the Godwines whispered into the dying ruler's ear and, in order to get some needed rest, he uttered the words they longed to hear. Whatever the case, death-bed speeches were taken with great seriousness during that era; and once the Godwines announced that Edward had expressed a last-minute change of heart about the succession, many people assumed that Harold was indeed the late ruler's preferred heir. Moreover, because of the dedication of Westminster Abbey only a week before, many of England's magnates were still in the capital. Thus it was an easy matter for Harold to hold an emergency meeting of the Witan within several hours of the Confessor's death.

During the course of that meeting a clamor for Harold to take the throne developed owing to the youthful age of Edgar the Aetheling, who was too inexperienced to lead England's forces should William invade in the near future. Archbishop Stigand probably spoke out in favor of Harold's accession, while no one seems to have upheld William's claim. The prospect of Harold Hardraada as England's next ruler, if actually mentioned at the time, was undoubtedly rejected out of hand. Thus, given the circumstances, the only viable option was to entrust the throne to Harold and hope for the best. In defense of the Witan's actions, Harold had been the kingdom's real ruler during the last thirteen years and had done a fine job.[35] Moreover, it now seemed likely that he was the Confessor's intended heir as well; and like Parliament in later centuries, the Witan never considered itself bound by decisions reached on earlier occasions. During the afternoon of 6 January, once the Confessor's body was laid to rest in the Abbey, Harold was crowned by the Archbishop of York during a hasty ceremony in the same church.

Shortly after ascending the throne Harold learned about Tostig's intrigues and his military alliance with Harold Hardraada. If a Norwegian attack on the eastern coast began about the same time William's troops landed on the southern shore, Harold's government would be forced to fight a two-front war. In that event it would be essential to have active support from the two northern Earls, Edwin and Morcar. Harold's chances of survival would be slight at best if they rallied to Tostig and Harold Hardraada or simply remained neutral. Therefore, during the early months of 1066, Harold travelled to York and met in private with Edwin and Morcar, who were young enough to be his sons. To obtain the support he needed so much, he agreed to marry their sister Ealdgyth, the widow of Gruffydd of North Wales. But in order to marry Ealdgyth, Harold had to divorce his "Danish" or common-law wife of many years, Edith Swansneck, who had borne him several children. Although an extremely painful step for him, apparently, the circumstances compelled him to take it.

Fortunately for Harold, Edwin and Morcar now considered themselves bound to his cause. Morcar in particular was eager to support Harold because of his determination to retain the earldom of Northumbria, which Tostig would doubtless recover should Harold Hardraada's cause be victorious. As a consequence when Norwegian forces landed on English soil, the two brothers made a valiant effort to defeat them.

After marrying Ealdgyth in the spring of 1066, Harold put England's military and naval forces on alert and waited for whatever might come. Optimistic and somewhat impulsive by nature, Harold was confident that he would prevail over his enemies in the end.

Meanwhile across the Channel in Normandy, William condemned Harold as both a perjurer and a usurper before assembling an army of approximately 7,000 men. Because of his reputation as a great commander--he had never lost a battle--and because he offered lands and other lucrative rewards to those who fought on his behalf, William had no trouble attracting recruits. Men from Brittany, Maine, Anjou, Flanders, Poitou, and of course upper and lower Normandy flocked to his banner; and so too did hundreds of adventurers from southern Italy, where men of Norman birth had gone fifty years before to oust the Saracens. William even secured pledges of help, but no actual assistance, from the Emperor Henry IV and King Sweyn Estrithson of Denmark, who probably considered him a useful counterweight against the aggressive designs of Harold Hardraada.

While completing his army's mobilization, William sent envoys to Rome to seek the Papacy's endorsement. Alexander II and his great adviser, Cardinal Hildebrand, the future Pope Gregory VII, were delighted with the chance to assist him. During earlier years the Papacy had called for reforms to eliminate the worst abuses in the Church, such as pluralism, absenteeism, and simony; and since 1059 William had actively supported the reform movement in his duchy. In that year he and his wife Matilda founded two convents, one for men and one for women, at Caen in lower Normandy. They had also granted offices to several foreign clerics, such as the great Lanfranc of Pavia, and by the mid 1060s the Norman church was stronger than ever. Unfortunately, deplorable conditions still prevailed across the Channel in England, where the average cleric was reputedly so ignorant he could barely read and write. The English laity venerated so many local saints that the Papacy refused to recognize them all; and worst of all, clerical marriage was far more prevalent in England than in most European countries. Finally, there was the serious problem posed by Stigand, who had been Archbishop of Canterbury since 1052 and a flagrant pluralist, who was still living with his wife and was widely rumored to have sold bishoprics and abbacies to the highest bidder. If only to secure Stigand's ouster, the Papacy felt compelled to support the Norman cause because William was a far more devoted son of the Church than England had produced in generations.[36] Without a moment's hesitation Cardinal Hildebrand gave his blessing to the enterprise, and within a week Pope Alexander II followed his lead. By sending William a papal banner he could display with his own flag, Alexander converted the campaign into something of a religious crusade.

While William was negotiating with the Papacy, Tostig and his troops appeared off the coast of southern England, which they plundered at will. At that juncture Tostig commanded a small fleet provided by Baldwin V of Flanders, who hoped to soften England up for a Norman landing that same year. After Tostig's troops occupied the Isle of Wight and seized money and provisions there, they sailed away and ravaged the coast around Sandwich, where they pressed additional men and ships into their service. But they soon learned that Harold was approaching with an army from the north, so they sailed away and soon dropped anchor near the mouth of the River Thames, where they were joined by Copsi, Tostig's most trusted associate during his decade as Earl of Northumbria. Copsi sailed down from the Orkney Islands, then a Norwegian outpost, with seventeen ships supplied by Harold Hardraada. Once the two squadrons merged into a combined fleet of some sixty vessels, Tostig and his confederates sailed up the eastern coast and pillaged Norfolk before entering the Humber estuary and going ashore during the first week of May. But shortly after they landed, an army led by Edwin of Mercia arrived and inflicted a stinging defeat on them. Half the invaders scattered in panic, while Tostig and the others rushed back to their ships and sailed away. Along the coast of Yorkshire they were held in check by Earl Morcar's troops. Ultimately Tostig's fleet, reduced to little more than a dozen vessels, reached the Firth of Forth, where Malcolm Canmore allowed them to anchor and await the arrival of reinforcements from Norway.[37]

Because of Tostig's return to Scotland, Harold must have felt genuine relief at his headquarters in Sussex. Perhaps Harold Hardraada would abandon his wayward brother, whose potential for mischief-making would then decline and probably disappear for good. Thus, the greatest need was to remain on guard in the south and prevent a Norman landing. Accordingly Harold kept his forces in Sussex and Kent on alert all that summer. However, by early September Harold's treasury was almost depleted while his men were running out of provisions. Moreover, his troops were anxious to return to their homes in order to bring in the harvest and prepare for the winter months ahead. Therefore on the 8th of September, Harold issued the order to demobilize, assuming that the end of the campaigning season almost was at hand and he was safe until the following spring.

Only ten days later Harold learned that Harold Hardraada had sailed across the North Sea and landed with approximately 10,000 men at the mouth of the River Tyne. To make matters worse, Tostig had left Scotland and joined the Norwegians there. At Tostig's suggestion they sailed down to the mouth of the Humber, a broader river than the Tyne and one with a navigable tributary, the Ouse, that the shallow boats of the period could use almost as far as York. By Tuesday, the 19th of September, the invaders had moved up the Ouse and disembarked at Riccall, ten miles southeast of Tostig's former capital.

The next day Edwin and Morcar arrived with the fyrd of northern England. That afternoon a great battle occurred at Fulford Gate, a short distance from York. It was a long and bitter struggle with heavy losses on both sides. However, the English casualties were greater than the Norwegians', and at the end of the day Edwin and Morcar withdrew, leaving the attackers in possession of the field.[38] Technically, therefore, the battle was a victory for the invaders, who were in a position to enter and plunder York. But because of Tostig's invaluable help and his hope of reestablishing his power in northern England, Harold Hardraada agreed to spare the city. Thereupon he moved his troops to Stamford Bridge, several miles east of York, and encamped along the banks of the Derwent River, near the ancient road that linked York with the eastern coast.

A day or two before the battle of Fulford Gate, Harold Godwine mobilized an army of 2,000 men and started northward to assist Edwin and Morcar. Within five days he and his troops covered the distance to England's northern capital, some 190 miles, and along the way they were joined by additional men who rode in from such scattered locales as Essex and Worcestershire. On Sunday the 24th they arrived at Tadcaster, several miles southwest of York. Early the next morning they swept through the city and arrived at Stamford Bridge so quickly that they enjoyed complete tactical surprise and almost won the encounter during their initial charge. But Harold Hardraada rallied his men and formed a compact square behind an almost impenetrable shield wall. He also sent a courier to Riccall, where a thousand men were standing guard over his moored ships. The Norwegian ruler hoped those men would arrive in time to turn the tide and win the battle for his side. But Harold Godwine used his archers so effectively, and his troops fought with such determination, that the invaders had no real chance.[39] By the late afternoon Harold Hardraada and Tostig were both dead and Viking resistance had collapsed altogether, giving the English a decisive victory. However, Harold Godwine lost many of his best troops, who would be difficult to replace that autumn. The Norwegian survivors, whom Harold permitted to sail away in peace, required only 24 of the 300 ships that had transported them across the North Sea.

Ironically, at almost the same moment the surviving Norwegians evacuated northern England, William and his troops landed on the coast of Sussex, some 250 miles to the south. From his flagship, the *Mora*, William went ashore about 9:00 o'clock on the morning of 28 September. Although Harold had managed to avoid a two-front war, he now had to face a far more capable and determined adversary on the soil of his own native county.

Luckily for Harold, William's voyage across the Channel had been delayed for six weeks by contrary winds. Assembled along the banks of the River Dives in western Normandy, William's fleet was ready to embark by 12 August, but for a month the winds blew steadily from the north and kept it bottled up in Norman waters. During that period William's patience must have grown thin, and he probably wondered how long he could retain control of his rowdy troops without action of some sort. Furthermore, because of the primitive sanitation facilities of the period, dysentery might infect his camp at any time, and during that era dysentery claimed more soldiers' lives than battle itself. As a consequence, William heaved a sigh of relief on 12 September, when the winds shifted to the west and it became possible to move the fleet from the Dives estuary to the mouth of the Somme, where he established a new camp at Saint-Valery, a much more sanitary camp. In addition the new camp offered the prospect of a shorter and quicker voyage across the Channel whenever the winds shifted again and allowed him to embark.

The winds finally shifted to the south during the afternoon of Wednesday the 27th of September. Shortly after supper that evening William gave the order to board ship, and because it would be a night crossing he directed each vessel to attach a lantern to its mast. About midnight he himself sailed out into the Channel on the *Mora* (i.e, Delay), which had been a gift from his wife Matilda, whom he left in charge of Norman affairs with help from two capable associates, Roger of Montgomery and Roger of Beaumont. Fortunately for William, it was a calm night without high winds or choppy currents. Horses often become violently sick at sea; and had the waters been turbulent, the Normans' journey across the Channel might have ended in disaster. As is was, William's voyage was a flawless operation except for a serious hitch that occurred after several Norman ships became separated from the main body of the fleet and anchored the next morning at Romney, Kent. When the crews of those ships went ashore, they were captured and put to death by the local people to William's fury.

Shortly after disembarking at Pevensey, William moved his troops to Hastings, several miles farther east. Hastings was a better anchorage than Pevensey, so it would be a good place to keep the fleet moored and ready for a quick voyage back to Normandy should that prove necessary. Moreover, the ruins of an ancient Roman fortress at Hastings could be strengthened to provide protection for the invaders, and the town itself was the terminus of the ancient road from the north, down which Harold and his troops were likely to advance in another week or two.

Because time was on the defenders' side--the Norman army would probably begin to dissolve after a month of inaction in England--William hoped to confront Harold in battle as soon as possible. To compel Harold to come south at once, William destroyed over twenty villages and harried the population of the surrounding countryside, hoping that a campaign of local terror would infuriate the English leader and cause him to appear much sooner than he would otherwise choose to do.

As for Harold, he was still in York on 1 October, when he learned of William's arrival in southern England. That the Normans had landed in his own county and were brutalizing his own people prompted the furious Harold to go and overwhelm them at once. Because the Norman army was considerably smaller than Harold Hardraada's host had been, and slightly less fearsome as a result, it seemed foolish to postpone another battle. Moreover, on the way south Harold would probably receive significant support from his brothers Gyrth and Leofwine, so he was likely to have a numerical advantage in the south. With what remained of the army he had led north only two weeks earlier, Harold set out on the morning of 2 October; and by covering almost forty miles a day, he and his men reached London by nightfall on the 6th. There Harold waited almost a week for the fyrd of southern England to arrive. By the morning of the 12th enough men had ridden in for him to leave the capital for Hastings, fifty-seven miles to the south, where he intended to clear the kingdom of foreign troops once and for all.

By dusk on the 13th Harold and his 8,500 men had reached the top of Senlac Hill, several miles north of Hastings. There they bedded down for the night, thinking they would mount their horses early the next morning and ride to the Norman camp. Exploiting the element of surprise again, they would destroy William's army just as they had annihilated the Norwegian horde at Stamford Bridge.

If that was their strategy, Harold and his men were unable to put it into effect. During the evening of October 13th, William's scouts reported that the English had arrived from the north and were now encamped at the crest of Senlac Hill. Two hours before dawn on the 14th, while the English were still asleep, William led his army out of Hastings to the knoll known as Telham Hill, which was only a few hundred yards south of the English position. When the English awoke with a start, they found the Normans almost upon them and about to launch a massive attack. With too little time to mount their horses, which were tethered several hundred yards to the rear, Harold and his men had no choice but to don their battle armor and form a tight shield wall similar to the Norwegian one at Stamford Bridge. Thus on 14 October, William turned the tables on Harold and compelled him to wage a defensive battle against his will. Moreover, on that day Harold had only a fraction of the archers he had commanded so effectively in the north, while William had considerably more horsemen than the English had used at Stamford Bridge. All those factors gave the Normans a clear advantage that William exploited brilliantly.

Yet when the first Norman charge began about 9:00 A.M. it was far from clear that the battle would end in a decisive Norman victory. The English troops fought bravely and with great valor; and as the day wore on hundreds of reinforcements arrived to take the place of those who fell. Moreover, William's task was unusually hard because he needed to win an overwhelming victory while capturing or killing Harold Godwine; otherwise the English leader would withdraw at the end of the day and rebuild his forces before returning to the scene under more favorable conditions. It was thus a do-or-die situation for William, whereas his enemies could survive a draw or a minor setback. Luckily for the Normans, their Duke had the ability, the vision, and the experience to be able to win the major victory his cause needed so badly.

During the course of the battle, which lasted until dusk, William demonstrated a willingness to improvise and change tactics as circumstances demanded, whereas Harold and his men stuck doggedly to a strategy they never altered. Probably the English expected their enemies to weaken themselves with repeated charges up Senlac Hill toward their shield wall. Then, as Norman strength ebbed away, the English would break ranks and destroy their opponents while pursuing them headlong down the hill during the final retreat. It was a reasonable strategy, but Harold had too little control over his men to implement it successfully.

After a shower of Norman arrows about 9:00 A.M., the Norman infantry moved up the hill to the English line but failed to penetrate the shield wall there. A period of vigorous but inconclusive combat with swords and poleaxes followed, and then the Normans retreated back down the hill while being pelted with sticks, stones, spears, and similar objects from above. Within minutes the Norman infantry's place on the slopes was taken by several hundred horsemen. But the Norman cavalry also failed to breach the English shield wall and ultimately returned to the base of the hill in considerable confusion. At that point the left wing of the English army broke ranks on its own initiative and pursued the retreating troops, which enabled William to lead a counter charge and inflict heavy losses on Englishmen who were no longer protected by the shield wall at the crest of the hill.

During the early afternoon the Norman cavalry advanced twice more, only to be repulsed each time by the English, who fought with great determination. But on both occasions a portion of the English army pursued its opponents back down the hill, only to be overwhelmed by Norman units at the bottom. As a consequence, by mid afternoon the English casualties were far greater than William's, although the decisive victory the latter desperately needed still eluded him. William could not allow the battle to end with the English still holding the crest of the hill and with Harold and enough of his men alive to make an orderly retreat before regrouping for another battle several days later. William therefore decided to make one last effort to destroy the shield wall that was still intact at the hill's summit. To that end he ordered his archers to launch a stream of arrows at an unusually steep angle, hoping they would descend a few feet behind the shield wall and inflict heavy damage. That tactic broke the impasse because Harold was hit in the face at that juncture and fell to the ground in agony. Because Harold's brothers, Gyrth and Leofwine, were already dead or mortally wounded, English morale collapsed altogether; and when the Normans charged up the hill for the fourth and last time, the English shield wall broke completely apart. The English position was overrun within a few minutes; and although several of Harold's élite guards closed around him and fought manfully to save his life, the Normans discovered where he was lying and hacked his prostrate body to pieces.

With their main leaders dead, the surviving English troops fled in panic toward the north while a cavalry unit led by Eustace of Boulogne rode in hot pursuit. At a deep ravine known as the Malfosse, a second and much briefer encounter occurred, as the English who had sought to hide there were attacked by the Normans. Briefly Eustace and his men were thrown back, but William arrived on the scene and ordered them to fight with greater determination. Within half an hour this second battle ended in the same manner as the first--with almost all the English troops killed or captured and the Normans completely victorious.[40]

William devoted the next day to the burial of the dead and on Monday, the 16th of October he and his men returned to Hastings. Doubtless he hoped that England's surviving leaders would appear at his camp within several days and accept him as their rightful King. After all, God had clearly favored his cause and it was obvious now that he was the true heir of Edward the Confessor. But Harold Godwine's sons by Edith Swansneck had already disappeared into the West Country, hoping to raise more troops with which to continue the conflict, while Edwin and Morcar were about to enter London from the north with an army of unknown size. Because the Londoners had a reputation for great ferocity, William could not afford to march north and enter the capital at once. In fact, William had no way of knowing how many Englishmen were willing to accept him, and under the circumstances it would be hazardous to venture into the kingdom's interior, thereby lengthening his lines to a dangerous extent. Yet he could not afford to remain in the vicinity of Hastings, where food supplies were almost exhausted and the sanitation facilities no longer usable. Moreover, his troops needed to remain active in order to keep from quarrelling among themselves.

Therefore, on Friday the 20th, after posting a small regiment in the ancient fortress his troops had rebuilt, William marched out of Hastings with most of his men toward the east. After crossing the border into Kent, they arrived at Romney, where they punished the local people for killing the Norman troops that had landed there on 28 September. From Romney the Normans continued on to Folkestone, where they constructed another castle, and thence to the stone fortress at Dover that Harold Godwine had erected in 1065. Once that castle surrendered without a fight, William's connections with Normandy were strengthened and his position in southeastern England firmly established. Yet about that time several hundred Normans became seriously ill. After a week in Dover William left the sick to recuperate while he and his healthy troops pushed on to Canterbury, which opened its gates without a fight. Nevertheless, the ancient cathedral was set on fire and all its muniments destroyed. While still at Canterbury William himself fell ill and had to remain in his bedchamber for several weeks.

Meanwhile Edwin and Morcar, both Archbishops, and several other magnates met in London and recognized Edgar the Aetheling as England's rightful King. Despite his youthful age Edgar was the only candidate with any chance of rallying enough support to prevail against the Normans. But Edgar's backers knew his cause had little chance of success and left the door open for a later accommodation with William should that prove necessary.

The wisdom of hedging their bets became apparent once Winchester admitted a Norman garrison. Still living quietly in that ancient city was Edith, the widow of Edward the Confessor and a surviving sister of Harold Godwine. Edith's opinions still commanded respect, and during a well-publicized ceremony she swore fealty to William as England's legitimate ruler.

By the end of November William was well enough to resume his efforts to gain popular acceptance. From Canterbury he moved toward the northwest, hoping to cross the River Thames at Southwark and enter the capital without opposition. But at Southwark he found London Bridge held against him by several hundred heavily armed citizens. Because he was unwilling to risk his troops in another pitched battle, he vented his anger by setting fire to Southwark before marching further west, where he hoped to find another bridge or a shallow place where he and his army could ford the river on foot. Then they could double back and take the city from the west without heavy losses.

While marching through Surrey and Berkshire, William's men lived off the land and inflicted such heavy damage on villages and fields that it was still visible at the time of the Domesday Survey of 1085-1086. On reaching Wallingford the Duke agreed to meet with Archbishop Stigand, who had concluded that Edgar the Aetheling's cause was hopeless and was therefore willing to swear homage to William. After the Normans forded the Thames and arrived at Berkhamstead in western Hertfordshire, a large number of magnates rode in and followed suit. These included Edgar the Aetheling himself, the Archbishop of York, the Bishops of Hereford and Worcester, and a delegation of London merchants, all of whom urged William to take the throne at once. He assented, although he postponed his entry into the capital until a small castle was built within its walls to shelter him and his élite guards.

By 21 December, when William finally rode into London, preparations for his coronation were underway. That lavish ceremony took place in the Abbey on Christmas Day and was an elaborate occasion, greatly eclipsing Harold's hasty investiture the previous January. Once again the anointing was performed by Archbishop Ealdred of York, who was assisted by the Norman prelate Geoffrey of Coutances. Archbishop Stigand was relegated to the sidelines once again, as he and most observers doubtless expected.

Several days after the coronation William began a progress through East Anglia, hoping to build popular support there. He was also anxious to inspect the region's defenses because he feared a Norwegian attack under its new ruler, King Olaf, Harold Hardraada's son. At Colchester, Norwich, and other towns near the coast, William built additional castles and stationed large garrisons. While in East Anglia he accepted submissions from several leading thegns, who included Thorkill of Arden, in Warwickshire, and Eadric the Wild, who enjoyed great power along the Anglo-Welsh border. It was at that point, apparently, that the two northern Earls, Edwin and Morcar, finally rode in and swore allegiance to the Conqueror. Nevertheless, William had serious doubts about their loyalty and replaced Morcar as Earl of Northumbria with Tostig's old associate Copsi. Copsi had appeared before him at Barking and made such a favorable impression that William authorized him to rule the far north in his name. However, when Copsi was assassinated during the autumn of 1067, probably by Morcar's retainers, William felt compelled to reappoint Morcar to his old position.

For several months after the battle of Hastings, William sought to rule England with help from cooperative Englishmen. Because the Norman element in England never exceeded 25,000 out of a total population of 1,500,000 or more, William had no recourse but to use hundreds of Anglo-Saxons for governmental purposes, especially at the local level. Moreover, it should always be remembered that he hoped to maintain continuity with the past and always claimed that he was England's rightful King by virtue of hereditary right and not by military conquest alone. As a result he intended to make few if any changes in the country's political and social institutions; and he assumed that, by using dependable Anglo-Saxons in important administrative positions, general acceptance of his regime would follow quickly.

His hopes in that regard proved illusory. When in March 1067 he sailed back to Normandy for a long visit and some badly needed rest, dissatisfaction with the three regents he left behind burst into the open within days.[41] By the time William returned to England ten months later, his continued hold over the realm was precarious, and for the next few years he fought tenaciously to retain and strengthen his power. Even more than in 1066, when he won his most famous victory, his actual conquest of England took place between 1068 and 1071, when he waged one successful campaign after another and defeated the Anglo-Saxons once and for all.

In a short account like this, it is unnecessary to trace William's maneuvers during those bitter years. Suffice it to say that after suppressing a dangerous rebellion in the West Country, where he captured Exeter in 1068 and built a castle within its walls, he was primarily concerned about the loyalty of the north. Indeed, he led armies into Yorkshire on three different occasions in 1068 and 1069. After his third and final trip to York, where he spent the Christmas season of 1069, he adopted a scorched-earth policy and burned countless houses and fields while killing thousands of cattle, sheep, and oxen. By that policy, which destroyed the region's ability to cause him further problems, he created a devastating situation for the local people, whose suffering led his memory to be reviled for centuries. For example, only a generation after his death Ordericus Vitalis, who otherwise regarded him as a great man, maintained that by February of 1070 Norman camps

> ... were scattered over a surface of one hundred miles; numbers of the insurgents fell beneath his vengeful sword, he levelled their places of shelter to the ground, wasted their lands, and burnt their dwellings with all they contained. Never did William commit so much cruelty; to his lasting disgrace, he yielded to his worst impulse, and set no bounds to his fury, condemning the innocent and the guilty to a common fate. In the fullness of his wrath he ordered the corn and cattle, with the implements of husbandry and every sort of provisions, to be collected in heaps and set on fire till the whole was consumed, and thus destroyed at once all that could serve for the support of life in the whole country lying beyond the Humber. There followed, consequently, so great a scarcity ... in the ensuing years ... that, in a Christian nation, more than a hundred thousand souls, of both sexes and all ages, perished of want.[42]

The misery that resulted from William's harsh northern policy must have weighed heavily on his mind. As he lay dying in 1087, he allegedly said:

> "I persecuted the native inhabitants of England beyond all reason. Whether nobles or commons, I cruelly oppressed them; many I unjustly disinherited; innumerable multitudes, especially in the county of York, perished through me by famine and sword .... I am stained with the rivers of blood that I have shed."[43]

Despite William's own remorse, modern historians consider him a merciful ruler, at least by the standards of his era. Henry R. Loyn, for example, notes that he executed only one English magnate, Waltheof Earl of Northumbria, between 1071 and 1076.[44] Waltheof was a leader of the last rebellion against William, the so-called Earls' Revolt of 1075-1076. Because of the Conqueror's exceptional generosity to him after Hastings, William therefore had every right to be furious at Waltheof's treachery, and during the spring of 1076 he refused to intercede and spare his life.[45]

Like Mr. Loyn, Professor Douglas maintains that even if William's rule was harsh and cruel, it "was never blindly tyrannical." Douglas concedes that while William was brutal on many occasions, he was not "simply a self-regarding tyrant ... nor was he regarded as such by those he ruled."[46] A harsher view of William's character has been advanced by Professor Barlow, who contends that the Conqueror "had some evil passions, and his lust for power, his ferocity, and his avarice were hardly subdued by religion .... When he was opposed or unheeded his anger knew no bounds."[47] Of course it is also true that William's ferocious temper, which was widely known, caused most of his subjects to refrain from dangerous plotting that had almost no chance of success.

In regard to Professor Barlow's charge of avarice, that unpleasant character trait was almost universal among the era's successful rulers. Long before modern times, Europe's monarchs knew that, in order to be strong, they had to be rich. Occasional Kings, whether through laziness, stupidity or both, failed to supervise their financial agents and allowed their revenues to fall into disorder. Edward the Confessor had been that sort of ruler; and during his last decade on the throne, the total revenues of the English crown had been only £5,000 a year, or approximately fifteen per cent *less* than the annual income of Harold Godwine and his three brothers Tostig, Gyrth, and Leofwine.[48] Whenever the royal revenues fell substantially below the combined incomes of the country's two richest noblemen, especially if the latter were related and willing to work closely together, the monarch was confronted by a potentially dangerous situation.

William the Conqueror understood the relationship between political and financial power far better than Edward the Confessor, and during the years after Hastings the royal revenues increased dramatically. By 1087, when William died, the crown possessed a landed estate worth between £14,000 and £17,650 a year, or approximately three times what the Confessor had enjoyed each year.[49] That dramatic increase of the royal revenues made possible the emergence of what one historian has termed "a strong, purposeful monarchy" for the first time in almost a century;[50] and it was accomplished primarily through a steady enlargement of the royal demesne with estates confiscated from the heirs of those who died while opposing William and his followers. For example, the lands of Harold Godwine and his brothers Gyrth and Leofwine were added to the royal demesne within a month of Hastings; and during later years so were the estates of the three Earls--Waltheof, Roger, and Ralph--who participated in the baronial revolt of 1075-1076. Because lesser men also engaged in conspiracy from time to time and forfeited large tracts as a consequence, the crown owned between fifteen and twenty per cent of all the land in the kingdom by the 1080s.

While expanding the crown lands so rapidly, William was conferring valuable estates on important subjects who had helped him capture the throne. Undoubtedly the individual who gained the greatest rewards was his half-brother Odo, Bishop of Bayeux, who had supplied a hundred ships for the invasion force of 1066. Within a few years of Hastings, Odo was named Earl of Kent and granted lands in seventeen counties with a combined worth of almost £3,250 a year.[51] After Odo, the greatest recipient of English estates was probably Roger of Montgomery, who provided sixty ships for the invasion flotilla but remained in Normandy to help Matilda supervise political affairs during the Duke's absence. The English lands granted to Roger, who soon became Earl of Shropshire, were scattered over twelve counties and had a collective worth of almost £2,100 annually.[52]

It would be tedious to list all the other beneficiaries of William's largesse. Suffice it to say that by the mid 1080s there were some 200 major landholders in the realm, all but two of whom were of foreign birth and twenty-nine of whom collectively held "almost half the territorial wealth of England."[53] By that juncture the distribution of land had been completely transformed. On the eve of the Conquest, the ownership of land had been widely dispersed, some 2,000 families controlling almost all of the kingdom's arable land with the exception of the estates owned by the crown and the Church. During the Conqueror's reign the land-owning class not only shrank by ninety per cent in terms of numbers, but it also became a group of men who were almost exclusively of foreign extraction. At the time of the Domesday survey of 1085-1086, the only native Englishmen who retained estates of sufficient value to qualify as true members of the landed aristocracy were Thorkill of Arden and Coleswain of Lincoln, neither of whom controlled lands worth over £125 per year.[54]

The English aristocracy was also transformed after Hastings by being linked to the King in a closer and more intimate way. During the century before the Conquest, the greatest English landowners had been only loosely bound to the crown because they were believed to own their estates outright. Although they had paid occasional taxes on their lands, there was little else they had to do to retain them. But during the Conqueror's reign, all of that changed at a stroke. William preached the novel theory that the estates he conveyed to his followers still belonged to him and his successors on the throne. His subjects could use all the lands they received from him for their own purposes provided they fulfilled whatever conditions he established at the time he bestowed one or more manors on them. In most cases, those conditions included almost all of the following: (1) service in his armed forces, along with a specified number of armed tenants from their lands, for up to forty days each year without recompense;[55] (2) performance of guard duty in a royal fortress as circumstances required; (3) attendance and the provision of full and accurate information about local conditions whenever the royal council, or Curia Regis, met in formal, deliberative session; (4) enforcement of the law and periodic royal edicts in their localities; (5) payment of a substantial relief, or primitive inheritance tax, whenever a new tenant-in-chief sought possession of the estates his late father or another deceased relative had held from the crown; and (6) payment of financial levies that the King and the Curia Regis agreed were necessary to meet emergency situations.[56] Because William imposed such specific obligations on the holders of virtually all estates within the realm, it is generally held that he was responsible for the establishment of feudalism in England.

Political necessity explains William's establishment of feudalism in his new realm. A practical and pragmatic man, William knew that he and his followers were hated by most of the English people. Indeed, there were so many assassination plots against him and his supporters that his first response was to establish a new "murder fine" for which there was no English precedent. By that "murder fine" all the inhabitants of a district would be held responsible and fined a large sum if any Normans in their midst were killed and the local authorities failed to punish the culprits severely. In essence, William realized that he and his lieutenants must maintain a united front; otherwise they would probably be picked off and killed separately. It was primarily to strengthen the loose bonds between the crown and its leading subjects that William soon moved well beyond his initial "murder fine" and established feudalism within a decade of Hastings. Thus, it can be said that feudalism served three principal functions. First, it gave the King adequate resources to govern the realm and defend it from foreign attack; second, it provided the crown with full and dependable information about local conditions, thereby promoting effective control over the countryside; and third, it encouraged meaningful cooperation between the new alien aristocracy on the one hand and the central government on the other, on the assumption that they would probably sink or swim together.

By establishing conditional tenures and promoting greater unity between the landed aristocracy and the crown, William introduced the most important element of the feudal order, which had developed on the continent long before it came into being in England. A second basic element of the feudal order--castles--also appeared in England substantially later than on the continent; and in virtually the same way the sudden spread of castles throughout the countryside was a consequence of the Norman Conquest.

As noted earlier, there were only four or five true castles in England on the eve of the Conquest.[57] But as soon as William landed at Pevensey on 28 September 1066, he erected a makeshift castle there; and once he arrived at Hastings, he converted the ruins of its ancient Roman fortress into another castle. During succeeding weeks he built yet another castle at Folkestone and began the construction of Canterbury and Rochester Castles. In addition, just before entering London for his coronation, he began the construction of the great stone fortress that was known as the Tower of London by the time it was completed in 1097. During his final years he built even more castles, including Windsor, Nottingham, and Carisbrooke Castles, although at a slower pace than during the frenzied years 1066-1071. By the time he died in 1087, he had erected twenty-three castles in all.

Considerably more castles were built by his leading followers. On the Sussex coast Roger of Montgomery erected imposing castles at Chichester and Arundel; while his son Roger, who dominated central Lancashire, began the construction of comparable fortresses at Clitheroe and Penwortham. The Conqueror's half-brother Roger, Count of Mortain, is credited with the construction of Montacute Castle in Somerset, Launceston Castle in Cornwall, and Berkhamstead Castle in Hertfordshire. But aside from William himself, the greatest of all castle builders was William Fitz Osbern, who built six castles in all--three in Monmouthshire and one each in Hampshire, Gloucestershire, and Herefordshire.

Most of the castles constructed before 1100 were built in the countryside, but a significant number were erected in urban areas, on sites long occupied by private dwellings. How many houses were pulled down to clear a site for the Tower of London is unknown, but at Gloucester some thirty houses were destroyed to make room for a fortress that would dominate that town and its inhabitants. At Shrewsbury over fifty dwellings were destroyed for the same purpose, while

Norwich and Lincoln lost 113 and 166 houses, respectively. The case of Lincoln is particularly instructive and tells us a great deal about the social and economic harm that resulted from this aspect of the Conquest.

In Lincoln on the eve of the Conquest, there seem to have been 970 houses in all. But after the castle's construction, there were only 804, which suggests that at least a thousand people were displaced out of a total population of around 6,000. Whether all those displaced persons moved away from Lincoln or secured lodging with local relatives, at the cost of serious overcrowding, is unknown. Probably a large proportion packed up and went elsewhere because Lincoln's population dwindled from that juncture and numbered only about 4,500 by 1086.[58]

If the erection of a castle within its walls led Lincoln to enter a period of decline, other towns stagnated after being sacked by William's troops. York, Stafford, and Chester all suffered that fate, and at Chester the resulting decline was especially dramatic. During the early 1060s some 487 houses in Chester were subject to periodic taxation, but by 1086 that number had dropped to 282.[59] These figures suggest that Chester's population fell from 3,019 to 1,748, or by slightly more than forty percent.

Most of England's towns struggled during the last years of the eleventh century, but those within several miles of the southern coast flourished owing to greater trade with the continent. London, Rye, Winchester, and several other southern towns prospered more than ever before from their commercial activities, which indirectly contributed to the stagnation of towns farther north, which became increasingly dependent on their southern competitors. Of course, during almost all periods of English history, the south was the most prosperous part of the kingdom, although that fact should not be exaggerated. In a general way, the economy of the entire country suffered as a consequence of the bitter fighting that occurred between 1066 and 1071, when the Conquest was finally complete.

To make matters worse for the English people, the 198 or so Norman families that dominated the countryside after Hastings seem to have been harsher landlords than their Anglo-Saxon predecessors had been. Of course, William himself was a stronger and more forceful ruler than Edward the Confessor; and after 1066 he demanded much more from his English subjects than previous rulers had required. Moreover, William expected greater taxation and military support from his transplanted Norman subjects in England than he had demanded from them on the opposite side of the Channel. As a result Norman landholders in England often complained about feeling pinched and wrung, and in most cases they found effective ways to pass their new obligations on to their English tenants. Because of this, the standard of living of almost all the surviving Anglo-Saxons declined significantly.[60]

In other ways also, the Conquest amounted to a major setback for the English people. Most of William's followers remembered Normandy with great fondness and used their newly acquired wealth to improve manor houses, castles, and parks on the continent. By that "gold drain," which had an adverse effect on the English economy, they provided much more work for Norman artisans than for their English counterparts. Great clerics from the continent operated in virtually the same way. Odo of Bayeux, and Geoffrey of Coutances were probably the richest of all Anglo-Norman prelates by the 1080s. As previously noted, Odo of Bayeux, William's half-brother, received the earldom of Kent as well as estates worth almost £3,250 a year. As for Geoffrey of Coutances, who held that great bishopric from 1049 until his death in 1093, he also became extraordinarily rich after Hastings, receiving over 275 English manors in all.[61] Both men sent vast sums of money across the Channel to enrich their Norman sees. Indeed, the wealth flowing out of England after 1066 played a major part in the renovation of both Coutances and Bayeux Cathedrals. In addition, valuable objects of all sorts were removed from England's churches and shipped abroad by Geoffrey's men. As Professor Le Patourel has written, Geoffrey exported

> ... a continuous stream of ornaments, vestments, and fittings of all kinds--chalices, crosses, reliquaries, candelabra; chasubles, dalmatics, albs and copes; alter linen and tapestries, bibles, missals, and other essential books; embroideries and orphreys with emeralds and gems from England.[62]

Among English monasteries, Ely and Abingdon Abbeys suffered especially heavy losses of books and manuscripts, but dozens of other religious houses that resisted the Norman take-over were despoiled almost as badly. The Norman convents that profited from this massive plunder marvelled at the quality and quantity of the many valuable artefacts that flowed in their direction.[63]

Whether William was aware of the outright plunder of the English church during the early years of his reign is unclear. Even if he knew about it, he did nothing to stop it, probably because he himself had engaged in similar actions during his first few months in England. In Professor Barlow's words,

> ... William showed his rough side immediately [after his coronation] by robbing the churches, especially the monasteries, of much of their treasure in order to embellish a victory parade through Normandy and reward his own churches for their successful prayers on his behalf.[64]

If the Conquest had a harsh impact on economic and religious conditions, which did not fully recover until the 1120s, it was even more detrimental to the literary and linguistic life of the English people. During the century between the 960s and the 1060s, England could boast the strongest vernacular tradition of any country in Europe. The great epic poem *Beowulf*, which extended to almost 3,200 lines, took final shape about the year 1000, which was only a few years after the appearance of important shorter poems like "Judith" and "The Battle of Maldon." In addition, since at least the time of Alfred the Great (871-899), English had been widely used for original works of history and minor prose works like "Apollonius of Tyre" and the "Blickling Homilies." During the half-century preceding the Conquest, the most important government directives of the period, the famous writs of the Anglo-Saxon Kings, were written in the vernacular as well.

But after the Norman Conquest the importance of the vernacular declined dramatically, although Old English continued to be used by the middle and lower classes. However, the foreign aristocracy that dominated the countryside after Hastings preferred to use its own native language--Norman French--while clerics who arrived from the continent depended chiefly on Latin and made little effort to learn English. As a consequence the vernacular ceased to be used for important purposes after the 1080s. Official charters were now issued almost exclusively in Norman French, and no more writs in the native language seem to have been issued after 1085. As early as 1079 the "D" version of the Anglo-Saxon Chronicle, which had been kept for generations by the monks of York and Worcester, came to an end, while the version that was kept at Canterbury was discontinued in 1118. The last surviving version of the Anglo-Saxon Chronicle, the one compiled at Peterborough Abbey, ended in 1154. In the meantime almost no literary works in the vernacular were produced; and that unhappy state of affairs continued until the latter part of the thirteenth century, when the vernacular began to assert itself again, although its progress was slow and unsure for several more generations.[65]

Just as the use of the native language declined after 1066, so did the status and political rights of women. During the last century of the Anglo-Saxon era, women enjoyed a greater degree of freedom and independence than existed in any other medieval kingdom. Although it is probably wrong to maintain that Anglo-Saxon men and women lived together before Hastings "on terms of rough equality with each other,"[66] it is nevertheless true that Anglo-Saxon women enjoyed greater political and economic rights than their Norman successors. Before 1066 Anglo-Saxon women were allowed to own and manage landed estates, and they occasionally participated in the deliberations of the Witan as near-equals with men. In addition a few exceptional women, such as Emma of Normandy and Edith Godwine, wielded considerable influence over long periods of time.

But with the Norman Conquest the political and economic rights of women declined dramatically. Despite his deep personal devotion to his wife Matilda, by whom he had many children and to whom he was unusually faithful, William the Conqueror believed in the inherent inferiority of women, whose views he saw no reason to seek. He never summoned them to attend the Curia Regis, the successor of the Anglo-Saxon Witan; nor did he permit them to serve as tenants-in-chief of the crown because he was convinced that women were incapable of discharging the military obligations that tenants-in-chief were required to perform from time to time.[67]

Partly because of William's policies, there was an obvious change in the public attitude toward women. Before the Conquest most writers had extolled the wisdom and piety of females, especially nuns. But after Hastings, women were portrayed in literature simply as weaker and less capable than men, and their "delicate nature" was emphasized as never before.[68]

Despite William's disregard for women's abilities, females tended to be somewhat safer from sexual assaults as a result of his attitude toward them. He detested the crime of rape and often had repeat offenders castrated. In addition he imposed heavy fines on men convicted of other sexual offenses against women, and those fines were usually doubled whenever the victim was a nun.[69] In addition William hated the practice of "Danish marriages," by which young men of prominent families, on entering puberty, were allowed he take common-law wives until they were ready to be united with "proper" wives for political or other reasons with the blessing of the Church. Danish marriages were inherently unfair to such women and their children, who could be cast aside with little if any provision for their well-being. Because of his own illegitimate birth, William hated such irregular unions and wanted them abolished. In that attitude he received strong support from the clerical hierarchy; and by the end of his reign Danish marriages had almost vanished from the English scene.

William also hoped to bring an end to slavery, which he also deplored and the Bishops railed against from time to time. Although he abolished slavery on the royal demesne by converting royal slaves into serfs, most of his richer subjects refused to follow his lead. In the Domesday survey of 1085-1086, some 26,000 slaves were enumerated in the counties of southern and western England, especially Worcestershire, Gloucestershire, and Cornwall. Farther north there were no slaves at all in Yorkshire and Lincolnshire, where the institution withered and died somewhat earlier. At the end of William's reign, slaves still comprised almost three per cent of the country's total population, which nevertheless amounted to a steep decline from Edward the Confessor's time, when they are thought to have comprised at least ten percent of all the English people.[70] Largely because of William's positive example, slavery gradually disappeared from the English countryside during the century after his death. When his great-grandson Henry II died in 1189, it was a distant memory in the land.[71]

In helping to abolish slavery, William was influenced by the leading prelates of the era, whose opinions he respected and frequently solicited. He was especially mindful of the views of Bishop Wulfstan of Worcester and Archbishop Lanfranc of Canterbury, who received that great office when Stigand was finally deposed in 1070. Born in northern Italy, Lanfranc studied theology with the great Berengar of Tours before becoming an Abbot in Normandy in 1045. Eighteen years later William transferred him from Bec to his new monastic establishment at Caen, which he and Matilda had founded in 1059. A cultured man of great ability, Lanfranc was arguably the most important Archbishop of Canterbury between Theodore of Tarsus (669-690) and Thomas Cranmer (1533-1556).

Lanfranc's contributions were so numerous they can only be summarized here. First, he reorganized the chapter of his own cathedral, for which he formulated a clear set of rules and procedures, and encouraged the other Bishops to do the same. Second, he promoted higher standards of education and conduct for both the regular and the secular clergy, and during his primacy Cluniac monasticism spread into all parts of the realm with his encouragement.[72] Third, he worked to suppress evils like absenteeism, nepotism, and simony, and made inroads against the continuing practice of clerical marriage. Fourth, he held seven different religious councils for Canterbury province, almost all of which adopted new canons to govern the affairs of the Church, which were soon much better regulated as a result. Fifth, he promoted the move of cathedral churches from hamlets and small villages to more populous towns, which enhanced the prestige of the Church in general.[73] Sixth, he encouraged the other English prelates to appoint Archdeacons, middling officials who operated as liaisons between the Bishops on the one hand and ordinary parish priests on the other. And seventh, he used a large portion of his own revenues to establish several important charitable institutions in the precincts of Canterbury, including a leper hospital, a hospice for the care of the aged poor, and the new collegiate church of St. Gregory's, which maintained a large grammar school for the education of local children.[74]

In his work of reform Lanfranc enjoyed strong support from William, who considered a prosperous, dynamic Church an essential prop of royal power. As a consequence, William himself presided over several sessions of the seven religious councils that met between 1072 and 1086. In addition William succumbed to Lanfranc's pleas in 1072 and authorized a new system of church courts in England. Henceforth all cases involving ecclesiastical causes and persons were to be tried before the Bishops and Archdeacons in their own courts, and not before the shire, hundred, baronial, or any other courts.[75]

It is not altogether clear why William agreed to the establishment of a separate system of church courts, which undermined the legal unity of the realm and gave the clergy a judicial system virtually independent of the royal will. Perhaps it was because the local courts were already burdened with thousands of cases stemming from the sudden transfer of millions of acres of land. But more likely it was because of Lanfranc's desire for arrangements that would stress the unique role of the clergy in society and emphasize their essential difference from the laity. Whatever the case, William issued the famous writ of 1072 that established the separate church courts, which looked to Rome as the final arbiter in disputed cases until Henry VIII's time.

Perhaps William felt compelled to issue that writ because of the way he had already feudalized the Church and established military quotas on the bishoprics and richer monasteries. As a consequence they were now compelled to assist the crown whenever a foreign war threatened. That new system seems to have annoyed the clerical hierarchy, whose support William wanted to retain, even at the cost of granting them extraordinary power over their own affairs.

As noted in an earlier part of this essay,[76] several English monasteries had been required on the eve of the Norman invasion to assist the central government with armed troops in the event of a serious crisis, as had been the practice on the continent for generations. Within several years of his great victory in 1066, William vastly expanded that system by incorporating all the richer abbeys within it as well as all the bishoprics and both archbishoprics. For example, the Abbots of Peterborough and Glastonbury received quotas of sixty horsemen each, whereas the Abbots of Hyde, Abingdon, and Bury St. Edmunds were required to supply between twenty and forty mounted knights. Tavistock and Westminster were obligated to provide fifteen knights each, while dozens of lesser houses were assessed between five and ten knights apiece. The military quotas of the Bishops and Archbishops were just as varied. Four prelates--those of Canterbury, Winchester, Lincoln, and Worcester--were required to supply sixty horsemen each. The Bishop of Salisbury was directed to provide thirty-two, while his counterparts in London, Bath, and York, received quotas of twenty each. In the case of Chichester, only two horsemen were required.[77] All in all, the English Church was required to supply a total of 780 knights, or about the same number William had received from the Norman aristocracy and Church together before Hastings.

With the establishment of those clerical assessments, feudalism came to full maturity in England, and English society became feudalized in all important regards. As a consequence, it was a stronger society than ever, with a government ready and able to defend the realm from massive foreign attacks. Indeed, the single most important result of the Norman Conquest was the extraordinary strengthening of the kingdom's defenses and the closer relationship that developed between the monarch on the one hand and his leading subjects, lay and clerical alike, on the other. Because of those developments, the English people were spared the horrors of another brutal occupation comparable to the one William and his followers imposed on them between 1066 and 1075. In that strange paradox exists the most fundamental meaning of the Norman Conquest for the English people during the centuries that followed.

For Further Reading

C. T. Chevallier, ed. *The Norman Conquest: Its Setting and Impact.* New York, 1966. Four important essays by such master historians as Frank Barlow, David Douglas, Dorothy Whitelock, and Charles H. Lemmon.

Frank Barlow, *William I and the Norman Conquest.* London, 1965. A brief study, especially suitable for students and general readers.

Frank Barlow, *Edward the Confessor.* London, 1970. A thorough study although perhaps a bit too sympathetic to its subject.

Frank Barlow, *The Norman Conquest and Beyond.* A collection of Professor Barlow's published papers, many of great importance.

David C. Douglas, *William the Conqueror: The Norman Impact upon England.* London, 1964; repr. 1977. Still the best full-scale biography; especially good on the Norman background.

David C. Douglas, *Time and the Hour: Some Collected Papers.* London, 1977. A collection of Professor Douglas's published papers, many of great value.

Sir Frank Stenton, *William the Conqueror and the Rule of the Normans.* London, 1908; repr. 1966. An old study by a great scholar; still well worth reading.

Sir Frank Stenton, *Anglo-Saxon England,* 3rd ed. Oxford, 1971. A massive study first published in 1943. Pages 525-687 are particularly relevant to the origins of the Norman Conquest and its consequences.

James Campbell, ed., *The Anglo-Saxons.* London, 1982; repr. 1991. Chapters 7-9 (by Eric John) pertain to the late Anglo-Saxon period and the Norman Conquest. Well written and lavishly illustrated.

Eric John, "Edward the Confessor and the Norman Succession." *English Historical Review,* vol. 94 (1979). Important.

Eric John. "The *Encomium Emmae Reginae*: A Riddle and a Solution." *Bulletin of the John Rylands Library,* vol. 63 (1980). An interesting theory about the events leading up to Edward the Confessor's return from the continent in 1041.

Philip Grierson, "A Visit of Earl Harold to Flanders in 1056." *English Historical Review,* vol. 51 (1936). A plausible explanation for Edward the Exile's decision to return to England in 1057 after a long absence.

Robin Fleming, "Domesday Estates of the King and the Godwines: A Study in Late Saxon Politics." *Speculum,* vol. 58 (1983). Shows how Godwine wealth grew steadily between 1045 and 1065 and eventually exceeded that of the crown itself. Very important.

P. H. Sawyer, *From Roman Britain to Norman England.* London,

1978. A useful survey that stresses social developments.

David Bates, *William the Conqueror.* London, 1989. A book of less than 200 pages, up-to-date, and intended for students and general readers.

Maurice Ashley, *The Life and Times of William I.* London, 1973. A lavishly illustrated book with a short, readable text.

Alan Lloyd, *The Making of the King: 1066.* New York, 1966. A good example of popular history, but very sound.

Henry R. Loyn, *The Norman Conquest,* 2nd ed. London, 1967. An excellent study of less than 200 pages. Judicious and well balanced.

David Howarth, *1066: The Year of the Conquest.* New York, 1978. A popular attempt to describe the events of 1066 primarily in social terms. Not notably successful because the author, a journalist, failed to grasp the meaning of several key events.

R. Allen Brown, *The Normans and the Norman Conquest.* New York, 1968. An important book by a leading scholar, but too hostile to the Anglo-Saxons, whose defeat at Hastings was far from inevitable, as Brown maintains.

W. L. Warren, "The Myth of Norman Administrative Efficiency." *Transactions of the Royal Historical Society,* 5th series, vol. 34 (1984). Argues that between 1066 and 1100, the sophisticated Anglo-Saxon system of government became ramshackle because Norman administrative methods were little more than ". . . a matter of shifts and contrivances." An important corrective to previous studies that exaggerated the Normans' genius for government.

James Campbell, "Observations on English Government from the Tenth to the Twelfth Century." *Transactions of the Royal Historical Society,* 5th series, vol. 25 (1975). A spirited defense of the Anglo-Saxons, which probably contributed to Warren's article above.

Sally P. J. Harvey, "Domesday Book and Anglo-Norman Governance." *Transactions of the Royal Historical Society,* 5th series, vol. 25 (1975).

David Bates, "The Origins of the Justiciarship," in R. Allen Brown, ed.,

Proceedings of the Battle Conference on Anglo-Norman Studies, IV (Woodbridge, Suffolk, 1981).

Henry R. Loyn, "The King and the Structure of Society in Late Anglo-Saxon England." *History*, vol. 42 (1957). Emphasizes the personal, non-territorial nature of English kingship during the century before the Conquest.

J. O. Prestwich, "The Military Household of the Norman Kings." *English Historical Review*, vol. 96 (1981). An important article, but stresses the period 1087-1154.

Marjorie Chibnall, *Anglo-Norman England 1066-1166*. Oxford, 1986. A useful survey that analyzes the changes in English government and society that occurred during the century after Hastings.

O. G. Tomkeieff, *Life in Norman England*. London, 1966. A good survey of social life in England during the six generations after Hastings.

R. Welldon Finn, *The Norman Conquest and its effect on the economy, 1066-1086*. London, 1971. A thorough study.

J. C. Russell, "Demographic Aspects of the Norman Invasion," in Richard H. Bowers, ed., *Seven Studies in Medieval English History and Other Historical Essays*. Jackson, Mississippi, 1983. An important study of the effects of the Conquest on England's population.

Richard Glover, "English Warfare in 1066." *English Historical Review*, vol. 67 (1952). Important.

John H. Beeler, "The Composition of Anglo-Norman Armies." *Speculum*, vol. 40 (1965).

C. Warren Hollister, *Anglo-Norman Institutions on the Eve of the Norman Conquest*. Oxford, 1962. A major study, extremely valuable.

Ella S. Armitage, *The Early Norman Castles of the British Isles*. London, 1912. Still the standard work.

Frank M. Stenton, "The Changing Feudalism of the Middle Ages." *History*, vol. 19 (1935).

Frank M. Stenton, "English Families and the Norman Conquest." *Transactions of the Royal Historical Society*, 4th series, vol. 26 (1944).

J. C. Holt, "Feudal Society and the Family in Early Medieval England: I. The Revolution of 1066." *Transactions of the Royal Historical Society*, 5th series, vol. 32 (1982).

C. Warren Hollister, "The Greater Domesday Tenants-in-Chief," in J. C. Holt, ed., *Domesday Studies*. Woodbridge, Suffolk, 1987. An important study of changes in land ownership after 1066.

Peter A. Clarke, *The English Nobility under Edward the Confessor.* Oxford, 1994. A thorough analysis of the landholdings of the Godwines and other important families before 1066.

John Le Patourel, "The Norman Conquest of Yorkshire." *Northern History*, VI (1971). A useful article for the effects of the Conquest on a single county.

William E. Kapelle, *The Norman Conquest of the North: The Region and Its Transformation, 1000-1135.* Chapel Hill, N. C., 1979. A thorough study.

Christine Fell, *Women in Anglo-Saxon England and the impact of 1066.* Bloomington, Indiana, 1984. Rather brief.

Margaret Gibson, *Lanfranc of Bec.* Oxford, 1978. A careful life of the great archbishop. Essential for an understanding of religious developments in England after 1066.

Helen Clover and Margaret Gibson, eds. *The Letters of Lanfranc, Archbishop of Canterbury.* Oxford, 1979. An important source.
Frank Barlow, *The English Church 1000-1066,* 2nd ed. London, 1979. Thorough and important.

Frank Barlow, *The English Church, 1066-1154.* London, 1979. A valuable account of the Church during the Anglo-Norman period.

Veronica Ortenberg, *The English Church and the Continent in the Tenth and Eleventh Centuries: Cultural, Spiritual, and Artistic Ex-*

changes. Oxford, 1992. An important study that holds that the English Church was not as isolated from Latin Christendom as was formerly believed.

Ordericus Vitalis, *The Ecclesiastical History of England and Normandy*, 3 vols., ed. and trans. by Thomas Forester. London, 1853. An important source.

Ordericus Vitalis, *The Ecclesiastical History of Orderic Vitalis,* 3 vols., ed. and trans. by Marjorie Chibnall. Oxford, 1969. A new, critical edition.

David Douglas and George W. Greenaway, eds., *English Historical Documents 1042-1189*. New York, 1953. A good selection.

Whitelock, Dorothy, David Douglas, and Susie I. Tucker, eds., *The Anglo-Saxon Chronicle*. New Brunswick, N.J., 1961. An excellent edition of the most valuable of all sources for the Norman Conquest.

Frank Barlow, ed., *The Life of King Edward who rests at Westminster*, 2nd ed. Oxford, 1992. A critical edition of a contemporary biography of Edward the Confessor that was probably commissioned by his wife, Edith Godwine. Her attempt to portray Edward as a saintly man, thereby justifying her failure to have children by him.

Sir Frank Stenton, ed. *The Bayeux Tapestry*. London, 1957. An outstanding study of the famous pictorial depiction of the main events in England and Normandy between 1064 and the battles of Hastings and the Malfosse in 1066. With 150 illustrations.

Notes for *The Norman Conquest*

[1] R. Allen Brown, *The Normans and the Norman Conquest* (New York, 1968), p. 203.

[2] Sir Frank M. Stenton, *Anglo-Saxon England* (Oxford, 1943), p. 677. The same statement occurs on page 686 of the third edition of that book, which appeared in 1971.

[3] David C. Douglas, *William the Conqueror: The Norman Impact upon England* (London, 1964; repr. 1977), p. 342.

[4] During the century before the Conquest, English social customs were similar to those of Scandinavia. As a consequence young Englishmen of high station, on reaching puberty, often took a "Danish wife," with whom they lived without the Church's blessing until they were ready to make a "proper marriage" for political or economic reasons. Although "Danish wives" were treated honorably, they were little more than glorified concubines who could be cast aside without trouble and whose children occupied an indeterminate status, with much weaker claims to the wealth and titles of their fathers than the children of "proper wives."

[5] Edward is generally known as the Confessor because he became increasingly religious during his final years and spent much of his time with Abbots and other clerics from the continent, such as the great John of Fécamp, who visited England in 1054. But Edward was not trained in childhood to be a churchman, as was long believed, although it was assumed from 1012 until 1041 that he would never occupy the English throne.

[6] Eric John, "The End of Anglo-Saxon England," in James Campbell, ed., *The Anglo-Saxons* (London, 1991), p. 216.

[7] Ralph of Mantes, or Ralph the Timid, was the second son of Edward's sister Goda (or Godgifu), who married Drogo, Count of the Vexin about 1025. Ralph and his older brother Walter, who was Drogo's principal heir, were thus grandsons of King Ethelred II.

[8] Swein apparently raped an Abbess and murdered several men. To atone for his sins he eventually made a pilgrimage to Jerusalem but died on the homeward trip in 1052.

[9] Eric John, "The *Encomium Emmae Reginae*: A Riddle and a Solution." *Bulletin of the John Rylands Library, Manchester*, vol. 63 (1980), p. 93.

[10] A pallium was a wool collar or mantle that the Pope granted to a new Bishop or Archbishop, thereby showing that the new prelate's election was recognized by the head of the Church. Without a pallium, which the Pope could withhold in unusual circumstances, the new prelate's election would be considered irregular, thereby casting serious doubt on that prelate's authority.

[11] William II of Normandy (1028-1087) was the son of Emma of Normandy's nephew Robert "the Devil," who died in 1035, and a peasant girl named Harleve, his "Danish wife" at the time. A "Danish wife" was little more than

a glorified concubine who lived with a young man of high station until he was ready to make a "proper marriage" for social, political, and economic reasons. Needless to say, the children of a man and his "Danish wife" had fewer rights than the children of a union that had been blessed by the Church. In later years, William of Normandy did everything in his power to destroy the institution of "Danish marriages," which he abhorred on personal grounds.

[12] Douglas, *William the Conqueror,* p. 76.

[13] It appears that the order to blind Alfred and his friends was given by King Harold I (1035-1040) and not by Earl Godwine. See J. C. Fuller, *The Decisive Battles of the Western World,* vol. I (London, 1954), p. 357.

[14] According to Eric John, Edward would have killed Earl Godwine in 1051 "if he could have got hold of him." See Eric John, "Edward the Confessor and the Norman Succession." *English Historical Review*, vol. 94 (1979), p. 249.

[15] Goda's first husband, Count Drogo of the Vexin (d. 1035), was the father of her sons Walter and Ralph.

[16] David C. Douglas, "Edward the Confessor, Duke William of Normandy, and the English Succession," in David C. Douglas, *Time and the Hour* (London, 1977), pp. 142-147.

[17] After the Norman Conquest, the bishopric of Dorchester was moved to Lincoln.

[18] Briefly, in 1058, Stigand did enjoy papal recognition because Pope Benedict X sent him a pallium. But Benedict was driven from office that same year; and after he was declared to have been a false Pope, all his acts were voided, which left Stigand without papal recognition once again.

[19] The best brief description of Harold's personality has been given by Professor Barlow, who holds that he "... passed through the dangers of the world with watchful mockery .... [He] was secular in outlook and pagan in morals; and it may be that the Danish side of his character was dominant for he lived with a mistress until his promotion to the throne, had an unbaptized son buried near the altar of Christ Church, Canterbury, and displayed characteristic Viking virtues. " See Frank Barlow, *The English Church 1000-1066*, 2nd ed. (London, 1979), p. 59.

[20] The judgment of William of Jumièges, Archdeacon of Lisieux and

chaplain to William the Conqueror; quoted in Alfred H. Burne, *The Battlefields of England* (London, 1950), p.120.

[21] Victoria Ortenberg, *The English Church and the Continent during the Tenth and Eleventh Centuries* (Oxford, 1992), pp. 233, 235. See also Peter A. Clarke, *The English Nobility under Edward Confessor* (Oxford, 1994), p. 23, for the grant of a Sussex estate worth £86 per year to Fécamp Abbey.

[22] For the steady growth of Godwine wealth during those years, see Robin Fleming, "Domesday Estates of the King and the Godwines: A study in Late Saxon Politics." *Speculum,* vol. 58 (1983), pp. 987-1005.

[23] According to Professor Barlow, the King was consumed "by paroxysms of rage" when the Godwines returned from abroad in 1052. See Barlow, *Edward the Confessor,* p. 240. If true, Edward is bound to have been annoyed when William did nothing to assist him against his enemies, and the always observant Harold is unlikely to have been ignorant of the royal anger.

[24] During 1047, as noted earlier, Henry I assisted William and helped his troops win the critical battle of Val-ès-Dunes. But after William's marriage to Matilda of Flanders and his nomination to be King Edward's heir-apparent, the French King concluded that his vassal's strength was increasing much too fast. As a consequence Henry I, in an effort to play the balance of power, turned against William in 1052 and formed an alliance with William's arch-enemy, Geoffrey Martel, Count of Anjou. From the conclusion of that alliance until 1060, when Henry I and Count Geoffrey both died, William was too insecure in his own duchy to be able to spare any time for the changing political situation in England.

[25] The two clerics who sought to persuade Edward the Exile to return to England in 1054 were Ealdred, Bishop of Worcester, and Aelfwine, Abbot of Ramsey.

[26] Philip Grierson, "A Visit of Earl Harold to Flanders in 1056." *English Historical Review,* vol. 51 (1936), pp. 90-97 and especially p. 96. Most of this is conjectural, of course, but it seems logical that the Emperor, a young and ambitious ruler, would have been glad to see Edward the Exile on the English throne one day, given the way his father had assisted him for so many years.

[27] Douglas, *William the Conqueror,* p. 171.

[28] *Ibid.,* p. 172.

[29] William of Poitiers was unaware that Dover Castle was not built until the

next year.

[30] David C. Douglas and George W. Greenaway, eds., *English Historical Documents 1042-1189* (New York, 1953), p. 218.

[31] John H. Beeler, "The Composition of Anglo-Norman Armies." *Speculum,* vol. 40 (1965), p. 409.

[32] For England's drift towards feudalism before the Norman Conquest, see J. C. Holt, "Feudal Society and the Family, I: The Revolution of 1066." *Transactions of the Royal Historical Society,* 5th series (1982), p. 202.

[33] C. Warren Hollister, *Anglo-Saxon Military Institutions on the Eve of the Norman Conquest* (Oxford, 1962), pp. 114, 117-122. See also K. M. E. Murray, "Faversham and the Cinque Ports." *Transactions of the Royal Historical Society,* 4th series, vol. 18 (1935), pp. 53, 60.

[34] Tostig probably felt some hostility toward Harold even before the events of October and November 1065. Peter Clarke has noted that after their father's death in 1053, Harold wound up with lands worth £2,846 per year, or over half of the family's total holdings. By contrast, Tostig held lands valued at only £492 a year according to Domesday Book, although this may have been a slight underestimate. See Clarke, *The English Nobility under Edward the Confessor,* p. 24.

[35] According to Professor Barlow, while Harold "... was Edward's second-in-command the kingdom was in safe hands." See Frank Barlow, *William I and the Norman Conquest* (London, 1965), p. 53.

[36] Perhaps it should be noted that William's good relations with the Papacy began only after Pope Nicholas II gave belated recognition to his earlier marriage to Matilda of Flanders. Pope Leo IX had prohibited that marriage in 1050, presumably because William and Matilda were too closely related to each other. But the marriage occurred anyway; and in 1059, after several children were born to them, Nicholas II agreed to recognize it, provided they did penance for disobeying the earlier papal ban by founding two new convents at Caen, which they did within a year. Thereafter, William and the papacy often worked well together, although William was quick to defy the Supreme Pontiff whenever he felt it in his self-interest to do so.

[37] Dorothy Whitelock, David Douglas, and Susie I. Tucker, eds., *The Anglo-Saxon Chronicle* (New Brunswick, N.J., 1961), pp. 141-142. For a good modern account of Tostig's activities during this period, see Brown, *The Normans and the Norman Conquest,* pp. 142-143.

[38] According to Professor Stenton, "The battle of Fulford ... was ... a murderous and protracted struggle." The English losses were so great in fact that Edwin and Morcar were unable "to take any effective part in the campaign of Hastings." See Sir Frank Stenton, "English Families and the Norman Conquest." *Transactions of the Royal Historical Society*, 4th series, vol. 26 (1944), pp. 2-3.

[39] It is possible that some of Harold's men fought on horseback at Stamford Bridge, at least during the first hour. If they did, this was probably the first time cavalry were used with any real success in the British Isles. See Douglas, *William the Conqueror,* p. 278; Hollister, *Anglo-Saxon Military Institutions*, pp. 136-37; and Richard Glover, "English Warfare in 1066," *English Historical Review*, vol. 67 (1952), pp.1-18 and especially p. 10.

[40] There are many good accounts of the battles of Hastings and the Malfosse. Two of the best are Charles H. Lemmon, "The Campaign of 1066," in C. T. Chevallier, ed., *The Norman Conquest: Its Setting and Impact* (New York, 1966), pp. 79-122; and R. Allen Brown, "The Battle of Hastings," in R. Allen Brown, ed., *Proceedings of the Battle Conference on Anglo-Norman Studies*, vol. 3 (Ipswich, 1980), pp. 1-19.

[41] William's regents for England in 1067 were Odo of Bayeux, Hugh of Montfort-sur-Risle, and William FitzOsbern.

[42] Ordericus Vitalis, *The Ecclesiastical History of England and Normandy*, 3 vols., translated and edited by Thomas Forester (London, 1853), II: 28. For a modern account of William's harrying of Yorkshire, see John Le Patourel, "The Norman Conquest of Yorkshire," *Northern History*, vol. 6 (1971), pp. 1-21, and especially pp. 7-9.

[43] Quoted in Maurice Ashley, *The Life and Times of William I* (London, 1973), p. 216.

[44] Waltheof became Earl of Northumbria shortly after Morcar threw in his lot with Herward, a rebel leader in the fen country around Ely and Peterborough. After William's troops suppressed that rebellion, Morcar was captured and sent across the Channel to Normandy, where he died in captivity some years later. Even before Morcar was captured, William granted the earldom of Northumbria to Waltheof, a powerful thegn of the region who had recently married the Conqueror's niece Judith.

[45] Henry R. Loyn, *The Norman Conquest,* 2nd ed. (London, 1967), pp. 109-110. Waltheof's two main associates, Roger FitzOsbern, Earl of Hereford, and Ralph the Breton, Earl of East Anglia, paid almost as heavily as Wal-

theof for their treason. Roger was condemned by William's councillors to life imprisonment and the loss of all his lands. In order to escape a similar fate, Ralph fled across the Channel to his castle at Dol, where he was protected by Philip I of France. However, many of Ralph's associates were captured in England before being ordered to leave the realm. For Earls Roger and Ralph, see David Bates, *William the Conqueror,* (London, 1989), p. 176.

[46] Douglas, *William the Conqueror,* pp. 315, 373-374.

[47] Frank Barlow, *The English Church 1066-1154* (London, 1979), pp. 54, 56.

[48] On this point, see Fleming, "Domesday Estates of the King and the Godwines," pp. 987-1005, passim.

[49] Bates, *William the Conqueror,* p. 125; Loyn, *The Norman Conquest,* p. 75.

[50] J. H. Round, *Feudal England* (London, 1909), p. 317.

[51] C. Warren Hollister, "The Greater Domesday Tenants-in-Chief," in J. C. Holt, ed., *Domesday Studies* (Woodbridge, Suffolk, 1987), p. 242.

[52] *Ibid.*

[53] David Douglas, *The Norman Achievement, 1050-1100* (Berkeley and Los Angeles, 1969), p. 112.

[54] Stenton, *Anglo-Saxon England,* 3rd edition, p. 626. See also Loyn, *The Norman Conquest,* pp. 171-172.

[55] All of William's tenants-in-chief together were required to provide a mobile military force of between 4,000 and 5,000 men. This force would serve as a cavalry wing for the national defense; whereas the traditional militia, the fyrd, which remained in existence for another century, continued to serve as the infantry. In addition, William and his immediate successors on the throne made occasional use of mercenary troops, as most contemporary rulers on the continent did.

[56] The famous feudal aids and incidents--payments extracted from the tenants-in-chief on the knighting of the King's eldest son, on the first marriage of the King's eldest daughter, and on the ransom of the King's own person--were not added until several generations after the Conquest.

[57] One of the earliest English castles, the fortress built at Hereford about 1048 by Edward the Confessor's nephew Ralph of Mantes, was destroyed in 1055 by the forces of Gruffydd of North Wales. Apparently it was not rebuilt before 1066. On that point, see Ella S. Armitage, *The Early Norman Castles of the British Isles* (London, 1912), p. 161. However, on the eve of the Norman Conquest, there were two surviving castles in Herefordshire as well as two in Kent, at Dover and Clavering.

[58] O. G. Tomkeieff, *Life in Norman England* (London, 1966; repr. 1967), p. 73. Somewhat higher figures for the number of inhabited houses in Lincoln in 1065 and 1080 are given by H. R. Loyn in *The Norman Conquest*, p. 176. But because Mr. Loyn contends that Lincoln lost between fifteen and sixteen per cent of all its inhabited houses during that fifteen-year stretch, the general picture is the same.

[59] Tomkeieff, *Life In Norman England*, p. 73.

[60] Stenton, *Anglo-Saxon England,* 3rd ed., pp. 686-687. See also R. Welldon Finn, *The Norman Conquest and its effects on the economy, 1066-86* (London, 1971), pp. 4-6; and also C. Warren Hollister, "Normandy, France, and the Anglo-Norman *Regnum.*" *Speculum*, vol. 51 (1976), p. 210.

[61] John Le Patourel, "Geoffrey of Montbray, Bishop of Coutances, 1049-93." *English Historical Review*, vol. 59 (1944), p. 152.

[62] *Ibid.*, p. 139.

[63] Vitalis, *The Ecclesiastical History of England and Normandy*, II: 6. For a modern view, see Veronica Ortenberg, *The English Church and the Continent in the Tenth and Eleventh Centuries*, p. 241.

[64] Frank Barlow, *The English Church 1066-1154*, 2nd ed. (London, 1979), p. 57.

[65] For a good account of the revival of English during the years 1270-1300, see Richard Bailey, "The Development of English," in David Daiches and Anthony Thorlby, eds., *The Medieval World* (London, 1973).

[66] Doris M. Stenton, *The English Woman in History* (London, 1957), p. 28.

[67] In this regard William was clearly inconsistent because he allowed men in holy orders to be tenants-in-chief of estates the Church held from the crown. Professional clerics were not expected to fight, although they did have to supply a certain number of armed men from their estates for the royal army. That women might have been allowed to do the same thing never seems to

have occurred to William and his followers.

[68] Christine Fell, *Women in Anglo-Saxon England and the impact of 1066* (Bloomington, Indiana, 1984), p. 149.

[69] *Ibid.*, p. 124.

[70] David Harrison, *England Before the Norman Conquest* (Ipswich, 1978), p. 375. See also Douglas, *William the Conqueror*, p. 311; and Loyn, *Anglo-Saxon England and the Norman Conquest*, pp. 350-352.

[71] David Pelteret, "Slave raiding and slave trading in early England," in Peter Clemoes, ed., *Anglo-Saxon England*, vol. IX (Cambridge, 1981), p. 113.

[72] The first English monastery to adopt the Cluniac Rule was Lewes Abbey, in 1077.

[73] Between 1070 and 1087 the bishopric of Dorchester became the bishopric of Lincoln; the seat of the ancient bishopric of Sarum was transferred to Salisbury; and the diocese of Selsey was move inland to Chichester, an especially important move because Selsey soon disappeared beneath the waters of the English Channel.

[74] For a scholarly study of Lanfranc's life and career, see Margaret Gibson, *Lanfranc of Bec* (Oxford, 1978), especially pp. 162-187. See also Frank Barlow, *The English Church, 1066-1154,* pp. 34-56.

[75] Douglas, *The Norman Achievement*, pp. 137-138.

[76] See above, p. 22.

[77] Douglas and Greenaway, eds., *English Historical Documents 1042-1189*, pp. 895-896, 898, 904-905.

Magna Carta and King John*

Few people today have more than a nodding acquaintance with Magna Carta, the most famous document in English history. Some know that King John agreed to its provisions in June of 1215, while others remember from a history course in high school or college that its main purpose was to subject the King to the rule of law without making him a constitutional figurehead. Professional scholars and serious history buffs are probably aware that Magna Carta was an unusually long document for the Middle Ages, consisting of sixty-three clauses and approximately 3,500 words in all.

In this essay we shall consider the circumstances that caused the barons to compile Magna Carta and threaten King John with deadly force unless he accepted it. But first it would be worthwhile to consider how historians have evaluated the document during the last century or so.

In 1896 William Stubbs praised Magna Carta as "a revelation of the possibility of freedom to the medieval world."[1] An equally favorable view of the charter was expressed by Sir Frederick M. Powicke a generation later.

> Much of it had long been needed, some of it restated earlier legislation, all of it was consistent with tradition.... It was a statement of common law no less than a piece of common sense.[2]

In a similar vein Professor Sidney Painter commented in 1947:

> If one lays aside the helter-skelter order in which the clauses are arranged, the charter is very ably drawn. Compared to such later documents as the Provisions of Oxford [of 1258], it is incredibly clear and precise. Moreover, it shows an intimate and accurate knowledge of the working of the English royal government.[3]

That tradition of admiration for Magna Carta was challenged in the 1960s by J. C. Holt. In a pioneering study of the original northern op-

---

* The notes for this chapter begin on p. 120.

position to King John, Professor Holt maintained of the charter:

> As a new departure it was fumbling, half-blind. Its provisions often constituted little more than crude propaganda, or vague and platitudinous generalities, or administrative tinkering at once naive and impractical. If at any stage it was drawn from a single coherent plan, this had long been lost in the complex interchange of arguments which preceded it.[4]

Four years later Professor Holt published an important study of Magna Carta itself, in which he dismissed the document as a hopeless failure that sought to reestablish trust between King John and his barons but actually "... provoked a war. It pretended to state customary law... [but] promoted disagreement and contention."[5]

An equally hostile view of Magna Carta has been advanced by Frank Barlow. In his famous survey of the Anglo-Norman period, Professor Barlow contends that:

> ... in substance the charter is curiously disappointing. It displays no real understanding of the problems of government, and in fact exerted no detailed influence on the development of the royal administration .... It was an inadequate judgment on the past and an impracticable guide for the future.[6]

Just as there has been a dramatic shift in the scholarly attitude toward Magna Carta, there has been an equally radical shift in the scholarly perception of King John, his goals and abilities. Until World War II almost all historians agreed with Stubbs' hostile view of that hapless monarch.

> He was the very worst of all our kings .... Polluted with every crime that could disgrace a man, false to every obligation that should bind a king, he had lost half his inheritance by sloth, and ruined and desolated the rest .... In the whole view there is no redeeming trait; John seems as incapable of receiving a good impression as of carrying into effect a wise resolution.[7]

During recent years historical research has softened Stubbs' portrayal of John not by denying his character flaws, which were many and substantial, but by shifting the emphasis to the selfish and grasping nature of his political opponents; by stressing the underlying dissatisfaction that had developed during previous decades; by emphasizing the steep inflation of the era, which would have perplexed even a great ruler; and by giving more attention to the aggressive designs of Philip Augustus of France (1180-1223), who was bent on destroying the Angevin empire and annexing Normandy and England's other continental possessions. Because of the many problems he faced, John is now seen as a bold and imaginative ruler who came within an inch of succeeding. Indeed, Professor Barlow has written that "John's problems were immense and his near-successes brilliant."[8] This view is shared by John's leading biographer, W. L. Warren, who considers him a monarch "of consummate ability";[9] whereas C. W. Hollister maintains that he was "... a person of keen intelligence and skill ... a highly talented man, perhaps in certain respects even a genius."[10]

However, the revisionist approach toward Magna Carta and King John failed to sweep the field and overwhelm the opposite point of view. Indeed, only two years after the appearance of Warren's biography of the monarch, H. G. Richardson and G. O. Sayles maintained in an important book that:

> ... the major count against John is that he was not prudent or considerate enough to live on good terms with his barons and that he provoked them to civil war over an issue not worth an armed conflict. In lacking the wisdom to concede in due time what must inevitably be conceded, he lacked the essential quality of a wise ruler and, indeed, of a righteous ruler, for political wisdom is the righteousness of princes.[11]

* * *

John became England's ruler in April of 1199, on the death of his older brother, Richard I, who had fathered no children by his wife, Berengaria of Navarre. Thirty-two years of age at his accession, John was the eighth and youngest child of his warring parents, Henry II and Eleanor of Aquitaine. Although not expected to inherit the throne, he nevertheless received a sound education for the era, largely at the hands of Ranulf Glanvill, Henry II's famous Justiciar, and William Marshal, the most celebrated fighting man of the period. From them he learned much about government and warfare and probably acquired his deep love of books.

Although John's tutors were honorable men, his character owed little if anything to their example. As Stubbs correctly noted, he grew up to be a treacherous and deceitful man and assumed his subjects were basically the same. He feared treason everywhere and tended to be wary and suspicious. Because he had few friends and rarely felt at ease with England's barons, he preferred the company of men of lesser station, especially his mercenary captains from the continent, which led to baronial resentments that grew stronger and more dangerous as the years wore on. Even worse, John was a bully who violated the rights of individuals who were down on their luck, while his grasping actions kept him from inspiring confidence or affection. Englishmen might fight in defense of the monarchical form of government but not to save John from his enemies, whose loyalty and good will he forfeited through greedy and short-sighted policies.

Paradoxically, John enjoyed considerable support at the beginning of his reign and could not have become King without it. This was the case because his twelve-year-old nephew, Arthur of Brittany, had an equally strong claim to the throne.[12] Although most of the Norman barons preferred a surviving brother's candidacy to that of a younger nephew, magnates in other parts of the Angevin empire usually preferred a nephew's claim, while in England itself the issue was still in doubt. To make matters worse, Richard I, while on crusade, had issued the famous Declaration of Messina of 1191, in which he recognized Arthur as his rightful heir should he die before returning to England. But in the years after 1196 Richard ignored his own declaration and favored John's accession, despite the latter's attempt to seize the throne before his return.[13]

At any rate, when Richard I died on 6 April 1199, a tense situation developed and a war for the throne was narrowly avoided. In Anjou, Maine, Touraine, and Brittany, the principal barons rallied around Arthur and proclaimed his accession. Luckily for John, who was on the continent at the time, his claim was loudly supported by his elderly mother Eleanor, who still wielded considerable influence. Of greater importance, John had the backing of his old tutor, William Marshal, who often extolled John as his favorite squire. In April 1199 Marshal was touring his Norman estates in the company of the elderly Archbishop of Canterbury, Hubert Walter.

A great Archbishop and an even greater royal official, Hubert Walter had serious reservations about John's fitness for the throne. Indeed, he predicted that England would fall into ruin if John ever wore the crown. But William Marshal convinced the Archbishop that Arthur's accession would be an even greater tragedy for England because Arthur was stubborn and impulsive as well as completely ignorant of English affairs. In addition Arthur was likely to be a puppet of Philip Augustus, his guardian since 1196. As a consequence the Archbishop suppressed his doubts about John's character, and together he and Marshal returned to England and won the support of Geoffrey fitz Peter, who had been appointed to the great office of Justiciar the previous year.[14]

Meanwhile, John was obtaining pledges of assistance from several other barons, including William de Briouse, one of the most powerful Englishmen of the era. Descended from a wealthy Conquest family, Briouse held valuable lands in Sussex, Devonshire, and South Wales, where he was lord of Brecon, Radnor, and Abergavenny. His eldest son, Reginald, was married to a daughter of the Earl of Hertford, while a younger son, Giles, would soon become Bishop of Hereford. Additionally Briouse had close ties with the Earls of Derby and Hereford and also with William Marshal, who held several Irish estates from him.

A bold and forceful man, Briouse always favored quick and determined action. He was at Richard I's camp in southern France when that monarch died, but he rode north at once and convinced John to assert his claim to the throne in an effective way. Together they rode to Chinon, the most important castle in Touraine, which was a critical link between the northern and southern parts of the Angevin empire.[15] There was a major treasury at Chinon and the castle was held by a pragmatic Englishman, Robert of Thornham. Just as Briouse predicted, Robert handed over the castle to John, who took possession of its treasury before galloping off to Fontrévault to attend his brother's funeral. Thence he travelled to Rouen, where Archbishop William of Coutances crowned him on 25 April and several leading barons girded him with the ducal sword. A month later John sailed across the Channel, still accompanied by Briouse, who was his boon companion during these early years. Once in England John approved the preparations already underway for his coronation on 27 May. That elaborate ceremony in the Abbey was conducted by Archbishop Walter, whose sermon stressed John's "election" to the throne in the hope of restraining any violent or impulsive actions on his part.

During the coronation festivities John heaped generous rewards on those who had helped him capture the throne. Archbishop Walter was given the great office of Lord Chancellor;[16] while Geoffrey fitz Peter was retained as Justiciar and raised to the peerage as Earl of Essex. As for William Marshal, he was created Earl of Pembroke, appointed castellan of Gloucester and Bristol Castles, and granted additional lands in the marcher lordship of Striguil. Somewhat lesser rewards were conferred on Briouse, who became sheriff of Gloucestershire and Herefordshire and received several estates in Warwickshire. Two years later he also received the valuable honour of Limerick in southern Ireland, for which he had to pay 5,000 marks, which was well beyond his means, as John doubtless knew.[17]

After the coronation and a quick trip to Canterbury to worship at the shrine of Thomas à Becket, John rode to Northampton for a Great Council on 7 June. The major topic debated during that Great Council was the danger posed by Philip Augustus, who was still bent on destroying the Angevin empire. Although Philip Augustus had concluded a five-year truce with Richard I in January of 1199, the French monarch was a shrewd and calculating man who was quick to seize any opportunity that occurred. Accordingly, John informed the Great Council that he intended to return to the continent to meet a possible French attack, and he urged the barons to accompany him with their retainers. Any baron who preferred to remain safely in England would be expected to pay the crown a scutage of two marks for each knight's fee in his possession. This marked the beginning of John's efforts to obtain considerably more taxation from his barons on a recurring basis, which provoked so much discord during the next fourteen years that it must be seen as a major cause of Magna Carta.[18]

From Northampton John rode south to Shoreham and sailed across the Channel to Dieppe. He was at Rouen on St. John's Day (24 June); and all that summer, while waiting for a French attack, he made sustained efforts to win the loyalty of Guillaume des Roches, an early supporter of Arthur of Brittany. Shortly after Richard I's death in April of 1199, Guillaume had recognized Arthur as the rightful ruler of Maine, Touraine, Anjou, and Brittany, and John desperately hoped to win his support. Within several months his efforts bore fruit, and that autumn he appointed Guillaume his constable for Maine, Touraine, and Anjou.

Because of John's successful appeal to Guillaume, Philip Augustus realized that John was firmly seated on the English throne and in command of the affairs of the Angevin empire. Accordingly, the French monarch opened negotiations with John, and in May of 1200 the two rulers signed the Treaty of Le Goulêt. By that treaty Philip Augustus obtained several small districts along the Norman border, which he had seized from Richard I during the 1190s, as well as an enormous relief (or inheritance tax) of 20,000 marks for all the provinces of the Angevin empire. Although Arthur was recognized as the titular Duke of Brittany, he was instructed to honor and obey John as his feudal overlord. On his part John agreed to sever England's ties with the Counts of Boulogne and Flanders, traditional enemies of the French crown.

Despite his concessions to Philip Augustus in the treaty, John had every right to consider it a great victory for himself and England. However, the enormous relief of 20,000 marks he pledged to pay the French crown required him to impose additional taxes on his richer subjects, even those in the far north. During past decades the people of England's northern counties had been almost exempt from royal taxation, which might drive them into the willing arms of the Kings of Scotland, whose desire for the region had been briefly realized during the the civil war of the 1140s and early 1150s between King Stephen and his cousin the Empress Matilada.[19] John's heavier taxation of the north helps explain why his popularity plummeted there and why the movement that led to Magna Carta originated in Yorkshire although it quickly spread into central England and East Anglia.[20]

Despite his imposition of heavier taxes and the grumbling it inspired, John ruled England with considerable success during his first year, and his reign gave promise of a favorable outcome. But then, during the summer of 1200, he made a serious blunder that provoked an unnecessary war with France and caused the barons to question his ability to rule.

In 1174 at the age of seven John had been betrothed to a great heiress, Isabelle of Gloucester, whom he finally married in 1189. That long-deferred marriage proved unsuccessful and produced no heir to the throne, although John fathered at least five children by other women. By 1200 he had decided to secure an annulment from Isabelle, which proved an easy matter because they were cousins and no papal dispensation had ever been obtained for their union.[21] During the summer of 1200 the Archbishop of Rouen granted the desired annulment so John could remarry and hopefully father a son to follow him on the throne in due course.

After being freed from his wife, whose dowry he refused to return, John arranged to marry a daughter of King Sancho of Portugal. But while travelling through western France on his way to Portugal, he stopped over at the court of Audemar, Count of Angoulême. Several months earlier Audemar and his brother, the Viscount of Limoges, had signed an alliance with Philip Augustus, which threatened the Angevin empire by weakening a vital link between Poitiers in the north and Bordeaux in the south. John hoped to strengthen that link and gain the brothers' support, which he could do by marrying Audemar's twelve-year-old daughter Isabel, whose youthful beauty he greatly admirred. Audemar voiced no objection, and on 24 August 1200 John and Isabel became man and wife. Within six weeks John took her to England and had her crowned as his consort in Westminster Abbey.

All of this was deeply resented by a powerful French baron, Hugh IX, Lord of Lusignan and Count of La Marche. An old friend of Isabel's father, Hugh IX had hoped to marry Isabel and thereby gain possession of Angoulême on Audemar's death. A formal marriage treaty had been drawn up several years earlier, and Hugh IX and Isabel had been officially betrothed before John appeared on the scene. However, in August of 1200, it was an easy matter for Isabel's father to get the marriage contract voided by stressing his daughter's tender age at the time of her betrothal to Hugh. On his part, Hugh was incensed by what had happened, as John clearly realized. In vain he tried to appease Hugh by arranging for him to marry a prominent ward of his own, an heiress known to history only as Matilda. But Matilda's fortune was too small to appease Hugh's bitter disappoint over the loss of Isabel and Angoulème.

Hugh's disappointment seems to have been fanned by his brother Ralph, Count of Eu, in eastern Normandy. During the winter of 1200-1201 Hugh and Ralph were openly critical of John's actions, and their complaints soon reached John's ears at Westminster. During the spring of 1201 he retaliated by ordering the seizure of Ralph's many estates. He also decreed that La Marche should be confiscated from Hugh and assigned to his new father-in-law, Audemar.

Determined to gain vengeance on John, Hugh and Ralph journeyed to Paris during the autumn of 1201 and appealed to Philip Augustus for justice. That prompted the French ruler to plan a new assault on the Angevin empire. Within weeks he developed closer ties with Arthur of Brittany, to whom he offered his daughter Marie's hand in marriage. In addition he cultivated cordial relations with the Counts of Flanders and Boulogne, whom John had abandoned in the Treaty of Le Goulêt, and he simultaneously laid the groundwork for military alliances with the Counts of Blois and Tours. After completing all those moves, Philip Augustus summoned John to appear before him in Paris in April of 1202 to answer the charge of oppressive treatment that Counts Hugh and Ralph had levelled against him.

Deeply alarmed, John made a show of cooperation and pledged two castles, Tillières and Boutavanat, as security for his good intentions. But ignoring the fact that Philip Augustus had summoned him to appear in Paris as Duke of Aquitaine, he refused to travel to the French capital on the grounds that, as Duke of Normandy, he was obliged to appear before his French suzerain only on the eastern border of that province. Philip Augustus treated that subterfuge as a pretext for war, and on 28 April he declared John to be a contumacious vassal whose disobedience justified the confiscation of all his French fiefs. Within another week Philip's troops seized the two castles John had pledged as security for his cooperation. Moreover, Philip raised a large army with which to drive John's forces out of Normandy and other parts of northern France. Thus John's heavy handed treatment of Hugh and Ralph had effectively nullified the great victory he won at Le Goulêt less than two years before and led to the outbreak of a completely unnecessary war.

Because the events of that war have been explained in great detail by Professor Powicke,[22] it is unnecessary for us to recount them here. However, it should be noted that during the first year of the war, a French victory was far from certain. John was in fact a more experienced general than Philip Augustus or his son, the Dauphin Louis, who inherited the French throne two decades after these events as Louis VIII; and had John demonstrated resolution and a strong sense of purpose, he would probably have prevailed in the end. Indeed, during the early stages of the war, he won an impressive victory that augured well for his chances.

Several months after the war began, John was at Le Mans, the capital of Maine, when Eleanor of Aquitaine arrived at Mirebeau Castle, eighty miles to the south. From Mirebeau Eleanor planned to move to Le Mans and merge her forces with John's army in another two weeks. But before she could leave the castle, her fifteen-year-old grandson, Arthur of Brittany, arrived with an army, hoping to capture or starve her into submission. When John learned of that development, he conferred with his old friend William de Briouse, who once again called for swift action; and together they set out for Mirebeau and seized Arthur on 1 August. In addition, several hundred Frenchmen were taken prisoner, including the Viscount of Châtelleraut and Geoffrey of Lusignan.

Within several days John imprisoned Arthur at Falaise in lower Normandy, the birthplace of William the Conqueror. At the same time he sent twenty-two of Arthur's leading supporters across the Channel to Cornwall, where they were starved to death at Corfe Castle within six weeks. Those important developments consolidated John's power over Maine and Anjou, to Philip Augustus's bitter disappointment; and John and his young wife Isabel are said to have spent a joyous Christmas season at Caen, in western Normandy, where they allegedly "lay in bed every day until dinner-time."

During the spring of 1203 John transferred Arthur from Falaise to Rouen, where on 3 April the boy disappeared under mysterious circumstances and was never seen again. Doubtless he was killed at that point, but exactly how and when he died has never been determined. Some contemporaries believed that John stabbed him in a drunken fury and threw his body off the ramparts of Rouen Castle. Others claimed that he took his nephew down river to a deserted place, where he murdered him before weighting his corpse with a heavy stone and tossing it into the Seine. Whatever the case, all the evidence points to John's responsibility for the boy's death, and rumors to that effect spread quickly.

One man who clearly assumed that John had murdered his nephew was Guillaume des Roches, one of the boy's earliest supporters. As already noted, John had made a successful appeal to Guillaume during the summer of 1199 before appointing him constable of Maine, Touraine, and Anjou. But by the summer of 1203 Guillaume was convinced that Arthur was dead, and at that point he renounced his allegiance to John and swore allegiance to Philip Augustus. That was a serious blow to John's cause because Anjou was the original hub of the Angevin empire, whereas Touraine was the main link between its northern and southern parts. Although Chinon and several other castles in Touraine held out until the summer of 1205, Guillaume's defection led Maurice of Craon and several other wealthy barons to abandon John and swear homage to the French ruler. Surprised and angered by that turn of events, John sailed back to England in a fury in December of 1203.

Another man who held John responsible for Arthur's death was William de Briouse, who had helped John capture the boy at Mirebeau. Briouse was at Rouen when Arthur disappeared and may well have witnessed his murder.[23] It was about that time that Briouse turned his back on John and ceased to be his boon companion. When John returned to England in December of 1203, Briouse took refuge on his estates in South Wales and rarely, if ever, appeared at court again.

For John, Briouse's retirement from court was a major setback because he was dilatory about most matters except legal cases, which he always wanted settled promptly, and he needed forceful advisers who would encourage him to take bold action. He was especially reluctant to adopt decisive military courses because he understood the hazards of battle all too well. In 1202 he would probably have avoided Mirebeau altogether had Briouse not goaded him into going and seizing his nephew there.

At any rate, even before John's return to England in 1203, Philip Augustus had begun the siege of Château Gaillard, a massive fortress twenty miles upriver from Rouen. Built in 1197-1198 at the enormous cost of £11,000, Château Gaillard was the strongest castle in western Europe, having been constructed with special features Richard I had observed at Acre and other fortified places in the Holy Land while on crusade. As long as the English controlled Château Gaillard, they were likely to retain possession of Rouen, the capital of Normandy. But if the castle ever fell, their days of power in northern France would be numbered.

The siege of Château Gaillard began in September of 1203, and the English garrison, led by Roger de Lacy, held out for six months. Before his return to England in December, John sent a letter urging Roger and his troops to persist until English reinforcements arrived. On reaching London the King talked repeatedly about raising a new army and going to the garrison's assistance. But without Briouse there to goad him to bold action, he frittered his time away in idle amusements, and on 6 March Roger and his starving troops surrendered.

After the fall of Château Gaillard, all of Normandy was threatened with a French takeover. Only immediate help from England could save the duchy now, but still John remained inert. As a consequence the garrisons of half a dozen Norman castles, including Falaise, Bayeux, Caen, and Bonneville-sur-Touques, sensed that further resistance was useless and threw down their arms. At Avranches and Mont Saint-Michel, there were determined attempts to repel the forces of Guy de Thouars, but they ended in failure. Meanwhile in upper Normandy the burghers of Arques, Verneuil, and especially Rouen decided to continue their opposition, still hopeful of English aid. When that prospect faded, the mayor and aldermen of Rouen opened the city gates to Philip Augustus on 24 June. The municipal officers of Arques and Verneuil followed suit within a week, which meant that England's connection with Normandy was severed after a century and a half.

John's loss of Normandy led to a further decline of his prestige, particularly among barons who held estates on both sides of the Channel. Those magnates were now forced to choose between two unhappy alternatives--whether to remain John's vassals in order to retain their estates in England, or whether to transfer their allegiance to Philip Augustus in order to retain their Norman properties. The only man allowed to serve both Kings was William Marshal, the highly respected Earl of Pembroke. In April of 1205 Marshal swore allegiance to Philip Augustus in order to keep the great honour of Longueville and other Norman properties. John was afraid to offend a man of Marshal's eminence by seizing his English, Irish, or Welsh estates. Yet John cannot have been happy about the Earl's decision to cooperate with Philip Augustus and eventually took harsh steps against him, which deprived the English ruler of another adviser comparable to Briouse in ability.

Of course John seized the English estates of Norman barons who renewed their allegiance to the French crown during the summer of 1204. One Norman magnate who lost all his English lands, worth over £500 a year, was Robert, the son of Ernis. By May of 1205 Robert's estates, which included the honour of Berkampstead and the manors of Depden and Hatfield Peverel in Essex, had been conveyed to John's Justiciar, Geoffrey fitz Peter, who thereafter paid the crown a yearly rent of £100 for them.

While depriving Normans of their estates in England, John felt compelled to grant many of them to Ranulf de Blundeville and several other English magnates who had forfeited extensive lands on the French side of the Channel.[24] At the same time John took steps to organize a belated expedition to the continent, hoping to relieve the ongoing siege of Chinon and other castles as a preliminary step toward the recovery of Normandy itself. But during a Great Council at Portsmouth in the spring of 1205, Archbishop Walter and William Marshal spoke out strongly against such an expedition. The Archbishop had never had any faith in John's character or leadership, and Marshal was reluctant to do anything that would offend Philip Augustus and prompt him to seize his Norman properties. Once those two magnates criticized John's plan, several northern barons declared that they were under no obligation to accompany the crown with their retinues to the continent. They owed the King military service only in England, they declared loudly, a novel view that would be reiterated in the barons' "Unknown Charter of Liberties" of January 1215, which might be considered a preliminary draft of Magna Carta.

Confronted by such determined opposition at Portsmouth, John was unable to raise an army, so French forces fought on almost unopposed. On 23 June 1205 the great castle of Chinon fell to the enemy, and its respected castellan, Hubert de Burgh, was captured and imprisoned. Girard d'Athée, the castellan of Loches, was no more successful in repulsing the French, who subsequently crossed the Loire in numbers and overran Poitou. Then the French wheeled toward the north and entered the semi-autonomous duchy of Brittany, which submitted after a fierce struggle. Thereafter it accepted as its hereditary Duke a cousin of Philip

Augustus himself, Pierre de Dreux.

Shortly before Brittany capitulated, John decided to lead a campaign that might draw strength from the Bretons' fear of outright absorption by France. But it was already too late when he embarked for the continent on 26 May 1206. His troops won several quick victories while the French were still bogged down in Brittany. In fact, the English took renewed control of Poitou before striking across the Loire in September and occupying Anjou. But then the French came howling out of Brittany and forced John's troops back across the Loire. A desultory campaign followed, until John and Philip Augustus agreed to hold peace talks at Thouars. On 13 October they concluded a two-year truce, which John intended to use to rebuild his forces and replenish his treasury. When the truce expired in 1208 he planned to launch a successful campaign and recapture most of his lost empire.

To finance a large army and a fleet of transport ships to ferry it across the Channel, John decreed in 1207 the collection of taxation equal to a thirteenth of the total value of his richer subjects' chattels, or movable goods.[25] That decree produced a revenue of well over £60,000, but it also provoked bitter complaints, especially in the northern counties. Roald, the constable of Richmondshire, was so outspoken that John dismissed him as castellan of Richmond Castle, an office Roald recovered only by sending the King a "free gift" of 200 marks and four palfreys (i.e., fine horses). Even more outspoken was the King's half-brother Geoffrey, a natural son of Henry II and the Archbishop of York for many years. A difficult and unaccommodating man, Geoffrey denounced John's attempt to tax clerical wealth, for which he was ordered to leave the realm. He died five years later on the continent.

Partly because of his half-brother's complaints, John gave an unusually warm to his German nephew, Otto of Brunswick, who made a ceremonial visit to England in 1207. There were tournaments and other lavish festivities at Windsor and Westminster in honor of Otto, who was a leading contender for the great office of Holy Roman Emperor.[26] John hoped that Otto would support him in a new campaign against Philip Augustus; and he therefore gave his nephew 6,000 marks shortly before he returned to central Europe. But despite John's eagerness for a new war against France, internal problems prevented a resumption of the conflict until 1213.

During the years 1206-1213, most of John's time and energy were required by two great quarrels--the first with his old supporter, William de Briouse, and the second with the greatest Pope of the Middle Ages,

Innocent III.

As already noted, William de Briouse lost faith in John at the time of Arthur of Brittany's death in 1203. Thereafter Briouse appeared at court only on rare occasions, to John's great annoyance. In December 1205 the King sought to regain Briouse's support by granting him three Welsh castles, Grosmont, Skenfrith, and Llantilio. But that stratagem failed, and during the spring of 1207 John decided to punish his old supporter severely. That summer he replaced Briouse as bailiff of Glamorgan and Gwynllwg with Fawkes de Breuté; and early in 1208 he named another Frenchman, Gerard d'Athies, to succeed Briouse as sheriff of Gloucestershire and Herefordshire. During the spring of 1208 John even ordered him to hand over his eldest son, William de Briouse the Younger, as a hostage for his future behavior. Unfortunately, when royal agents arrived to take custody of the younger Briouse, his embittered mother, Matilda, made a nasty remark. Referring to the fate of Arthur of Brittany, she declared that she would never surrender her son to a man who had killed his own nephew. When that statement was reported at Westminster, John flew into a rage and vowed to ruin the whole family. Thereupon Briouse and his wife fled with their children to Ireland, where they received shelter from William Marshal, Earl of Pembroke and Lord of Leinster. Almost at once John's new justiciar in Ireland, John de Grey, Bishop of Norwich, insisted that Marshal surrender the entire family to his men so they could be sent back to England for trial and possible execution. But Marshal refused to comply, claiming it would be immoral for him to hand over his own feudal overlord to an avowed enemy.[27]

In 1210 John led an expedition across the Irish Sea and attempted to capture the Brdebriouses. During the King's stay in Ireland, William de Briouse became separated from his wife and children. Eluding capture, Briouse sailed back to Wales, where he found a safe haven. As for Matilda and their children, they fled northward and crossed the straits from Ulster to the Scottish lowlands, where they soon fell into the hands of English agents. In desperation Matilda promised to pay the King 40,000 marks for a full pardon that would cover the whole family. From Wales Matilda's husband travelled to Bristol, abased himself before the King, and solemnly swore to uphold Matilda's promises. Then he returned to Wales, ostensibly to raise the first installment of their huge fine, which was twice the relief John had paid for the Angevin empire in 1200. In the end Briouse fled to France, where he died a broken man in 1211. That left Matilda and William Briouse the Younger at John's mercy because Matilda was unable to raise even the first installment. When she begged for mercy and more time, John was unmoved and had her and her eldest son imprisoned at Windsor. He directed his castellan there to withhold all food and drink from them, and they soon died of starvation.

While John was still in Ireland, Llywelyn ap Iorwerth and several other Welsh chieftains invaded western England. Incensed, John retaliated with an invasion of his own during the summer of 1211 and defeated Llywelyn and his troops during a short campaign in North Wales. Before peace was restored, the city of Bangor was burned and its Bishop imprisoned. In order to obtain a truce, the Welsh chieftains surrendered twenty-eight of their teenage sons as hostages. John imprisoned those boys at Nottingham Castle; and the next summer, after Llywelyn invaded western England a second time, burning towns and executing English prisoners, John had all his Welsh hostages executed on 14 August. That cruel incident, along with his harsh treatment of the Briouses and the murder of Arthur of Brittany less a year before the starvation of more than twenty of Arthur's supporters at Corfe Castle, helps to explain John's evil reputation. No amount of historical revisionism can eradicate those blots from his record. Although it was a brutal age, John's cruelty exceeded that of his contemporaries.

John's evil reputation also resulted from his long quarrel with Innocent III, who was elected to the papal throne only a year before John's accession in England. Medieval chroniclers always assumed that, in the event of a serious disagreement between the Papacy and a secular ruler, right was invariably on the side of the former. But in actual fact, John was correct when he and Innocent III became locked in a bitter quarrel over a disputed episcopal election.[28]

The argument between John and Innocent III began shortly after the death on 13 July 1305 of Hubert Walter, who had held two great offices. To succeed Walter in the post of Lord Chancellor, John's choice fell on Walter de Grey, a priest and Chancery clerk of limited ability and no great experience. But Walter de Grey had offered 5,000 marks for the position, so John named him Lord Chancellor for life in October of 1205.[29] For the even greater position of Archbishop of Canterbury, John turned to John de Grey, Walter de Grey's uncle and a much abler and more experienced man. Since 1200 John de Grey had doubled as Bishop of Norwich and the King's personal secretary, and he would doubtless have made a satisfactory, perhaps even a distinguished, Archbishop.

But unfortunately for John, the choice of a new Archbishop in 1205 proved exceptionally difficult because John's prestige was at a low ebb after the loss of Normandy the year before. Probably because of that the Bishops of Canterbury province demanded a voice in the election of the next primate. During past centuries archiepiscopal elections had always been conducted only by the surviving members of the cathedral chapter at Canterbury after they informed the King that a vacancy existed and received his authorization to proceed. (In his authorizing letter the King invariably included the name of his own candidate, whose later "election" was thus a mere formality.) Not only did the Bishops of Canterbury province demand a voice in the election, but so too did the suffragan or assistant Bishops, with even less justification.

Given those unwarranted demands, which could not be ignored, it is hardly surprising that John postponed the election until the following December. During the interval he hoped to find arguments to silence the claims of the Bishops and suffragan Bishops, and then he expected to secure John de Grey's election without further delay.

Although John's strategy was sound, the younger monks at Canterbury had still another view of the matter. Indeed, they were determined to avoid another Archbishop in the tradition of Hubert Walter and his predecessor, Archbishop Baldwin, both of whom had been harsh taskmasters. Therefore, several weeks before John's four-month delay was due to expire, the younger monks held a secret, unauthorized election and chose their easygoing sub-prior, Reginald, for the vacant position. Then they sent Reginald to Rome with instructions to remain silent about everything that had occurred. In particular, Reginald was instructed to conceal that he was the younger monks' choice unless there was no other way to prevent the election of John de Grey. But because Reginald was elated by the prospect of becoming Archbishop, he ignored his instructions and sought papal recognition almost as soon as he arrived in the Eternal City.

When news of Reginald's efforts to secure papal confirmation reached John at Westminster, he rushed to Canterbury with a regiment of heavily armed men. On 10 December he summoned the monks of the cathedral chapter to appear before him. They stoutly denied that they had elected Reginald or anyone else to be their Archbishop, and then they bowed to John's command and elected John de Grey to the vacant position. The Bishops and suffragan Bishops were allowed no role in these proceedings, and John subsequently ordered them to withdraw their appeal to Rome and make no such appeals in the future. Shortly before Christmas of 1205, John sent a large delegation, including six older monks from Canterbury, to Rome to secure papal confirmation of John de Grey's election.

But Innocent III was concerned by the delay in filling the vacancy and even more by John's confiscation of all the archbishopric's revenues since Archbishop Walter's death in July. The appeal already filed by the dissatisfied Bishops of Canterbury province also raised questions in his mind. At any rate, the Pope refused to rubber-stamp John de Grey's election, as John had thought he would do.[30] Rather, he sent a messenger to Canterbury and directed the cathedral chapter to send another sixteen monks to the Curia, with full authority to hold an election in Rome should that prove necessary. Shortly afterward Innocent announced that he would take the matter under advisement and make careful inquiries of his own. He would announce his decision on 21 December 1206 at the latest.

Undoubtedly Innocent should have recognized John de Grey's election in the end. Never before had an English ruler failed to secure the election of his own candidate to be Archbishop of Canterbury, who was by tradition the King's leading adviser. But Innocent was an aggressive Pontiff, intent on strengthening the power and prestige of his position. Since his consecration in 1198, he had intervened more often in the affairs of Europe's secular rulers than any of his predecessors. Perhaps he did not actually hope to create a Christian commonwealth headed by the Papacy, as was long believed; but certainly he expected to be considered a first among equals with power to punish any King or Prince who ignored his decrees and the Church's interests. Given Innocent's high opinion of himself and his office, it was almost inevitable that he would decide the matter in a way unacceptable to John.

On 30 March 1206, Innocent nullified John de Grey's election on the grounds that the Bishops of Canterbury province had already asked for a formal ruling on the validity of Reginald's election. Thus it would be improper to hold another election while that earlier question was unresolved. Shortly afterwards the Pope dismissed the claims of the Bishops and suffragan Bishops to have a voice in the election of a new Archbishop because that right belonged to the surviving members of the cathedral chapter alone. Some months later, after the sixteen additional monks from Canterbury arrived in Rome, Innocent voided Reginald's election on the grounds that the election had been held in private by a minority of the cathedral chapter, the older and wiser monks having been deliberately excluded. Then Innocent ordered all the Canterbury monks who were still in Rome to meet in his presence chamber and hold another election. When that election occurred on 21 December 1206, the poll was evenly divided between Reginald's supporters and those who wanted John de Grey. Once that result was announced, Innocent proposed a compromise candidate of his own--Stephen Langton--who was elected with only one dissenting vote, doubtless because he had the Pope's energetic backing.

In some ways Langton was an even better choice for Archbishop than John de Grey. A native of Lincolnshire, where he had been born some fifty years before, Langton had taken doctorates in theology and the liberal arts at the university of University of Paris, where he became a famous professor. His lectures on religious and moral issues were known throughout Europe, and he wrote one of the greatest of all medieval hymns, "Veni, sancte spiritus." But his most important contribution was to divide the books of the Bible into chapters for easier reference. Langton was a popular preacher as well as an eminent professor and Biblical expert, and by 1205 Innocent had taken favorable notice of him. In June of that year the Pope summoned him to Rome and elevated him to the College of Cardinals.

Because John sent a letter congratulating Langton on his elevation to the College of Cardinals, Innocent had every reason to believe that John would welcome him as Archbishop. But John had never met Langton, whom he knew only by reputation. Furthermore, while Langton had been a prebendary of York Minster for some years, he had never occupied high office in England, causing John to consider him too inexperienced for the great position of Archbishop. Finally, Langton had not been John's nominee for the office, and the King was determined to keep the Papacy from exercising anything more than a final veto over the selection of a new Archbishop, as previous Popes had done. Certainly Innocent had no right to tell John whom he must employ in such an important office. Accordingly, John lodged a strong protest in a letter to the Curia and declared that he would never accept Langton's election because he knew nothing about the man.

On 26 May 1207, Innocent wrote a blistering reply in which he essentially accused John of hypocrisy.

> We are surprised ... that a man of so great a name, a native of your own kingdom, could have remained unknown to you at least in reputation, especially since after his promotion to the cardinalate you wrote to him that, though you had planned to summon him to the service of your household, you rejoiced at his elevation to the greater office.[31]

Then, after summarizing Langton's many achievements, Innocent commanded John to recognize the new Archbishop's election. Before the King could make another protest, Innocent consecrated Langton at Viterbo on 17 June.

When John learned of the Pope's action, he fell into a violent rage. After shouting that anyone who recognized Langton's election would be treated as a public enemy, he vented his anger on the hapless monks at Canterbury. On 14 July a royal force, headed by two of John's household knights, arrived at the cathedral compound. One of those knights, probably Fulke de Cantilupe, assailed the monks as traitors to the King and ordered them to leave the realm at once. If they refused, he and his men would set fire to the buildings and burn all the monks alive. Although thirteen monks were too ill to leave their beds in the infirmary, sixty-seven bowed to the King's wishes and sailed across the Channel to Normandy, where Langton, who had just taken rooms at the large Cistercian monastery at Pontigny, arranged for them to be scattered among several different abbeys in northwestern France.

Meanwhile John had transferred a number of monks from St. Augustine's Abbey, Canterbury, to the cathedral compound, where they conducted the daily rites in the cathedral. John put those monks under the supervision of Cantilupe, who also took charge of the cathedral's revenues, most of which he funnelled directly into the King's coffers.

On learning of John's actions, Innocent III reacted with his customary vigor. On 27 August 1207, he wrote to the Bishop of Rochester, Gilbert de Glanvill, and directed him to excommunicate Cantilupe and another of the King's household knight, Reginald of Cornhill, as well as any other men who were involved in the illegal management of the cathedral's revenues. That same day the Pope sent letters to three other Bishops, William of London, Eustace of Ely, and Mauger of Worcester, whom he trusted above all others. Those three prelates were directed to go and confer with John. If they failed to persuade him to relent, they were

> ... to publish throughout England the general sentence of Interdict, permitting no ecclesiastical office except the baptism of infants and the confession of the dying to be celebrated there. This sentence you must yourselves fully observe, and by ecclesiastical censure you must cause it to be inviolably observed by all.[32]

During the winter of 1207-1208, John tried frantically to prevent the publication of the Interdict. In February 1208 he sent a safe-conduct to

Langton's brother, Simon, who was urged to come to England at once for confidential talks. Discussions occurred at Winchester during the first half of March, but neither side would yield an inch. Simon Langton, speaking on behalf of his brother and the Pope, held out for John's unconditional submission; but the King reiterated his earlier statement that he would never accept Langton as Archbishop. Thereupon Simon Langton returned to the continent, leaving the three Bishops no choice but to publish the Interdict, which they did in their cathedrals on Palm Sunday, 23 March. Then they packed their bags and fled to the continent.

Once the Interdict took effect the next day, most of the other Bishops published it in their cathedrals on the following Sunday. The only two prelates who refused to comply out of loyalty to John were Peter des Roches of Winchester and John de Grey of Norwich. In gratitude the King returned all their cathedral's revenues to them on 5 April, which amounted to a partial reversal of his declared policy of seizing all clerical wealth in the kingdom during the aftermath of the Interdict's publication. John was determined to punish clerics of all ranks and degrees who failed to perform the regular and occasional services of the Church (i.e., baptisms, weddings and funerals), their most important function in his view. Furthermore, he knew that if he failed to use financial or other pressure to make them perform that function, his subjects might grow sullen and resentful, causing him to face mounting pressure from all sides to surrender to the Papacy in regard to Langton.

Just as John feared, religious services came to a halt in most places during the spring of 1208, causing Innocent to feel confident that John would accept Langton in a year or less. When in 1200 Innocent had imposed an Interdict on France as a way of forcing Philip Augustus to agree to a reconciliation with his estranged wife, Ingeborg of Denmark, the Papacy achieved its goal in only eight months.[33] However, that earlier struggle involved no constitutional issues comparable to those involved in John's dispute with Rome. John knew that a dangerous precedent would be set if he submitted to Innocent's demands regarding the selection of a new Archbishop, and as a consequence he was prepared to hold out indefinitely. Luckily for John, he had strong support from his barons, who also sensed that an important constitutional principle was at stake. Indeed, they urged him to continue the struggle until Rome gave assurances that the rights and dignity of the English crown would be respected.[34]

By the spring of 1209 Innocent was becoming impatient and warned John of sterner measures if his resistance continued. When the Pope's threats produced no results, Innocent directed Langton to excommunicate John at the appropriate moment.

John seems to have known by August of 1209 that he was about to be excommunicated, which caused him to become more alarmed than ever. This was the case because excommunication was a particularly dangerous form of censure in the Middle Ages. It forbade the named individual to participate in any of the services of the Church and isolated him from all other individuals except his immediate family and clerics seeking to persuade him to repent. Furthermore, in most parts of Europe excommunication was tantamount to outlawry, and those who assisted or socialized with an excommunicated person ran the risk of being excommunicated themselves. Because of his deep alarm John held a Great Council at Marlborough in September of 1209 and ordered each magnate in attendance to swear fidelity to himself and his two-year-old son, Prince Henry.

Langton had no particular desire to excommunicate John; and with papal approval he sailed across the Channel in October and spent a week at Dover, hoping to negotiate with the King. But John refused to appear, so Langton returned to France and published the decree of excommunication in November. At that point the Bishops of Salisbury, Bath, Lincoln, and Rochester fled across the Channel and joined the other prelates in exile on the continent. Because John had recently sent John de Grey to be his Justiciar in Ireland, the only Bishop still toiling away at his duties was Peter des Roches of Winchester, whose loyalty to John never waned.[35]

Despite the collapse of the English episcopate during the autumn of 1209, baronial opposition to the King began to mount, especially in the north. The original leader of that opposition seems to have been Roger de Lacy, sheriff of Yorkshire and Cumberland, who had been castellan of Château Gaillard when it fell to the French in March of 1204. Shortly before Christmas of 1209 John expelled Roger from his two shrievalties and sent him off to fight in Wales, where he died two years later to the fury of his son and heir John.

If Roger de Lacy and several other northern barons were alarmed by John's dispute with the Papacy, the average magnate felt no cause for concern. In fact, most of the kingdom's magnates applauded John's defiance of the Pope, which enabled John to transfer the burden of taxation from their estates to those of the Church. From 1209 until 1213, when John finally came to terms with Rome, he derived more money from the clergy than any other English ruler before the time of Henry VIII during the sixteenth century.

Of course, whenever a Bishop fled abroad or was ordered to go into exile, the King was entitled to confiscate his revenues for the duration. This proved extremely lucrative for John because the archbishopric of Canterbury was worth over £2,200 a year at that time, while the archbishopric of York and the bishopric of Winchester were worth about £1,000 each, and the bishoprics of Ely, Norwich, and Lincoln approximately £600 each. John also made heavy assessments on the parish priests of adjacent counties from time to time. For example, in 1211 he ordered the rectors and vicars of York province to pay him slightly more than £3,700.

Because John considered the Interdict a papal declaration of war on him, he felt justified in seizing the estates of wealthy monasteries, which their Abbots recovered only by handing over large sums to royal agents. The Abbot of St. Albans paid 1,100 marks for the lands of his rich house, while the Abbot of Rufford contributed 300 marks to that end. It appears that John received the largest sums from the houses of the Cistercian order, which were enjoying record profits from the wool trade by the thirteenth century. In 1210 John ordered all sixty-eight Cistercian monasteries in England to pay him 40,000 marks, or an average of 581 marks each. Sums like these help to explain how John secured over £100,000 from the Church by 1213.

Because of the ease with which he extorted huge sums from the Church, John's appetite was whetted, and he soon demanded equally large sums from the laity. Of course, his goal was simply to amass a huge war chest in order to subsidize foreign allies and hire huge numbers of mercenary troops with which to recover Normandy, Anjou, and the other provinces he had lost to Philip Augustus in 1203-1204.

The smallest and most vulnerable group in the kingdom during that age were the Jews, who had lived in England on royal sufferance since the Norman Conquest. Because the Jews were restricted to moneylending and often charged yearly interest of forty or even fifty percent, they were hated and often assaulted by their neighbors, causing John to realize he could exploit them in total safety. As early as 1206 he allowed wealthy landowners to default on their financial obligations to Jewish moneylenders provided they accompanied him to the continent with their retinues. Even worse, in 1207 or 1208 he formally cancelled Warin de Montchesney's heavy debts to a Jewish moneylender once Montchesney agreed to pay 2,000 marks to the crown immediately; while in 1211 he cancelled Gilbert de Gant's debt of 1,500 marks to another Jewish moneylender provided he deposited 1,200 marks in the

Exchequer within two years.

The climax of John's harsh policy toward the Jews came in January of 1210. During that month Jews throughout the realm were suddenly imprisoned and their records confiscated. Once those records were analyzed, several Jews were brutally punished as a way of intimidating their co-religionists. Isaac of Canterbury was hanged and all his goods sold for the Exchequer's benefit, while Isaac of Norwich saved his life only by handing over 10,000 marks to royal agents. At Bristol the head of the Jewish congregation, whose name is unknown to us, was also imprisoned and ordered to pay 10,000 marks. That bold and courageous man refused to part with a single penny, even after being threatened with torture. Thereupon royals agents knocked out one of his teeth each morning for a week. On the eight morning, after losing seven teeth, he capitulated and agreed to pay the sum demanded. As a result of those brutal incidents, which were widely reported, Jewish families were softened up for a general tax later that year. When in October of 1210 John imposed a heavy tallage on the Jewish minority, royal agents collected over 65,000 marks for the King's war chest.

Rich widows were equally defenseless, and John took unscrupulous advantage of them too, which led to a special clause in Magna Carta, as we shall see. Even before he launched his attack on the Jews, John demanded large sums from rich widows who preferred to remain single or wished to choose new husbands to suit themselves. Only a year after his accession he obtained forty marks from Emma, the widow of Henry de Montfort of Berkshire, for a royal license "to marry whom she will and to have her dower in peace." As the years wore on, the price of such licenses rose sharply, particularly in the case of aristocratic widows. In 1205 the dowager Countess of Warwick paid £1,000 and sent John ten palfreys in order to remain unmarried and have custody of her children and the revenues from their inherited estates. During that same year another widow was required to pay 2,000 marks to the same end; while in 1212 Hawisa, the thrice-married Countess of Aumale, was required to pay 5,000 marks in order to avoid remarriage against her will.

Just as John's exploitation of wealthy widows grew more oppressive as the reign continued, so did his treatment of officials who failed to perform their duties to his total satisfaction. In 1207 he amerced, or fined, Thomas of Moulton, sheriff of Lincolnshire, 200 marks for incorrect information he had allegedly supplied the Curia Regis. The next year Thomas was arrested and fined another 1,000 marks, this time for falling behind in his monthly payments to the crown. In 1209 a popular northern baron, Robert de Ros, was amerced 300 marks because a prisoner in his custody had escaped; while in 1212 the Vavasour brothers of Yorkshire, Robert and Malgar, were amerced 1375 marks for several minor offenses committed during earlier years. Undoubtedly the official most heavily amerced was Hugh de Neville, chief justice of all royal forests in England. In 1211 Hugh was fined 1,000 marks for failing to notify the King before allowing a royal favorite, the Bishop of Winchester, to establish a deer park in his diocese; and two years later Hugh was ordered to pay 6,000 marks because two prisoners in his custody had escaped and "for other [similar] offences." Although Hugh's second fine was reduced to 5,000 marks in 1214, he was not appeased. During the spring of 1215 he actively supported the campaign that led to Magna Carta, just as Robert de Ros did.

That John amerced officials whose service displeased him in any way seems ironic in view of his practice of selling offices to mediocre men of limited experience. During that era most of Europe's rulers sold governmental offices in order to raise funds, but rarely for the high prices John charged or to men of such obvious mediocrity. Reference has already been made to the way he sold the Lord Chancellorship in 1205 to the undistinguished Walter de Grey. Thomas of Moulton, another undistinguished man whom John amerced in both 1207 and 1208 for a variety of infractions, had somewhat earlier purchased the shrievalty of Lincolnshire for 500 marks and five palfreys as well as a pledge to pay an additional 300 marks into the Exchequer from his yearly tax collections in that county. Similarly, John sold the shrievalties of Yorkshire and Northumberland to the unfit William de Stuteville for £1,500. Because many other examples of this sort could be cited, it is difficult to agree with his defenders' claim that the central government functioned with greater efficiency during his reign.[36]

Because of John's practice of selling offices, it was almost inevitable that he would traffic in the sale of justice too. During the course of his reign, and especially during the years 1204-1213, he travelled the realm continuously, hearing cases and settling disputes of all kinds. Some historians give him high marks as a judge and hold that he administered the law more effectively than his father or older brother, who had spent most of their time on the continent.[37] Although John was right to oppose judicial delays and speed up the wheels of justice, he was required to promise in Article 45 of Magna Carta that he would never again appoint "... justices, constables, sheriffs or bailiffs who do not know the law of the land and mean to observe it well." Moreover, in Article 17 of the charter he agreed to reestablish the Court of Common Pleas, which he had suspended in 1209 to the anger of the common lawyers, whose work he sought to perform in the new Court of King's Bench with assistance from other novices like himself. Finally, John annoyed almost all of the barons by making heavy use of the writ *praecipe quod reddat,* which was an easy way for well-to-do petitioners to transfer cases from a baronial court to the new Court of King's Bench.[38] The barons were upset by the sharp contraction of their legal jurisdiction, which led to a steady drop in their revenues and fears about their courts' continued existence; and in Article 34 of Magna Carta this matter was settled to the barons' satisfaction.

Most historians assume that the barons were chiefly concerned to defend their own financial interests and thus less objective than John in settling cases, but that assumption seems unwarranted. In dozens of instances John dispensed the law to suit himself and exacted large bribes in return for economic and political favors. For example, in 1207 he dismissed charges brought against Gerard de Furnival by a private citizen in return for a cash payment of £1,000 to the crown. A more complex but revealing case involved the Yorkshire baron William de Mowbray. In 1200 a bitter dispute erupted between Mowbray and his neighbor, William de Stuteville, who was attempting to gain possession of many of Mowbray's estates. In desperation Mowbray turned to the King and offered 2,000 marks to have the suit settled to his satisfaction. Thereupon John considered the matter and, on 21 January 1201, rendered a judgment directly contrary to Mowbray's interests. By that judgment Stuteville was awarded the manor of Brinklow as well as nineteen of Mowbray's forty or so knight's fees. Mowbray was dismayed, especially when John demanded payment of the entire sum he had pledged for a "satisfactory" judgment; and in 1215 Mowbray was a leading member of the baronial faction that forced him to accept Magna Carta.

One of John's favorites, whom he permitted to bend the law to his own ends, was William Briwerre. Indeed, Briwerre accumulated great wealth in less than a decade and might be compared to an American robber baron of the late nineteenth century. In 1204 John permitted Briwerre to dispossess the five sisters of John de Bidun, who had held the valuable honour of Lavendon, in Buckinghamshire. In fact, John himself transferred the lands in question to Briwerre, which he justified by citing the late John de Bidun's unpaid debts to the Exchequer. During the same year Briwerre secured control of extensive lands in Ongar hundred, Essex, which had been held during earlier years by Bishop de Lucy of Winchester (d. 1204). And shortly thereafter Briwerre profited in similar fashion by seizing Walter Croc's estates in Wiltshire.

That John did nothing to restrain men like Briwerre and even assisted them on occasion provoked growing fears among the ranks of the landed class. As a leading student of the period has noted, the grasping actions of John's favorites

> ... alarmed conservative moralists, many aristocrats, and jealous colleagues at court, who saw them as "new men" threatening the traditional social order.... Old landed families had good reason for their fears that King John was threatening their lawful rights of inheritance.[39]

Most men were even more worried about John's policy of charging considerably higher reliefs, or inheritance taxes, than his predecessors on the throne. During the years 1154-1199 the crown had rarely charged more than twice the yearly income of an estate as the relief owed by an adult heir seeking confirmation of his legal title. But during John's time the reliefs charged on such landed estates tripled before rising to even higher levels. In 1212 John de Lacy was ordered to pay 7,000 marks for estates worth approximately 1,500 marks a year; and two years later William Fitz Alan was assessed a relief of 10,000 marks on properties of approximately equal value.

Apparently John did not expect to collect such enormous reliefs. Rather, his actual goal was to put landowners like John de Lacy, whose father Roger had been the last English castellan of Château Gaillard and a victim of John's Welsh policy in 1211, under a staggering financial obligation to the crown because of serious doubts about his loyalty. Then, if de Lacy ever ignored a royal command or conspired against the King, he could be ruined at a stroke. But the policy itself provoked serious criticism, and in Article 2 of Magna Carta the reliefs the crown could assess on inherited estates were limited to nominal amounts.

Because of all the financial expedients John used, which included the collection of heavier and more frequent scutages than any previous ruler,[40] he was in an unusually strong position by 1212. Indeed, it appears that by January of that year, John had at least 200,000 marks in his castle treasuries at Bristol and Nottingham. That enormous sum made him momentarily the richest ruler in English history, richer even than William the Conqueror or the first Tudor monarch, Henry VII, who is usually described as the best businessman ever to occupy the

English throne. John's enormous financial horde was intended, as noted earlier, to finance a successful campaign against Philip Augustus and thereby achieve the reconquest of Normandy and the other lost provinces of the Angevin empire. Certainly John's goal was not to make himself an absolute ruler, although his financial success may have raised that specter in many minds. This was the case because John had trampled the rights of hundreds of individuals while accumulating so much wealth. He had repeatedly demonstrated favoritism and petty vindictiveness. He had violated customary rights of inheritance and quarrelled with the Pope while driving most of the country's prelates into exile and seizing their estates. But by the time John reached the zenith of his financial success, the kingdom was rife with dissatisfaction and his political position began to crumble.

During the summer of 1212 serious plotting against John began, and within several weeks a dangerous conspiracy against his life was afoot in Yorkshire and the northern midlands. While at Nottingham on 16 August, John was shaken by reports that he was about to be assassinated or handed over to his Welsh enemies, who were still furious about his execution of twenty-eight of their teenage sons. The next day he sent letters to the sheriffs in which he offered large rebates to those who owed substantial debts to Jewish moneylenders. In addition he instructed the sheriffs and six knights from each county to confer with him during a Great Council in the near future. Doubtless he wanted to discover the identity of the conspirators but, in Professor Holt's words, he also hoped "... to test feeling and initiate action."[41]

Within several weeks John managed to suppress the conspiracy of 1212. The leading plotters were summoned to appear before the shire courts, and those who failed to respond to the third and final summons were outlawed. Robert fitz Walter, one of the King's wealthiest subjects, fled across the Channel to France, while another ringleader, Eustace de Vesci, took refuge at the court of his father-in-law, William the Lion of Scotland. Shortly after de Vesci fled northward, royal agents took possession of his stronghold, Alnwick Castle in Northumberland. Another important conspirator, Robert de Vaux, who was still smarting from a large fine he had been assessed two years before, was imprisoned shortly after the plot of 1212 collapsed. He soon offered to pay an additional 2,000 marks for his freedom, but John ruled that a fourth of that amount must be handed over before his release, which suggests that he remained in captivity for several years, his barony being a relatively poor one. Another plotter, John de Lacy, had to surrender two castles, Pontefract and Donington, while still another conspirator, Richard de

Umfraville, had to hand over Prudhoe Castle and four of his teenage sons as hostages for his future behavior. All in all, at least a dozen men were required to surrender at least one castle and one or more of their sons to retain their freedom.

Shortly after suppressing the conspiracy of 1212, John heard reports that Philip Augustus was about to launch a massive attack on England, which he hoped to conquer as an appanage for his son, the Dauphin Louis. Those reports aroused John's deepest fears and caused him to consider a *rapprochement* with the Pope out of political necessity. In November of 1212 John sent a delegation headed by Alan Martel and Philip of Worcester to Rome to explore the possibility of a negotiated settlement. But that delegation accomplished nothing, mainly because Stephen Langton was present at the Curia at the time. Langton still enjoyed Innocent's confidence, and he was determined that John should accept a number of precise conditions before he and England were reconciled with the Church. When Langton returned to Pontigny in January of 1213, he took with him a bull of deposition that he was directed to publish whenever Rome instructed him to do so.[42]

Shortly after Langton's departure from the Eternal City, Innocent sent a special legate, Pandulf, to meet with Philip Augustus in Paris. Pandulf was directed to persuade the French monarch to launch a holy war against England on behalf of the suffering Church. Philip Augustus was delighted by the Pope's invitation to attack his old enemy and soon ordered the construction of a large fleet at Damme, the port used by the rich merchant oligarchy of Bruges in the Low Countries. However, Pandulf also had secret instructions to negotiate with John without informing the French crown.

After a brief stay in Paris Pandulf crossed the Channel to England and held private talks with John during the last week of February 1213. On that occasion the legate warned John to conclude a satisfactory agreement with Rome by 1 June. If he failed to do so, Innocent would direct Langton to publish the bull of deposition that was now in his possession at Pontigny. As John well knew, the publication of that bull might trigger a massive uprising in England, greatly increasing the chances of a successful foreign attack on the realm.

Because Innocent had suggested terms that John considered unreasonable, the latter hesitated for six more weeks. But on 8 April Philip Augustus held a Great Council at Soissons and ordered his nobles to meet him at Rouen within thirteen days, fully armed and ready to move up the coast to Damme, where they would embark for England. When that news was reported in London a week later, John realized he had no choice. He must conclude an agreement with Rome in order to keep the bull of deposition from being published, and possibly to get the Interdict and the bull of excommunication withdrawn. If John and the Pope composed their differences, he would be in a much better position to repulse the French attack, which might even be cancelled as a result. Because of the dire situation John invited Pandulf to return to England for serious negotiations at last. On 13 May John and the legate concluded a solemn accord in the presence of four important witnesses--the Earls of Salisbury, Ferrers, and Warenne and John's old ally, the Count of Boulogne. By that accord of 13 May, which the witnesses pledged to guarantee, John finally accepted Stephen Langton as Archbishop; and once Langton crossed the Channel during the coming summer, he would absolve John of all his sins and withdraw the bull of excommunication at once. However, at John's insistence, it was agreed that the King's customary rights concerning clerical elections would be scrupulously honored by the Papacy in the future.[43] Secondly, John promised that all the Bishops who had lived in exile since 1208 would be allowed to return from the continent, and the crown would restore their lost income according to a precise schedule.[44] Third, John would return to the English Church all the revenues he had confiscated from it since 1208 according to a definite agreement to be negotiated in the next few months. Once that agreement was concluded and partial restitution made, the Interdict would be lifted, although that might not occur for another year.[45] Fourth and last, John would allow Robert fitz Walter and Eustace de Vesci, the ringleaders of the unsuccessful plot of 1212, to return and recover their estates in England.[46]

Because the Interdict's withdrawal was still more than a year away and the Archbishop was not expected to arrive in England and absolve John of his sins until July, the King felt the need for another measure that would stress his improved relationship with the Papacy. Back in 1194, in order to speed his release from captivity, Richard I had resigned England to the Holy Roman Emperor, who granted it back to him at once as an imperial fief conditional on the payment of an annual pension of £5,000. Perhaps John should take a similar step. If he resigned England into the Pope's hands and received it back as a papal fief, he would become a leading papal vassal, and Innocent would be obligated to assist him against enemies like Philip Augustus. Moreover, such a step was unlikely to be viewed as craven or dishonorable by his subjects. During recent years that very step had been taken by the rulers of Denmark, Sweden, Poland, Aragon, and Sicily, all of whom were considered strong and honorable monarchs by their people.

At any rate, on 15 May 1213 John appeared before Pandulf at the Templars' house outside Dover. On that occasion John performed the customary acts of feudal homage, thereby recognizing the Pope as his feudal overlord. As a symbol of his vassalage to the Papacy, John agreed to send Rome a yearly payment of 1,000 marks, 700 for England and 300 for Wales.[47] John's theoretical surrender of his dominions to the Papacy was applauded by most of the English barons, who were relieved that his quarrel with Innocent III was finally over. Two years later on the eve of Magna Carta, several of John's bitterest opponents even claimed credit for the maneuver, which they considered a prudent move.

While taking those steps to secure papal support, John was readying his fleet for action. Since 1207 John had expanded his fledgling navy and developed it into an effective fighting force. Because of the loss of Normandy and its harbors in 1204, John was aware of the importance of naval power if he was to have any chance of defeating Philip Augustus and reestablishing the Angevin empire. During the spring of 1213 he used his growing fleet to prevent French troops from landing on the southeastern coast. After mobilizing his warships, he placed them under the command of his half-brother, William Longsword, Earl of Salisbury. At the same time he gathered large forces in the fields around Dover and sent several thousand marks to the continent, hoping to persuade the Count of Flanders to join an anti-French coalition.

On 22 May the French army marched out of Rouen and within a week reached Damme, where dozens of barges were waiting to ferry it across the Channel to England. But on 28 May the English fleet set sail from Portsmouth; and two days later, while the French army was off besieging the nearby city of Ghent, a pitched battle occurred at Damme. The Earl of Salisbury and the Count of Boulogne sank or badly damaged most of the barges anchored in the harbor. Before sailing away they spread additional havoc by cutting loose all the vessels moored in the river. It was a disastrous setback for Philip Augustus, who felt compelled to cancel his attack on England before returning to France with his demoralized troops.

Elated by the outcome, John was soon considering the possibility of a new offensive against his old enemy, who seemed more vulnerable than at any time since 1206. The more John thought about the manner, the more optimistic he became, On 15 July he sent an embassy to the continent to meet with his nephew, the Holy Roman Emperor Otto IV, and such rulers in the Low Countries as the Dukes of Brabant, Limburg, and Lorraine and the Counts of Namur and Holland. John was confident that Otto and the others would join him in a great coalition against Philip Augustus in the near future.[48]

Shortly before that important embassy departed, Stephen Langton arrived in southern England. From Dover the Archbishop travelled on horseback to Winchester, where John appeared before him on 20 July. At the western door of the great cathedral, while the monks of the cathedral chapter chanted the Fiftieth Psalm, John swore on the Gospels that he would defend the Church and restore all its property; revive and abide by the laws of Edward the Confessor; and respect the rights of all his subjects, punishing no one without due process of law. Thereupon the Archbishop formally absolved him of his sins and publicly declared that his excommunication was over. Afterward they exchanged the symbolic kiss of peace and, according to a contemporary chronicler,[49] retired to the refectory and dined together "in joy and merriment."

If there was "joy and merriment" that day, it ended quickly. John never liked Langton, whom he accepted only out of dire necessity, while the Archbishop was even more suspicious of the King's character than Hubert Walter had been. The two men never worked harmoniously together, and within weeks there was obvious tension between them. On 25 August 1213, during a clerical synod in London, the coronation charter of Henry I was produced and debated at length, doubtless at Langton's urging. Because Henry I was the only previous monarch to have granted precise reforms to his subjects, John was deeply annoyed and made his displeasure with the Archbishop painfully evident.[50]

Innocent III was soon aware of the situation in England and appointed a new legate, Nicholas, the Cardinal-Bishop of Tusculum, whom John might trust and consult occasionally. Nicholas arrived in England on 26 September and developed a rapport with John that the latter loudly publicized as a way of embarrassing Langton. Like Pandulf before him, Nicholas conceded everything John wanted in regard to clerical elections, and with great fanfare the King promised to reimburse the Church for all its losses during previous years according to a recently negotiated schedule.[51]

Because of John's flamboyant show of cooperation, the Pope addressed a circular letter to the English people in October of 1213. Innocent instructed them to respect and obey his esteemed vassal John, whose person and dominions, along with those of his heirs forever, enjoyed the special protection of the Holy See. In the words of Professor Painter, the Pope's letter is clear proof that John had gained

"... a vigorous, determined, powerful, and none too discriminating ally."[52]

Assured of papal support and military aid from Otto IV and a number of rulers in the Low Countries, John continued to ready his forces for a massive attack on Philip Augustus during the summer of 1214. John's plan called for a two-front war, beginning in the late spring, which would force the French ruler to divide his troops. John himself would embark for Poitou by the end of March, and using it as a base, he and the Count of Toulouse, with whom he had recently concluded a military pact, would push up through Anjou and Maine into western Normandy. Somewhat later Otto IV, aided by the Dukes of Brabant, Limburg and Lorraine, the Counts of Boulogne, Holland, Flanders, and Namur, and an English army led by the Earl of Salisbury, would sweep through Hainault into northern France. In that way Philip Augustus would be caught in a trap and totally destroyed. Although strategically sound, John's plan was too ambitious for an age when travel and communications were so slow.

During the last week of January, John completed his preparations before appointing Bishop des Roches of Winchester to the great office of Justiciar, which had been vacant since Geoffrey fitz Peter's death several months before. He also named Peter de Maulay to be paymaster of his forces in Poitou. On 9 February, John set sail from Portsmouth in the company of dozens of barons, who included Ranulf de Blundeville, the powerful Earl of Chester. In 1204 Ranulf had lost all his Norman estates, which he hoped to recover by helping John to reestablish the Angevin empire.

When John and his followers landed at La Rochelle on 15 February 1214, they received a warm welcome from its citizens, whose prosperity depended on continued trade with England. Within a week more than a dozen castles within fifty miles of La Rochelle declared for John. He therefore made that city his campaign headquarters .

During his first ten weeks on the continent, John moved erratically through Poitou and central Aquitaine, trying to secure additional support for his cause. By 3 April he had reached Limoges, where Vicomte Guy swore fealty to him. Within a few more days he reached La Réole, in northern Gascony. Once he was confident the Gascons would remain loyal to him, he turned northward and concentrated on winning support in the counties of Angoulême and La Marche. By making extensive grants to baronial families like the Mauleons and the Thouars, his efforts bore fruit, but there was still the great house of Lusignan to conciliate. John could not allow the Lusignans, his bitter enemies since his diplomatic and marriage blunders of 1200, to remain disaffected. He therefore courted them assiduously and even concluded a marriage alliance with them. In the near future one of his daughters would marry a son of Hugh of Lusignan.

By that juncture John's financial reserves were almost depleted. On 26 May he sent a letter ordering his new Justiciar, the Bishop of Winchester, to collect a scutage of three marks per knight's fee and to send the proceeds to him at once. Barons and other men who held estates directly from the crown but had failed to accompany him to the continent were to pay the scutage without complaint; if they refused to do so, they would be severely punished on his return. Bishop des Roches attempted to carry out the King's command, but his agents encountered stiff opposition in most localities. In Essex, Hertfordshire, and Yorkshire not a single penny was collected, while in Norfolk and Suffolk the outcome was almost as dismal. The amount collected from the whole country was less than twenty-five percent of what it should have been.[53]

On the continent John was unaware of the firm resistance to his demand for additional taxation. Because his efforts had enjoyed considerable success since February, he expected the needed money to arrive soon. Moreover, he felt strong enough to cross the Loire and enter Brittany, whose current Duke, Pierre de Dreux, was a close relative of Philip Augustus. By the second week of June John was approaching the important city of Nântes, and at that juncture he captured the Duke's younger brother, Robert, which did not cause the Duke to switch sides, however. But the fact that John had the Duke's brother in his power caused Pierre to restrain his troops as the English marched out of Brittany toward the east.

Ultimately John and his army moved up the Loire, and on 17 June they captured Angers, the capital of Anjou. Two days later they surrounded the castle of Roche-au-Moine, which had been built by Guillaume des Roches after his defection to Philip Augustus in 1203. If the English could capture Roche-au-Moine, the road to Paris would lie open to them. Philip Augustus realized this and directed the Dauphin to mobilize an army in Touraine and go to the relief of the beleaguered fortress. Louis and his army arrived at Roche-au-Moine on 2 July, causing John's troops to retreat in haste. Because the Count of La Marche and most of his lieutenants were unwilling to fight against the Dauphin, John suspected that he would lose a pitched battle, which would virtually destroy his basic strategy. To avoid that outcome he fled toward the west, and within two days he took shelter at the abbey of Saint-Maxent. The next day he continued on to La Rochelle, where the Dauphin kept him pinned down all summer. Meanwhile developments of much greater importance were occurring in the Low Countries.

About the middle of June Philip Augustus left Paris for modern-day Belgium, hoping to keep John's allies out of northern France. Within a brief time Philip arrived in Hainault and mustered his army at the great castle of Valenciennes. Shortly afterward Otto IV left the Rhineland and, on 12 July, arrived at Nivelle, in southern Brabant, some forty miles away. During the next two weeks the rival commanders jockeyed for the best battle position. Although French numbers seem to have remained constant during those days, the troops in Otto's command almost doubled. An English force led by the Earl of Salisbury arrived, and so did dozens of regiments led by the Dukes of Brabant, Limburg, and Lorraine and the Counts of Flanders, Holland, Boulogne, and Namur. Half a century later a chronicler at Semones, in the Vosges Mountains, maintained that allied numbers grew to about 105,000 men in all, including 25,000 horsemen. But a modern authority, Georges Duby, considers that number far too high. Indeed, Professor Duby maintains that although Otto and his subordinates commanded slightly larger forces than Philip Augustus, both armies together contained only about 16,000 men.[54]

On Sunday the 27th of July, one of the truly decisive encounters of the Middle Ages, the celebrated battle of Bouvines, took place in western Hainault, a few miles outside the town of Tournai. The fighting began about noon when Otto IV ordered his men to attack the eastern end of the French line. Within a short time the opposing generals lost control of the action, and a series of confused mêlées took place. Under the circumstances controlled charges and counter-charges were impossible, and the fighting degenerated into an enormous, almost chaotic tournament. Because the French nobility always excelled in actions of that sort, they enjoyed a crucial advantage, which increased when the Duke of Brabant and his troops fled the field, thereby depriving John's allies of badly needed support. Otto IV had three horses killed out from under him, whereas Philip Augustus, who commanded the French centre, was also unhorsed and almost killed. In fact, shortly before the battle began Otto and the Counts of Boulogne and Flanders swore that they would keep on fighting until Philip Augustus was dead. Luckily for the French monarch, he enjoyed unwavering support from the Duke of Burgundy, the Counts of Beaumont, Bar,

Champagne, and Saint-Pol, and four important prelates--the Bishops of Beauvais, Léon, and Senlis, and the Archbishop of Rheims. The Bishop of Beauvais made an especially valuable contribution to the French victory. Armed with a heavy club, he knocked the Earl of Salisbury from his horse and took him prisoner. Salisbury was only one of many allied commanders who were captured that afternoon. Others who enjoyed that questionable distinction were the Counts of Boulogne and Flanders, nine lesser Counts, and at least twenty-five knights. How many men perished during the encounter has never been determined, but in percentage terms the casualty rate was probably high, perhaps thirty-five or forty per cent.[55]

Once the fighting ended about 5:00 P.M., Otto IV fled the field and made his way back to Germany, where he died four years later without an heir and was succeeded by his old enemy, Frederick of Hohenstaufen. As for the French monarch, he led his hundreds of prisoners in a vast triumphal procession to Paris and parcelled them out to his leading followers, who were allowed to ransom them for whatever sums they could get. William Longsword was assigned to the Duke of Brittany, whose younger brother Robert was still an English captive. Ultimately a swap was arranged, and Longsword and several other English commanders returned to their native land.

John was the last important Englishman to embark for his native country. Aware of the hostility that would confront him after this great new defeat, he remained in western France as long as he could. On 18 September he concluded a five-year truce with Philip Augustus at Chinon, after which the people of La Rochelle expected him to set sail momentarily. But knowing he would return to an empty treasury and almost no political support, he delayed his departure until 13 October. Thereafter he was confronted by such great political opposition in England that he never went abroad again.

When John reappeared at Westminster, dissatisfaction was rife and most of the barons felt it was past time for him to make major concessions. Yet only a small minority were willing to come out in open opposition to him; and had he played his cards skillfully, he might have emerged from the crisis almost unscathed. But once he reached the capital, he learned that the scutage his Justiciar had attempted to collect the previous May had been ignored in most places. Furious, he met with a group of defaulters in Norfolk on 4 November and insisted that they pay their full assessments immediately.[56] This may have enabled his agents to collect several hundred more marks from the cautious and faint of heart, but at a heavy political cost. The more courageous barons now realized that John was incorrigible. He could never be trusted to use his power prudently and with restraint. Limits must be placed on his authority if they were ever to feel safe in their persons and estates again.

On 20 November, after John left Norfolk for London, the principal malcontents reassembled and voted in favor of a joint campaign against the crown. The only baron definitely known to have been present at that meeting was Robert fitz Walter, who was elected to be the barons' chief spokesman.[57] Others who may have been in attendance that day included the Earls of Norfolk, Essex, Oxford, Hertford, Hereford, and Winchester; Eustace de Vesci, William de Mowbray, John de Lacy, Robert de Ros, Roger de Cressi, William Marshal the Younger, and the two surviving sons of William de Briouse, Reginald and his younger brother Giles, Bishop of Hereford since 1200, who had just returned from a five-year exile on the continent.

Many of the dissatisfied barons came from the northern counties, as had most of the conspirators of 1212. But the baronial party of 1214-1215 also drew strength from Lincolnshire, East Anglia and the Home Counties, which made it a more powerful faction than its predecessor. Still, the new baronial party never numbered over forty men in all, a hundred or so of their compatriots being reluctant to commit themselves out of fear of John's wrath.

Opposed to the baronial party were a number of dedicated royalists--prelates and laymen who were initially prepared to support John out of deep concern for the monarchical form of government but not for John himself. Included in this faction were the Bishop of Winchester and three other influential prelates: William de Sainte-Mère-Eglise, Bishop of London since 1198; Walter de Gray, the Lord Chancellor since 1205 who had become Bishop of Worcester in October 1214; and William de Cornhill, the newly consecrated Bishop of Coventry and Lichfield. Also in the royal faction were eight powerful Earls, of whom the most important were probaably Ranulph de Blundeville (Chester); William Marshal the Elder (Pembroke); William Longsword (Salisbury); and Geoffrey de Mandeville (Essex and Gloucester).

As the crisis deepened during the winter of 1214-1215, some of the King's defenders drifted away, probably because of the unwavering determination of their opponents. A case in point is the behavior of Ranulph de Blundeville, Earl of Chester, who had accompanied John to the continent in 1214. An extremely wealthy man, Ranulph believed in the need for unfettered royal power, although he may have had little personal regard for John. According to his recent biographer, Ranulph distanced himself from the King as the crisis unfolded, which caused John to become apprehensive. Ultimately he tried to recover Ranulph's support by granting him the castle and manor of Newcastle-under-Lyme, which he enjoyed for the service of only one knight.[58]

In much the same way William Marshal the Elder ceased to be quite as fervent in his support of unfettered royal power as the crisis continued. Marshal's son, William Marshal the Younger, was a leading member of the baronial faction, and in earlier years the older Marshal's relationship with John had been strained. In 1205 the Earl had opposed John's call for a campaign to recover Normandy, causing him to fall out of royal favor; and for the next seven years Marshal lived primarily in Ireland, where he further alienated John by refusing to hand over William de Briouse for punishment. After the discovery of the 1212 plot against John's life, Marshal returned to England and recovered his former influence. In October of 1213 he received a grant of the castle and manor of Haverfordwest in Pembrokeshire, for which he paid the crown 1,000 marks; and during the next few months he also became castellan of Gower, Cardigan, and Carmarthen Castles, which made him the most important magnate in South Wales.[59]

Despite all those rewards, by which John hoped to bind Marshal to the royal cause, the Earl emerged during the winter of 1214-1215 as the spokesman for what might be called a "middle group." That group included several capable officials, such as Hubert de Burgh and the Bassett brothers, Thomas and Alan. But of greater importance than any of those officials was Archbishop Langton, who desperately hoped to avoid a civil war. Such a conflict might result in thousands of casualties and tempt Philip Augustus to make another effort to conquer the realm for his son the Dauphin.[60]

During the first weeks of the crisis Langton met on numerous occasions with Robert fitz Walter and several other baronial leaders. He urged them to take their stand on the laws and coronation charter of Henry I, which they should entreat John to reissue and uphold. However, while the barons were willing to consider documents from Henry I's time, from which they drew ideas and inspiration, they refused to copy them blindly. In fact, the barons eventually produced a document that reflected their own interests and concerns.

Although Langton's role in the evolution of Magna Carta was limited, he worked closely with William Marshal. Indeed, he and Marshal exercised a positive influence and convinced the two extremist factions to exercise restraint. As a consequence the danger of civil war receded for a time during the spring of 1215 although it never disappeared altogether.

During the late winter of 1215, John did his best to avoid a major grant of concessions. He met with the baronial leaders in London on the Feast of the Epiphany (6 January), and on that occasion the document generally known as the "The Unknown Charter of Liberties" was presented to him. That short document might be viewed as a preliminary draft of Magna Carta, and it acquired its name after lying hidden in the French archives until 1863, although it did not become widely known to English historians until the 1890s. Probably compiled to satisfy Langton, who wanted to know the barons' exact demands, it contained clauses relating to scutage, overseas military service, the administration of justice, and the maximum reliefs heirs to large landed estates could be required to pay for confirmation of their legal titles. In many ways the relatively brief Unknown Charter was a more radical document than Magna Carta, which discarded five of its main demands in favor of many lesser ones.[61]

John was reluctant to reject the Unknown Charter out of hand, which would probably cause his opponents to mobilize their troops and declare war on him. He therefore played for time and asked to have until the last Sunday of April to devise an answer. The barons agreed but kept their retainers in readiness, to his deep disappointment.

Early in March John made a dramatic move calculated to ensure papal support should fighting erupt in the near future. On 4 March he took the cross as a crusader and hinted that he was about to embark for the Holy Land. Actually John had no intention of leaving England, but in that era crusaders were entitled to special papal protection for three years. Thus John's goal at that juncture was to deter his opponents from attacking him, and he hoped the barons would fail to see through his ploy. In fact, he suddenly felt so much safer that he dismissed most of his foreign troops, who returned forthwith to the continent.

Because the barons were not fooled by John's maneuver, they compiled a longer document with more demands to present to him during the scheduled meeting on 26 April. During March and early April so many additional grievances were compiled that the Unknown Charter increased from less than a dozen clauses to forty-nine, which are usually characterized as "The Articles of the Barons."[62]

While the Articles of the Barons were being drawn up, John met with a baronial delegation at Oxford on 13 April. That conference produced no results because the King was inflexible and refused to negotiate in good faith. Once John departed the barons reassembled at Stamford and began to organize for war. That alarmed the King, who responded with another hollow gesture. When the barons refused to be deterred and learned that John was claiming to be too ill to attend the scheduled meeting on 26 April, they gave their spokesman, Robert fitz Walter, greater authority and an exalted title--"Marshal of the Army of God and Holy Church."

Deeply frightened, John agreed to meet with another group of barons at Reading on 1 May. During that conference the barons' chief negotiators were Bishop Briouse of Hereford and Geoffrey de Mandeville, Earl of Essex and Gloucester. The discussion began on a chilly note but became more cordial when John promised not to launch a campaign against his own subjects. Moreover, he won points for himself by suggesting that the main differences between the crown and its opponents should be resolved by eight arbitrators, four named by himself and the other four by his critics. But he destroyed the good effect of that offer by insisting that Innocent III, his overlord and strongest adherent, have final authority with power to veto any agreements reached by the eight arbitrators. The barons felt they had no chance of receiving a fair judgment from Rome, so at that point the dye was cast. Civil war was no longer avoidable.

Technically the conflict began on 3 May, when the barons renounced their homage and allegiance to the crown. For nine more days John clung to the naive belief that hostilities could still be avoided. But on 12 May he directed the sheriffs to seize all the lands and chattels of his enemies. Two days later he ordered the transfer of his main opponents' estates to his own followers, which was another serious mistake on his part. Such a policy was unenforceable at the time and its announcement strengthened the barons' resolve to continue the struggle.

On 14 May, while travelling through the midlands, John learned that his enemies were negotiating with several aldermen of London for possession of the city. Should the capital fall into their hands, the rebels would become almost invulnerable to royal attack, provided they remained safely behind the city's walls. On Saturday the 16th John sent his half-brother, the Earl of Salisbury, into London to prevent its capitulation. The next day John instructed Bishop Cornhill of Coventry, who belonged to one of the city's leading merchant families, to leave at once for the capital to assist Salisbury's efforts. But that same day a group of baronial sympathizers left the city gates unlocked while most of the citizens were attending mass, and rebel forces entered and took control of the municipal government, replacing the mayor with a baronial sympathizer. Then they plundered the dwellings of several committed royalists and prominent Jewish moneylenders. Half a dozen houses were dismantled and their timbers used to buttress the city walls, which became impregnable until the introduction of gunpowder two centuries later.

Once the capital was safely in rebel hands several magnates who had previously remained on the fence announced their support of the baronial faction. These included William d'Albini and the powerful Count of Aumale. This development so soon after London's capitulation caused enormous dismay in the royalist camp and forced John to alter his strategy. Because he was in poor health at the time, suffering from a painful attack of gout, he decided to submit to his enemies' demands for the moment but later, when in good health again, to get the Pope to nullify whatever concessions he had made in the interium. Then he would raise an army and destroy his opponents for good. On 27 May he directed Archbishop Langton to arrange a truce and instructed all his followers to honor its terms. Two days later he sent a letter to Rome explaining his new strategy and entreating the Pope's continued support.

During the next ten days messengers travelled back and forth between the barons' camp at Staines, near Windsor, and the King's pavilion at Runnymede, a large meadow on the opposite bank of the River Thames. The two principal negotiators at that juncture were William Marshal for the royalists and Saer de Quinci, Earl of Winchester, for the barons. Within ten days the forty-nine clauses of the Articles of the Barons increased to sixty-three in the next draft of the emerging charter.

That draft of Magna Carta was ready for debate by 10 June, when there was a conference to review and discuss its main points. That meeting was followed by a second conference for additional discussion on 15 June, when John agreed in principle to all 63 clauses while calling for several important changes of wording and arrangement.[63] By 19 June a corrected version of the document was ready, and during a conference that day it was approved by both sides, after which John directed royal scribes to produce several dozen copies within four days, when they would be sealed and sent to all parts of the realm by special couriers.[64]

During the meeting on 19 June, several other significant steps were taken. First, the unpopular Justiciar, Bishop Peter des Roches of Winchester, was replaced with Hubert de Burgh, a baronial leader who commanded great respect on both sides. Second, several barons whose estates had been seized by the King in recent years recovered them. For example, the Earl of Huntingdon and Roal fitz Alan regained possession of Fotheringhay Castle and Richmond Castle, respectively. And third, on 19 June the barons renewed their homage to John, which they sealed by exchanging the symbolic kiss of peace with him.[65] Thus the "civil war" that had begun on 3 May was over after less than two months without any actual fighting. However, the peace that was established on 19 June was more illusory than real, given John's determination to repudiate it once he was in a position to do so.

Of course, the bitter fighting that broke out in September of 1215 should not be blamed on the limitations and shortcomings of Magna Carta. John never intended to abide by the document a day longer than circumstances compelled him to do so; and by the time the Pope nullified it at his request on 24 August, he was in better health and ready to take the field again.[66] At that point a true civil war began, and it produced heavy casualties on both sides until John died of dysentery at a northern monastery on 18 October 1216. At that point he was succeeded on the throne by his nine-year-old son, Henry III, whose government was headed by William Marshal until his death in 1219 and then by Hubert de Burgh until his ouster in 1232. They voluntarily reissued Magna Carta with improvements and deletions in 1216, 1217, and 1225; and in that way baronial confidence in the central government was finally restored.

Since the early 1960s most scholars have stressed the limitations and shortcomings of Magna Carta, as if the barons hoped to solve the fundamental problems of English government for centuries to come. Clearly their goal was far more limited than that. Their principal objective was to establish a just and lasting peace with John, one that would require him and later Kings to rule in a lawful way and restrict royal power enough for them to feel safe during the remainder of his lifetime, however long that might be. But they had no desire to transform the monarch into a constitutional figurehead, of which they had no concept at all. In fact, they recognized the need for strong central government and sensed how difficult it would be for a baronial clique to serve as the supreme executive authority, given their own rivalries and bitter resentments, which often prevented effective action.

That Robert fitz Walter and his supporters were anxious to conclude a satisfactory peace with John is proved by Articles 50 and 51.[67] By Article 50 the King promised to dismiss from office almost all of his foreign favorites, who had shown themselves to be his most resolute champions and afforded him dangerous police power. These included Guy and Engelard de Cigogné; Peter, Andrew, and Guy de Chanceux;

Geoffrey de Martigny and his younger brothers; Philip Marc and his brothers as well as their nephew Geoffrey; and the many relations of Gerard d'Athée. Article 51 buttressed Article 50 and reads in a modern translation: "Immediately after concluding peace, we will remove from the kingdom all alien knights, crossbowmen, sergeants and mercenary soldiers who have come with horses and arms to the hurt of the realm."[68]

In several scattered clauses John promised to make restitution for past injustices and to cancel policies that had caused his subjects undue suffering. For example, in Article 52 he pledged that if he had illegally deprived any subject of "... lands, castles, liberties, or his rights, we will restore them to him at once...." Along the same lines he promised in Article 31 that, "Neither we nor our bailiffs shall take other men"s timber for castles or other work of ours, without the agreement of the owner'; while in Articles 47 and 49 he committed himself to disempark any royal forests that had been established since his accession in 1199. Additionally he would restore "... all hostages and charters delivered to us by Englishmen as securities for peace or faithful service." Finally, in Article 55 John pledged that all fines and amercements "... imposed unjustly and contrary to the law of the land, shall be completely remitted...."

Because John's heavy and amercements had provoked so much dissatisfaction, clauses 20-22 defined how they should be imposed in the future. Because of its unusually precise wording, Article 20 deserves to be quoted in full.

> A free man shall not be amerced for a trivial offence, except in accordance with the degree of the offence; and for a serious offence he shall be amerced according to its gravity, saving his livelihood; and a merchant likewise, saving his merchandise; in the same way a villein [i.e., resident of a village or small town] shall be amerced saving his wainage, if they fall into our mercy. And none of the aforesaid amercements shall be imposed except by the testimony of reputable men of the neighbourhood.

Article 21 stipulated that Earls and other noblemen could be amerced only "... by their peers and only in accordance with the nature of the offence"; whereas Article 22 decreed that the same principle should apply whenever a cleric was amerced.

In view of John's long quarrel with the Papacy and Archbishop Langton's conciliatory role during the spring of 1215, it seems surprising that the affairs of the Church received so little attention in Magna Carta. As already noted, Article 22 referred to the amercement of clerics, but only three other clauses had any bearing on clerical matters. Article 1 stipulated that henceforth "... the English Church shall be free, and shall have its rights undiminished and its liberties unimpaired ...." At first glance it might seem that this was intended to protect the English Church from undue royal influence. But in actuality it meant that whenever important clerical positions fell vacant, elections to fill those vacancies were to be conducted in proper canonical fashion, to which the Papacy had formally agreed in May of 1213.[69] This interpretation is fully consistent with the wording of Article 46, which reads: "All barons who have founded abbeys of which they have charters of the Kings of England, or ancient tenure, shall have custody thereof during vacancies, as they ought to have." The only other clause that pertained to religious matters was Article 27, which decreed that whenever a free subject died intestate, his chattels were "... to be distributed among his relatives and friends, under the supervision of the Church, saving to everyone the debts which the deceased owed him."

Because John had often violated customary rights of inheritance, that important matter was addressed in clauses 2-5, 37, and 43. By far the most important of those clauses, Article 2, established maximum reliefs the King could demand from adult males who were seeking confirmation of their titles to estates held through knight service. From the heir or heirs of an Earl, the crown could henceforth require no more than £100 for the entire estate; and from the heir or heirs of a lesser nobleman, the maximum relief the crown could require was £5 for the whole property, which was a mere pittance compared to the huge sums John had often demanded.

Inheritance practices were also the subject of several clauses pertaining to women. Because Article 7 was written so concisely it also deserves to be quoted in entirety.

> After her husband's death, a widow shall have her marriage portion and her inheritance at once and without any hindrance; nor shall she pay anything for her dower, her marriage portion, or her inheritance which she and her husband held on the day of her husband's death; and she may stay in her husband's house for forty days after his death, within which period her dower shall be assigned to her.

A widow's right to remain unmarried was established by Article 8.

That article stipulated that a widow could live for an unspecified number of years without taking a new husband provided "... she gives security that she will not marry without our consent, or without the consent of the lord of whom she holds, if she holds of another." This amounted to an important gain for women, but otherwise they retained their inferior status under the law, as is evident from Article 54: "No one shall be taken or imprisoned upon the appeal [i.e., complaint] of a woman for the death of anyone except her husband."

In another respect, however, the status of women was improved by Magna Carta, albeit at the expense of the Jewish minority, which received no protections at all. Article 11 decreed that "... if a man dies owing a debt to the Jews, his wife may have her dower and pay nothing of that debt ...." Article 10 was almost as prejudicial to the Jews because it decreed that, "If anyone who has borrowed from the Jews any amount, great or small, dies before the debt is repaid, it shall not carry any interest as long as the heir is under age, of whomsoever he holds; and if that debt fall into our hands, we shall take nothing except the principal sum specified in the bond."

Articles 10 and 11, which violated Jewish interests so egregiously, seem to have had a detrimental effect on financial conditions throughout the realm. But several other clauses were designed to promote commercial activities. For example, Article 35 decreed that a uniform system of weights and measures should be used in all parts of the realm; while Article 41 stipulated that

> All merchants are to be safe and secure in leaving and entering England, and in staying and travelling in England, both by land and by water, to buy and sell free from all maletotes by the ancient and rightful customs, except, in time of war, such as come from an enemy country. And if such are found in our land at the outbreak of war they shall be detained without damage to their persons or goods, until we or our chief justiciar know how the merchants of our land are treated in the enemy country; and if ours are safe there, the others shall be safe in our land.

Article 30 buttressed Article 41 by decreeing that, "No sheriff or bailiff of ours or anyone else is to take horses or carts of any free man for carting without his agreement"; while Article 33 called for the removal of all fish-weirs and other obstacles to navigation on the Thames, the Medway, and "... throughout all England except on the sea coast." Finally, Article 13 established the right of the country's cities, boroughs, ports, and towns to enjoy without restriction "... their liberties and free customs."

It would have been strange indeed if taxation and scutage in particular had not been addressed in Magna Carta. John had caused deep resentment by imposing scutage more often, and at considerably higher rates, than any of his predecessors of the throne. Article 12 therefore stipulated that,

> No scutage or aid is to be levied in our realm except by the common counsel of our realm, unless it is for the ransom of our person, the knighting of our eldest son or the first marriage of our eldest daughter; and for these only a reasonable aid is to be levied. Aids from the city of London are to be treated likewise.

In Article 14 the membership of a special body to express "the common counsel of our realm" was defined, and the method by which it was to be summoned into being was explained in detail.

> And to obtain the common counsel of the realm for the assessment of an aid ... or a scutage, we will have archbishops, bishops, abbots, earls and greater barons summoned individually by our letters; and we shall also have summoned generally through our sheriffs and bailiffs all those who hold of us in chief for a fixed date, with at least forty days' notice, and at a fixed place; and in all letters of summons we will state the reason for the summons. And when the summons has thus been made, the business shall go forward on the day arranged according to the counsel of those present, even if not all those summoned have come.

Just as Article 12 stipulated that the King should require only reasonable sums for the three customary feudal aids, Article 15 ordained that noblemen should demand only reasonable amounts from their "free men" (i.e., free tenants) for those same purposes.

Several other aspects of the feudal and manorial systems were regulated by Magna Carta. Article 16 decreed that, "No man shall be compelled to perform more service for a knight's fee or any other free tenement than is due therefrom"; while the marriage of minor heirs in the custody of relatives or royal agents was the subject of Article 6, which ordained that the marriage of minor heirs should be arranged "without disparagement" (i.e., not to individuals of lower social rank).

Article 6 also decreed that during the month preceding the marriage ceremony, its time and place were to be made known to the heir's next of kin.

Although the controversial issue of overseas military service was removed from Magna Carta--it had been included in the Unknown Charter of Liberties--the later document devoted a clause to military service within England itself. Indeed, Article 29 of Magna Carta held that,

> No constable is to compel any knight to give money for castle guard, if he is willing to perform that guard in his own person or by another reliable man, if for some reason he is unable to do it himself; and if we [later] take or send him on military service, he shall be excused the guard in proportion to the period of his service.

Although most of the barons had opposed John's periodic demands for military service, they had been even angrier about by his frequent use of the writ *praecipe quod reddat*, by which royal agents had transferred cases from the baronial courts to the new Court of King's Bench. Whenever that happened the barons lost income; and many of the barons had become fearful that the steady contraction of their legal jurisdiction might lead to the eventual disappearance of their courts altogether. Article 34 of Magna Carta regulated that sensitive matter in their interest. In Article 34 John promised that, "The writ called *praecipe* shall not, in future, be issued to anyone in respect of any holding whereby a freeman may lose his court."

Legal issues of that sort account for several of the most important clauses in the charter. Articles 26 and 27 were devoted to the unpaid debts owed to deceased persons and how they might be recovered by their legal heirs; whereas Articles 18 and 19 dealt with the procedures to be used by local courts in settling disputed claims to land. Article 24 decreed that "the pleas of the crown" should not be conducted by sheriffs, constables, coroners, or other local officials without sufficient legal knowledge; whereas Article 38 stipulated that, "Henceforth no bailiff shall put anyone on trial by his own unsupported allegation, without bringing credible witnesses to the charge." In Article 45 John made his famous promise never to employ "... justices, constables, sheriffs or bailiffs who do not know the law of the land and mean to observe it well."

Undoubtedly the most important legal clauses of Magna Carta dealt with the royal courts and the King's role in the administration of justice. In Article 17 John agreed to reestablish the Court of Common

Pleas, which he had suspended in 1209, and to keep it permanently at some convenient place that was known to all. Article 32 was a royal pledge not to retain the property of a convicted felon for more than a year and a day; while Article 36 was a similar promise that the writ of life and limb would henceforth be granted freely to all who made formal application for it. In Article 40 John made a celebrated pledge that is often cited: "To no one will we sell, to no one will we deny or delay right or justice." Article 39 contained an even more famous promise that is often quoted in scholarly writings about the period.

> No one shall be taken or imprisoned or disseised [i.e., dispossessed of land] or outlawed or exiled or in any way ruined, nor will we go or send against him, except by the lawful judgement of his peers or by the law of the land.

The remaining thirteen clauses of Magna Carta addressed a variety of problems that defy easy categorization. Article 23 was a declaration that no individual or township would be forced to construct bridges over nearby rivers or streams "... except those that ought to do so by custom and law"; whereas Article 28 stipulated that, "No constable or any other of our bailiffs shall take any man's corn or chattels unless he pays cash for them at once or can delay payment with the agreement of the seller." In Article 25 John pledged that, with the exception of the rents from the crown lands, he would never again require the sheriffs to collect more revenue from their localities for yearly deposit in the Exchequer.[70] Articles 44, 48, and 53 pertained to the rules that governed the affairs of those who lived in the royal forests and lacked the ordinary protections provided by the common law; whereas Articles 56-59 applied to Welsh and Scottish matters of no constitutional significance. The last two clauses of the document, Articles 62 and 63, summed up the philosophy that underlay everything that had already been stated.

This leaves only two other clauses to be considered. Article 60 sought to extend the rights and privileges won by the baronial class to all free men, clerics and laymen alike. The framers of Magna Carta hoped to keep the document from being viewed as nothing more than a veiled assertion of aristocratic privilege. As a consequence Article 60 declared: "All these aforesaid customs and liberties which we have granted to be held in our realm as far as it pertains to us towards our men, shall be observed by all men of our realm, both clerk and lay, as far as it pertains to them, towards their own men."

Finally, Article 61 sought to provide an effective remedy for those who, in future years, felt they had been seriously abused by royal agents. Because the judges were answerable to the monarch alone, who could remove them whenever their rendered decisions contrary to the royal interest, it was necessary to provide another mechanism, one that would be free from the King's interference. Accordingly, in Article 61, the longest and most controversial in the entire document, John agreed to the election of a committee of twenty-five barons with an inner ring of four men, their election probably taking place on June 19th.[71] Those twenty-five barons and especially their four designated spokesmen were empowered to use all their resources

> ... to observe, maintain and cause to be observed the peace and liberties which we have granted and confirmed to them by this our present charter; so that if we or our justiciar or our bailiffs or any of our servants offend against anyone in any way, or transgress any of the articles of peace and security, and the offence is indicated to four of the aforesaid twenty-five barons, those four barons shall come to us or our justiciar, if we are out of the kingdom, and shall bring it to our notice and ask that we will have it redressed without delay. And if we, or our justiciar, should we be out of the kingdom, do not redress the offence within forty days from the time when it was brought to the notice of us or our justiciar, should we be out of the kingdom, the aforesaid four barons shall refer the case to the rest of the twenty-five barons and those twenty-five barons with the commune of all the land shall distrain and distress us in every way they can, namely by seizing castles, lands and possessions, and in such other ways as they can, saving our person and those of our queen and of our children until, in their judgement, amends have been made; and when it has been redressed they are to obey us as they did before.

Far more has been written about this article of Magna Carta than any other. Some historians maintain that it authorized the barons to create an alternative government, while others hold that it established the right of justifiable rebellion. In actual fact, the barons had neither of those goals in mind, and Article 61 is chiefly important as evidence of their deep distrust of John. The barons were well aware that he often broke his promises, and they hoped to find a way to compel him to abide by Magna Carta once they demobilized their troops and returned to their estates in the countryside.

Even if one disputes this view, it is revealing that, after John's death and the accession of his young son Henry III in 1216, Magna Carta was quickly reissued with Article 61 deleted, probably because it was no longer felt to be needed. Magna Carta was reissued again in 1217 and 1225, both times with Article 61 deleted. Because the 1225 version became standard during the late Middle Ages, the provisions of Article 61 were operative for less than three months--between 23 June 1215, when dozens of copies of the charter were sealed and distributed throughout the countryside, and early September, when a true civil war began. Whether the baronial committee could have functioned as effectively as Magna Carta's framers hoped is a moot question that will never be answered to general agreement.

If Magna Carta was important for its specific clauses, it was even more important for its general implication that the King must respect the laws and customs of the realm. In no article of the document was that stated explicitly; but all 63 clauses together suggested that royal authority was indeed limited. Law was not just an expression of the King's will, and the wishes of his greater subjects could no longer be ignored with impunity. If a later monarch resorted to despotic policies, he was likely to face the same intractable opposition that had come to a head during John's reign. Thus a prudent ruler should consult regularly and openly with his leading subjects, clerics and laymen alike, and certainly before he announced any major changes of policy or imposed heavy grants of taxation.

Unfortunately, even after the conclusion of Magna Carta, there was no constitutional mechanism to ensure that the country's later rulers would heed that rule. Article 61 of the document disappeared in less than two years, as we have seen; and despite the famous Provisions of Oxford of 1258, it was not until the seventeenth century that similar efforts were made to limit royal power. The next constitutional document of comparable importance was the Petition of Right of 1628, three years after Charles I's accession to the throne.

Why it took the English people so long to solve their basic constitutional problems is to be found in the sphere of political thought. As long as they conceived of their monarch as a divinely appointed ruler who derived his authority from God and was thereby answerable only to God, it was impossible for them to devise a successful way to restrict the ruler's actions. Only when they began to conceive of their monarch in a different light--as one who derived his power from the community and who was thus bound to rule in his subjects' interest, which implied that he could be opposed or even toppled if he ignored that basic obligation--only then were the English people able to establish the type of constitutional system that the framers of Magna Carta visualized imperfectly if at all. Without a doubt Robert fitz Walter and his associates had their gaze focused more strongly on the past then on the future. After all, at Stephen Langton's urging, they drew inspiration and not a few ideas from the laws and coronation charter of Henry I. Yet the barons who framed Magna Carta were far from reactionary and gave a strong, if unintended, boost to one of the greatest political developments of the next century--the emergence of Parliament. John himself, after discovering the 1212 plot against his life, took the first step toward adding an elective element to the Great Council of the realm. But Magna Carta buttressed John's move in several ways, even if the first burgesses and knights of the shire were not summoned until the 1250s and 1260s.[72]

As already noted, several clauses of Magna Carta cut deeply into the crown's ability to raise revenue. For example, after June of 1215 the King could no longer demand the enormous reliefs of recent years, which were now limited to maximums of £100 from an Earl and £5 from a lesser nobleman; nor was he able to impose heavy amercements, which were henceforth to be "reasonable" and in direct proportion to whatever offences royal officials were alleged to have committed. John also promised in Magna Carta that, aside from the rents from the crown lands, he would never again increase the amounts the sheriffs had to collect and pay into the Exchequer each year; and he additionally pledged that he would not demand a scutage or any financial aid other than the three customary ones without the consent of the General Council of the realm whose membership was defined in Article 14.[73] As a consequence, John's successor, Henry III, never experienced a full treasury like the one his father had amassed between 1207 and 1213, and in actual fact Henry III's government was often on the verge of bankruptcy. Although various explanations have been offered for the emergence of Parliament during the thirteenth century, the well-known theory advanced by F. W. Maitland before World War I still commands the greatest respect. In Maitland's words, "... the necessity of raising money forced the King to negotiate with all classes of his realm."[74] But the crown would not have found it so difficult to raise additional revenue, and thus no need to summon the first burgesses and knights of the shire, had the framers of Magna Carta not restricted the methods by which John had raised enormous sums between 1207 and 1213. Clearly the baronial faction of 1215 did not envisage the emergence of Parliament, but their actions nevertheless made that development much more likely. Because the "great inflation" that began around 1180 came to an end in the early 1220s,[75] thereby giving the crown a breathing spell for several decades, the time lag that occurred between Magna Carta and 1254, when the first knights of the shire were summoned, should not blind us to the close connection between the charter and the beginning of what ultimately became the world's most successful form of representative government.

Thus in a number of ways, Magna Carta brought an end to one era and initiated another. But it also left a number of important questions unanswered, and in some cases those questions were not resolved until the Later Stuart period.[76] Yet to stress the shortcomings of Magna Carta at the expense of its strengths seems shortsighted and unfair. The framers of the document were sailing in uncharted waters with few beacons to guide them. Like all pioneers they made their share of mistakes, but it is remarkable that they did their work so well, particularly when they were opposed at every turn by a treacherous monarch and his reactionary followers. Moreover, later generations extended Magna Carta's meaning, just as the rights enumerated in the first ten amendments to the American Constitution were later extended, until it became a charter of liberty for all social groups, not just a list of rights and privileges enjoyed by the rich and powerful. W. S. McKechnie was probably closest to the mark when he observed of Magna Carta that it "... stands directly in the line of development of English liberty and the reign of law; because it marks the first decisive step in the establishment of a system of government of great value to the whole of the civilized world."[77]

For Further Reading

W. S. McKechnie, *Magna Carta: A Commentary on the Great Charter of King John*, 2nd ed., rev. Glasgow, 1914. A classic study with a short chapter devoted to each clause of the document. Dated in some respects but still an indispensable work.

J. C. Holt, *Magna Carta*. Cambridge, 1965; repr. 1969. An outstanding work, although overly critical of Magna Carta's shortcomings.

J. C. Holt, *The Northerners: A Study in the Reign of King John*. Oxford, 1961; repr. with corrections, 1992. A pioneering study of the northern opposition that began with the conspiracy against John's life in 1212.

J. C. Holt, "The Barons and the Great Charter." *English Historical Review*, vol. 70 (1955). Very valuable.

J. C. Holt, "The Making of Magna Carta." *English Historical Review*, vol. 72 (1957). Also valuable.

H. G. Richardson, "The Morrow of the Great Charter." *Bulletin of the John Rylands Library, Manchester,* vol. 28 (1944). A careful study of the events between the grant of Magna Carta in June of 1215 and the outbreak of a true civil war in the following September.

J. A. P. Jones, *King John and Magna Carta*. London, 1971. A brief study with twenty-two pages of documents. Intended primarily for students._

Sidney Painter, *The Reign of King John*. Baltimore, 1949. Still the most comprehensive study of the reign. Balanced and judicious.

Sidney Painter, "Magna Carta." *American Historical Review*, vol. 53 (1947). Brief but with valuable insights.

Henry Elliot Malden, ed., *Magna Carta Commemoration Essays*. London, 1917. Nine important essays by outstanding scholars like W. S. McKechnie, J. H. Round, Paul Vinogradoff, Sir Frederick M. Powicke, and Charles McIlwain.

Edwin N. Griswold, ed., *The Great Charter: Four Essays on Magna Carta and the History of Our Liberty*. New York, 1965. Four essays by leading authorities, including Samuel Thorne and W.H. Dunham, Jr.

William F. Swindler, *Magna Carta: Legend and Legacy*. New York, 1965. A popular book for general readers.

Doris M. Stenton, *After Runnymede: Magna Carta in the Middle Ages*. Charlottesville, Va., 1965. A brief but useful introduction to the subject.

Faith Baldwin, *The First Century of Magna Carta: Why It Persisted as a Document.* Minneapolis, 1925. A long and thorough study.

Faith Baldwin, *Magna Carta: Its Role in the Making of the English Constitution.* Minneapolis, 1948. An equally thorough study.

W. L. Warren, *King John.* Berkeley and Los Angeles, 1961; repr. 1978. The best life yet to appear, although much too sympathetic. Includes an excellent translation of Magna Carta by Professor Harry Rothwell of the University of Southampton.

John T. Appleby, *John, King of England.* New York, 1959. Less scholarly than Warren's biography, but more critical and convincing.

Alan Lloyd, *King John.* Newton Abbot, 1973. Full and detailed but too sympathetic.

Maurice Ashley, *The Life and Times of King John.* London, 1972. A whitewash, but useful for its many illustrations.

Kate Norgate, *John Lackland.* London, 1902; repr. 1970. The first modern life of King John. Dated in many ways but still useful.

C. Warren Hollister, "King John and the Historians." *Journal of British Studies*, vol. 1 (1962). High praise for Warren's biography of the King, which appeared in 1961, and a quick summary of changing interpretations before that time.

John Gillingham, *Richard the Lionheart.* New York, 1978. An excellent biography of John's older brother, against whom John rebelled in 1193. Contains many unflattering statements about John before he ascended thhe throne in 1199.

John Baldwin, *The Government of Philip Augustus: Foundations of French Royal Power in the Middle Ages*. Berkeley and Los Angeles, 1986. A valuable study of the French ruler who opposed John for many years. Chapters 5 and 9 are especially useful for foreign policy.

Sir Frederick Maurice Powicke, *The Loss of Normandy 1189-1204: Studies in the History of the Angevin Empire,* 2nd ed., rev. Manchester, 1961. An indispensable work by a master historian. Too detailed for general readers.

J. C. Holt, "The Loss of Normandy and Royal Finance," in John Gillingham and J. C. Holt, eds., *War and Government in the Middle Ages*. Totowa, N.J., 1984. A valuable essay.

Georges Duby, *The Legend of Bouvines: War, Religion, and Culture in the Middle Ages*, trans. by Catherine Tihany. Berkeley and Los Angeles, 1990. A study of the great campaign of 1214 and its climactic battle.

Georges Duby, *William Marshal: The Flower of Chivalry*, trans. by Richard Howard. London, 1986. A brief sketch of the life of the great English leader.

David Crouch, *William Marshal: Court, Career and Chivalry in the Angevin Empire 1147-1219*. London, 1990. A more judicious work than Duby's; less hagiographical.

Sidney Painter, *William Marshal: Knight-Errant, Baron, and Regent of England*. Baltimore, 1933. Still the best life. Full and detailed.

Sidney Painter, *Feudalism and Liberty: Articles and Addresses of Sidney Painter*, ed. by Fred A. Cazel, Jr. Baltimore, 1961. Twenty-five short pieces by a great historian.

James W. Alexander, *Ranulf of Chester: A Relic of the Conquest*. Athens, Ga., 1983. A careful study of one of John's richest subjects.

Clarence Ellis, *Hubert de Burgh: A Study in Constancy*. London, 1952. A brief study of an important figure whose chief contributions came after Magna Carta.

C. R. Cheney, *Hubert Walter*. London, 1967. An excellent study of the great Archbishop and Lord Chancellor who died in 1205.

Charles R. Young, *Hubert Walter, Lord of Canterbury and Lord of England*. Durham, N.C., 1968. A shorter book than Cheney's, but still useful.

Sir Frederick Maurice Powicke, *Stephen Langton*. Oxford, 1928. An indispensable work. Based on the author's Ford Lectures for 1927.

David M. Knowles, "The Canterbury Election of 1205-6." *English Historical Review*, vol. 53 (1938). A useful article, but too sympathetic to Innocent III.

Helene Tillmann, *Pope Innocent III,* trans. by Walter Sax. Amsterdam, 1980. A comprehensive study.

Charles Edward Smith, *Innocent III: Church Defender.* Baton Rouge, La., 1971. Slight and too sympathetic.

Sidney R. Packard, *Europe and the Church under Innocent III.* New York, 1927. A brief but useful essay.

C. R. Cheney, *Pope Innocent III and England.* Stuttgart, 1976. A major study. Very valuable.

C. R. Cheney and W. H. Semple, eds. *Selected Letters of Pope Innocent III concerning England (1198-1216).* London, 1953. A valuable source.

C. R. Cheney, *The Papacy and England, 12th-14th Centuries.* London, 1982. A collection of Cheney's essays. Important.

C. R. Cheney, *From Becket to Langton: English Church Government 1170-1213*. Manchester, 1956; repr. 1965. A fine work.

Z. N. Brooke, *The English Church & the Papacy: From the Conquest to the Reign of John.* Cambridge, 1931; repr. 1968. Stresses the period 1066-1170. Only a sketch after Becket's martyrdom.

Doris M. Stenton, *English Justice between the Norman Conquest and the Great Charter 1066-1215.* Philadelphia, 1964. An important work, but too sympathetic to John.

Doris M. Stenton, ed., *Pleas before the King or His Justices, 1198-1212*, 4 vols. London, 1952-1967. An important source for legal developments during the era.

Ralph V. Turner, *The King and His Courts: The Role of John and*

Henry III in the Administration of Justice, 1199-1240. Ithaca, N.Y., 1968. A careful study.

Ralph V. Turner, *The English Judiciary in the Age of Glanvill and Bracton, c. 1176-1239.* Cambridge, 1985. A detailed work intended for other scholars. Important.

Ralph V. Turner, *Men Raised from the Dust: Administrative Service and Upward Mobility in Angevin England.* Philadelphia, 1988. Six important studies of leading figures of the era.

W. L. Warren, *The Governance of Norman and Angevin England 1086-1272.* London, 1987. A learned survey.

H. G. Richardson and G.O. Sayles, *The Governance of Mediaeval England from the Conquest to Magna Carta.* Edinburgh, 1963. A more detailed work than Warren's. Chapters 17-19 cover John's reign.

J. E. A. Jolliffe, *Angevin Kingship*, 2nd ed. London, 1963. An important book covering the years 1154-1216.

M. T. Clanchy, *England and Its Rulers, 1066-1272.* Totowa, N.J., 1983. A judicious survey. Useful for students and general readers.

Francis J. West, *The Justiciarship in England 1066-1232.* Cambridge, 1966. A careful study of that important office.

William A. Morris, *The Medieval English Sheriff to 1300.* Manchester, 1927; repr. 1968. Chapter 6 focuses on John's reign.

Sidney Knox Mitchell, *Studies in Taxation under John and Henry III.* New Haven, 1914. A pioneering work; still indispensable.

Sidney Knox Mitchell, *Taxation in Medieval England,* ed. Sidney Painter. New Haven, 1951. Also extremely useful.

Thomas K. Keefe, *Feudal Assessments and the Political Community under Henry II and His Sons.* Berkeley and Los Angeles, 1983. An important study.

Austin Lane Poole, *Obligations of Society in the XII and XIII Cen-*

turies. Oxford, 1946; repr. 1970. Six valuable essays. The Ford Lectures for 1944.

Hugh M. Thomas, *Vassals, Heiresses, Crusaders, and Thugs: The Gentry of Angevin Yorkshire 1154-1216.* Philadelphia, 1993. Interesting social history.

Peter Coss, *Lordship, Knighthood, and Locality: A Study in English Society c.1180-c.1280.* Cambridge, 1991. A study of social life in and around Coventry.

Frank Barlow, *The Feudal Kingdom of England 1042-1216,* 3rd ed. London, 1972. An outstanding survey. Chapters 8-10 cover the Angevin period (1154-1216).

John Gillingham, *The Angevin Empire.* London, 1984. A brief but valuable survey. Especially recommended to students and general readers.

Alfred Duggan, *Devil's Brood: The Angevin Family.* London, 1957. Deals mainly with the reign of Henry II and ignores the period after 1204.

Austin Lane Poole, *From Domesday Book to Magna Carta 1087-1216,* 2nd ed. Oxford, 1955; repr. 1958. A thorough and judicious book, if somewhat dated. Chapters 10-15 deal with the years 1154-1216.

Harry Rothwell, ed. *English Historical Documents 1189-1327.* New York, 1975. An extensive collection; very valuable.

R. Trevor Davies, ed., *Documents illustrating the History of Civilization in Medieval England (1066-1500).* New York, 1926; repr. 1969. Still useful.

G. W. S. Barrow, *Feudal Britain: The Completion of the Medieval Kingdoms 1066-1314.* London, 1956; repr. 1965. Covers Wales, Scotland, and Ireland as well as England. Only a cursory treatment of Magna Carta, however.

Robin Frame, *The Political Development of the British Isles 1100-1400.* New York, 1990. Useful, but even shorter than Barrow's survey.

Notes for *Magna Carta and King John*

[1] William Stubbs, *The Early Plantagenets*, 8th ed. (London, 1896), p. 150.

[2] F. M. Powicke, *Stephen Langton* (Oxford, 1928), p. 122.

[3] Sidney Painter, "Magna Carta," *American Historical Review*, vol. 53 (1947), p. 47.

[4] J. C. Holt, *The Northerners: A Study in the Reign of King John* (Oxford 1961; reprinted with corrections 1992), p. 2.

[5] J. C. Holt, *Magna Carta* (Cambridge, 1965; reprinted 1969), p. 1.

[6] Frank Barlow, *The Feudal Kingdom of England 1042-1216*, 3rd ed. (London, 1972), p. 425.

[7] William Stubbs, *The Constitutional History of England*, 4th edition (Oxford, 1896), II: 17.

[8] Barlow, *The Feudal Kingdom of England*, p. 395.

[9] W. L. Warren, *King John* (Berkeley and Los Angeles, 1961; reprinted 1979), p. 232.

[10] C. W. Hollister, "King John and the Historians," *Journal of British Studies*, vol. 1 (1962), p. 7.

[11] H. G. Richardson and G. O. Sayles, *The Governance of Medieval England from the Conquest to Magna Carta* (Edinburgh, 1963), p. 394. In another recent work, M. T. Clanchey not only criticizes John"s political and administrative skills but also contends that Magna Carta "... is impressive as legislation precisely because it concerns specific grievances, which are clearly defined and specifically listed." See Clanchy, *England and Its Rulers 1066-1272: Foreign Lordship and National Identity* (Totowa, N.J., 1983), p. 196.

[12] Born in 1187, Arthur was a posthumous child of John"s older brother Geoffrey (1158-1186), and his wife, Constance of Brittany, an important heiress. By Constance, Geoffrey also fathered a daughter, Eleanor, who was several years older than Arthur.

[13] According to Professor Holt, Richard"s attitude toward the succession

changed in 1196, when the nobles of Brittany made Arthur a ward of Philip Augustus of France. Once that happened, "... Richard began to treat John as his successor almost immediately." See Holt, "Politics and Property in Early Medieval England," *Past and Present*, no. 57 (1972), p. 23, and especially note 103._

[14] The Justiciar served as regent whenever the King was out of the realm and ranked even higher in the political and administrative hierarchy than the Lord Chancellor. Established shortly after the Norman Conquest, the office of Justiciar was abolished in 1232 by John"s son and successor, Henry III (1216-1272).

[15] The Angevin empire was a loose union of England and Normandy on the one hand and such nearby French provinces as Anjou, Brittany, Maine, Touraine, Poitou, and Aquitaine on the other. The Angevin empire came into being in 1154, when Henry II succeeded King Stephen on the throne.

[16] Walter had been the Justiciar from 1193 until 1198, when Pope Innocent III directed him to resign that great office as inappropriate for a cleric. He served as Lord Chancellor from 1199 until his death in 1205 and instituted the great series of records for which the Chancery soon became famous.

[17] John often required his subjects, even favorites like Briouse, to pay heavier taxes and entry fines than they could afford. As long as they were loyal, he allowed them to postpone those payments indefinitely. But if they criticized him in any way, he would demand whatever sums were still unpaid, thereby ruining them at a stroke.

[18] Scutage was a tax that originated a generation after the Norman Conquest, although it was collected irregularly until John"s time. In effect, scutage gave the King money to hire mercenary troops to replace the armed retinues of barons who preferred not to accompany him to the continent. Before 1189 the rate never exceeded £1 per knight"s fee; but because of inflationary pressures between the 1180s and the 1220s, mercenary troops suddenly became more expensive. This explains why John raised the rate from £1 to two marks (£1 6s. 4d.) per knight"s fee when he assessed his first scutage in 1199. Within a few more years he raised the rate again, to three marks (£2) per knight"s fee, which led to serious baronial grumbling. (An average baron in this period controlled some thirty knight"s fees, so the amount he owed the King for each imposition of scutage, if he declined to go with his retainers to the continent, was now considerably higher than in the past.) For a good discussion of scutage and John"s tax policies in general, see Sydney Knox Mitchell, *Taxation in Medieval England*, ed.

Sidney Painter (New Haven, 1951), pp. 287-300.

[19] During the "anarchy" of Stephen"s reign (1135-1154), David I of Scotland had sent an army across the border into Northumberland, Durham, Cumberland, and Westmorland. However, during the minority of David I"s successor, Malcolm IV, who ascended the Scottish throne in 1153 at the age of twelve, Henry II of England was able to oust those Scots and reestablish England"s sway over that contested region. On these points, see John C. Appleby and Paul Dalton, eds., *Government, Religion and Society in Northern England 1000-1700* (Stroud, Gloucestershire, 1997), pp. 17, 36-38.

[20] Not only did John tax the northern counties much more heavily than his predecessors, but while touring that region in the spring of 1201 he collected over 10,000 marks by levying fines for minor offenses that would have been ignored during earlier eras. On these points, see J. E. A. Jolliffe, *Angevin Kingship*, 2nd ed. (London, 1963), p. 81.

[21] John and Isabelle were both being great-grandchildren of King Henry I (d. 1135). Rather interestingly, they do not seem to have lived together at any point during the 1190s, nor was she present at John "s coronation on 27 May 1199.

[22] Sir Maurice Powicke, *The Loss of Normandy 1189-1204,* 2nd ed. revised (Manchester, 1961).

[23] According to the monastic chronicle known as the Annals of Margam, John killed his nephew during a drunken rage or or about Easter of 1203 before weighting his body with a stone and throwing it into the Seine. Because Margam was located in South Wales, it seems probable that this story was recorded by an inmate of Margam who heard it from Briouse himself.

[24] One of England"s richest men, Ranulf de Blundeville, Earl of Chester, lost French fiefs equal to seventy-one knight"s fees when Normandy fell to Philip Augustus in 1204. To compensate Ranulf for those lands, John granted him the honour of Richmond, in Yorkshire, which worth some £1,400 a year.

[25] Technically, the tax rate in 1207 was a shilling for each mark (13s. 4d.) of assessed value. Perhaps it should be noted at this point that John had collected additional scutages in 1204 and 1205, although he had not fought on the continent during either of those years. This helps to explain the barons" bitter opposition to repeated impositions of scutage and the thir-

teenth the King decreed in 1207.

[26] Otto was the son of John"s sister, Matilda, who had married Henry the Lion, Duke of Saxony. In June of 1208 Otto"s great rival, Philip of Swabia, was murdered by the Count of Wittelsbach, and at that point Otto"s elevation to the imperial throne became a certainty. He was crowned by Innocent III in Rome on 4 October 1209 .

[27] It should be remembered that as early as the summer of 1205, John was furious at Marshal because of his opposition in the Great Council at Portsmouth and his decision to swear homage to Philip Augustus for his Norman lands. Thereafter the King struck at Marshal and reduced his power in several ways. For example, John deprived him of the offices of sheriff of Sussex and castellan of Chichester and Cardigan Castles; placed the castle and forest of St. Briavells under Hugh de Neville, chief justice of all the royal forests in England; required him to surrender two of his sons as hostages for his future behavior; and even seized Chepstow and all his other castles in England and Wales as additional guarantees of his loyalty. Faced with such clear signs of the King"s hostility, Marshal retired in 1206 to his estates in southern Ireland, where he remained until 1213 or 1214.

[28] John was doubtless aware of the provisions of the Compromise of Bec of 1106 and the Concordat of Worms of 1122, which had ended the famous Investiture Contest that originated during the time of Pope Gregory VII (d. 1085) and the Holy Roman Emperor Henry IV (d. 1106). By those agreements it was affirmed that the election of high Church officials much be conducted in "proper canonical fashion" (i.e., by the group with the legal right to conduct such an election, normally the surviving members of a cathedral or monastic chapter). But whenever a high clerical official held one or more fiefs from the secular ruler, that secular ruler had the right to authorize when the election of a new occupant of that position would take place. This he normally did in a letter (usually called the *conge d"élire)* in which he inserted the name of the individual he favored for that vacant office. John clung tenaciously to that position from 1205 until May of 1213, when he and Innocent III finally came to terms and the latter agreed to respect it. In June of 1215 John even managed to get a clause to that effect included as the first article of Magna Carta, which seems a bit ironic given the fact that Magna Carta was the greatest list of concessions ever forced on an English ruler.

[29] According to Sidney Painter, Walter de Grey "... rarely acted in person during his tenure of [the] office [of Lord Chancellor]." See *The Reign of King John* (Baltimore, 1949), p. 64. That John sold such an important

post to a mediocrity like Walter de Grey lends support to the statement of H. G. Richardson and G. O. Sayles that John "... fulfilled, without any particular distinction, the duties expected of a king." See *The Governance of Medieval England*, p. 379.

[30] After the death of Bishop Godfrey de Lucy of Winchester in 1204, there was a disputed election at that cathedral, which John referred to Rome for papal mediation. On that occasion Innocent III threw his weight behind John"s candidate, Peter des Roches, one of the King"s main financial advisers, who wound up with the position.

[31] C. R. Cheney and W. H. Semple, eds., *Selected Letters of Pope Innocent III concerning England* (London, 1953), p. 87.

[32] Cheney and Semple, eds., *Selected Letters of Pope Innocent III,* p. 94.

[33] After the death of his first wife, Isabella, Philip Augustus married Ingeborg of Denmark in 1193. He soon developed a deep aversion to her and, after convincing several of his Bishops to annul the marriage on grounds of consanguinity, took another wife, Agnes, a daughter of the Duke of Meran. But Innocent III overturned the Bishops" ruling and in 1199 ordered Philip Augustus to take Ingeborg back. He refused, and on 15 January 1200 the Pope placed an Interdict on France. Like John in 1208, Philip Augustus fought the Interdict and expelled all the Bishops and Abbots who observed it, seizing their lands and goods in the process. But Philip Augustus backed down on 7 September 1200 and submitted to the Pope. Once he took Ingeborg back, Innocent III withdrew the Interdict. However, the Pope"s victory over Philip Augustus was more apparent than real. After a brief reconciliation with his first wife, Philip Augustus imprisoned her in a remote castle for thirteen years.

[34] Sir Maurice Powicke, *Stephen Langton* (1928), p. 100. It should also be noted that irregular church attendance by commoners of all ranks had worried the clerical hierarchy for more than a century. As early as the 1040s Bishops and Archbishops throughout central and western Europe had complained and tried to find ways to force their flocks to attend mass more often. Finally, in 1215, the Fourth Lateran Council required Christians in good standing to take communion at least once a year.

[35] As already noted, Archbishop Geoffrey of York was exiled in 1207 because of his opposition to the taxation of that year; while the Bishop of Hereford, Giles de Briouse, fled to the continent shortly after the Interdict was published because of the King"s overt hostility toward his family.

The Bishops of Exeter and Chichester died shortly before the Interdict took effect, and the Bishops of Durham and Lichfield followed them in death within another year. John saw no reason to fill any of those vacancies while the Interdict was in force.

[36] Rather interestingly, when one of John"s most important financial agents, Reginald of Cornhill, died in 1210, his son paid the crown 10,000 marks to escape the duty of rendering his father"s accounts for audit, which suggests sloppiness and/or dishonesty in the performance of his duties.

[37] Henry II spent approximately two-thirds of his time on the continent between 1154 and 1189, while Richard I was there almost 95% of the time between 1189 and 1199. From December 1203 until February 1214, John was in England continuously except for brief absences in 1206 and 1210, which together extended to only about six months.

[38] For the writ *praecipe quod reddat,* see Carl Stephenson and George Marcham, eds., *Sources of English Constitutional History* (New York, 1937), p. 84. As for the Court of King"s Bench, which emerged after John"s suspension of the Court of Common Pleas in 1209, it usually accompanied the King on his travels around the realm, which caused major problems for most plaintiffs, who wanted the Common Pleas or a similar court to be established at some convenient place that was fixed and known to all. This matter was addressed in Article 17 of Magna Carta, as already noted.

[39] Ralph V. Turner, "Exercise of the King"s Will in Inheritance of Baronies: The Example of King John and William Briwerre." *Albion,* vol. 22 (1990), pp. 397-398.

[40] John collected eleven scutages between 1199 and 1214, or one in every year except 1207, 1208, and 1212, thereby convincing the barons that he planned to convert an occasional tax into a yearly one, which they were determined to prevent. In addition he gradually raised the rate to £3 per knight"s fee, or triple what it had been during Henry II"s time, which fueled the barons" growing dissatisfaction. For other comments about John"s use of scutage after 1199, see p. 68 and alsofootnote 18 above.

[41] J. C. Holt, "The Prehistory of Parliament," in *The English Parliament in the Middle Ages,* ed. by R.G. Davies and J.H. Denton (Manchester, 1981), p. 7.

[42] In essence a bull of deposition was a papal invitation to the subjects of a

disobedient ruler to rebel. The Popes of the later Middle Ages claimed to be able to absolve the subjects of a wicked ruler of their oath of allegiance. Accordingly, the subjects of such a monarch would be guilty of no sinful acts if they overthrew him and placed a more upright individual on the throne.

[43] See above, p. 76 and also footnote 26 above. Essentially, John was still determined to control the time and outcome of all important clerical elections in England, just as his predecessors on the English throne had done for centuries.

[44] By that schedule, the Archbishop of Canterbury was to receive £2,500; the Bishop of Ely, £1,500; the Bishops of Lincoln, London, Hereford, and Bath, £750 each; and the Prior and monks of Canterbury, £1,000. On this point, see Cheney and Semple, eds., *Selected Letters of Pope Innocent III*, p. 135.

[45] In actual fact, the Interdict was not lifted until 2 July 1214, by which time John had paid 27,000 marks to the Church. Innocent III expected John to pay another 73,000 marks, which he failed to do. For John"s financial dealings with the Church, see Sydney Knox Mitchell, *Studies in Taxation under John and Henry III* (New Haven, 1914), pp. 108-109.

[46] Fitz Walter and de Vesci had convinced the Pope that John had sought to destroy them because of their loyalty to the Church, which was a complete falsehood. As a result of papal pressure, John agreed to their return, and on 27 May 1213 he issued safe-conducts to them. But before de Vesci returned from Scotland, John ordered the destruction of his castles at Alnwick, Northumberland and Malton, Yorkshire. See Holt, *The Northerners*, pp. 87, 94-5.

[47] John"s surrender of England and Wales to the Papacy, and his pledge to pay a yearly pension of 1,000 marks for them, were recounted in a charter that was ratified at St. Paul"s Cathedral on 3 October 1213.

[48] John knew that Otto was annoyed by French support of his main rival, Frederick of Hohenstaufen. Apparently John wanted to launch his attack on Philip Augustus in the autumn of 1213,but was unable to do so because of the opposition of a number of northern barons. Again they claimed that they were not required to fight in John"s levies on the continent, forcing him to remain in England until the following spring.

[49] Roger of Wendover.

[50] According to C. R. Cheney, John demonstrated "... obsessive repugnance to his [Langton"s] person" until his death in 1216. See Cheney, *Pope Innocent III and England* (Stuttgart, 1976), p. 346.

[51] By the schedule of 1213, John was required to pay 40,000 marks to the Church before the Interdict was lifted. However, as previously noted, the Interdict remained in effect until 2 July 1214, by which time John had handed over only two-thirds of that amount. Thereafter John was supposed to make yearly payments of 12,000 marks, half on All Saints" Day and the other half on Ascension Day, until the full sum of 100,000 marks was discharged. Although he made several other payments after July 1214, he made none at all after September 1215, when a true civil war broke out in England. All in all, the King probably repaid less than 25 per cent of the money he had confiscated from the Church between 1205 and 1213. On these points, see Mitchell, *Studies in Taxation,* pp. 108-109.

[52] Painter, *The Reign of King John*, p. 199. In the opinion of A. L. Poole, Innocent III thereafter ". . . abetted the king unswervingly, even in his most arbitrary conduct." See *From Domesday Book to Magna Carta 1087-1216,* 2nd ed. (Oxford 1955; repr. 1958), p. 458.

[53] Mitchell, *Studies in Taxation,* pp. 110-115.

[54] Georges Duby, *The Legend of Bouvines*, trans. by Catherine de Tihany (Berkeley and Los Angeles, 1990), pp. 19, 158.

[55] *Ibid*, p. 125. There are good brief accounts of the battle in Baldwin, *The Government of Philip Augustus*, pp. 215-218, and in Poole, *From Domesday Book to Magna Carta*, p. 467.

[56] William S. McKechnie, *Magna Carta: A Commentary on the Great Charter of King John,* 2nd ed. rev. (Glasgow, 1914), p. 31.

[57] Exactly why fitz Walter was chosen to be the barons" chief spokesman in November 1214 is unclear. Of course he was extremely rich, with extensive estates in East Anglia and Yorkshire. In addition he participated in the wine trade on a massive scale. Because of his deep involvement in the 1212 plot against John, he suffered a period of exile. But of greater importance, he had wielded considerable influence in London for some years as Lord of Baynard"s Castle, in which capacity he was a banneret of the city and honorary captain of its militia.

[58] James W. Alexander, *Ranulph of Chester* (Athens, Georgia, 1983), p. 31.

[59] For the sudden recovery of Marshal"s fortunes in 1212-1213, see Sidney Painter, *William Marshal* (Baltimore, 1933), pp. 176-177.

[60] In September 1215, three months after John agreed to Magna Carta, a true civil war broke out in England; and just as many people feared, Philip Augustus intervened and sent an army across the Channel. For a time the Dauphin held London, but William Marshal, Hubert de Burgh, and several other barons expelled him from the realm after John"s death in October of 1216.

[61] The "Unknown Charter" is printed in McKechnie, *Magna Carta*, pp. 485-486. There is a good discussion of it in W. L. Warren, *King John* (Berkeley and Los Angeles, 1961), pp. 215-217. Another scholar, William F. Swindler, has noted that, "On the whole the tenor of the Unknown Charter was in terms of fundamental principles which were inherent obligations of good kingship...." See Swindler, *Magna Carta: Legend and Legacy* (New York, 1965), pp. 75-76.

[62] The Articles of the Barons are printed in McKechnie, *Magna Carta*, pp. 487-493.

[63] Although it cannot be proved, John apparently hoped to weaken Magna Carta and minimize the barons" victory over him by scrambling articles that addressed the same or similar grievances throughout the document. Additionally, he seems to have insisted that the charter begin with a clause buttressing his right to hold clerical elections in the traditional canonical way. If John devised this face-saving stratagem as seems likely, the barons probably went along with it because they were much more interested in the essence than the appearance of their great victory over the crown.

[64] There are four surviving copies of Magna Carta, two of which remain in their original repositories, the cathedral archives at Salisbury and Lincoln, while the other two are among the treasured holdings of the British Library in London.

[65] It will be argued below, at a more relevant point, that the standing committee of twenty-five barons decreed by Article 61 of Magna Carta was elected on 19 June.

[66] Innocent III maintained in his bull condemning Magna Carta that the document was prejudicial to the King"s rights and honor. The Pope also

absolved John of his oath to abide by the charter and threatened to excommunicate all those who continued to insist that he should adhere to it.

[67] These articles, which had enjoyed pride of place in the "Unknown Charter of Liberties" of January 1215, were buried deep in Magna Carta, undoubtedly at John"s insistence.

[68] Holt, *Magna Carta*, p. 331. All subsequent references to Magna Carta"s clauses are to Professor Holt"s translation of the document, which is printed on pages 317-337 of his book.

[69] See p. 92 and also footnote 43 above.

[70] During the middle years of his reign, John had attempted to increase the sums the sheriffs paid into the Exchequer each year, but his efforts ended in failure.

[71] For matters pertaining to the committee of twenty-five barons, see C. R. Cheney, "The Twenty-Five Barons of Magna Carta," *Bulletin of the John Rylands Library, Manchester*, vol. 50 (1968), pp. 280-307.

[72] The original knights of the shire were summoned in 1254 and the first burgesses in 1265. In 1267 both groups met simultaneously with the six groups enumerated in Article 14 of Magna Carta.

[73] Perhaps it should be noted that after John"s death in 1216, the clause in which he promised never to command the sheriffs to collect additional revenues in their counties was eliminated from the earliest reissues of the document; but at the same time the maximum relief that the crown could require from an Earl was reduced from £100 to 100 marks.

[74] F.W. Maitland, *The Constitutional History of England*, ed. H. A. L. Fisher (Cambridge, 1908; repr. 1961), p. 70.

[75] On that inflationary period in general, see P. D. A. Harvey, "The English Inflation of 1180-1220," in R.H. Hilton, ed., *Peasants, Knights and Heretics: Studies in Medieval English Social History* (Cambridge, 1976), pp. 57-84.

[76] For example, the goal of Article 61 of Magna Carta, namely how to secure redress for royal offences committed against private subjects, was not achieved until 1701, when the Act of Settlement gave the common-law judges a degree of independence from the crown by forbidding the ruler to

dismiss them from office except on petition of both Houses of Parliament.

[77] McKechnie, in *Magna Carta Commemoration Essays,* ed. Henry E. Malden (London, 1917), p. 17.

The Wars of the Roses, I*

The Wars of the Roses were the longest political crisis in English history. A brutal conflict between two competing branches of the royal family, the Wars of the Roses burst into the open in the 1450s and continued intermittently for three decades, during which there were some twenty pitched battles, scores of ambushes and political assassinations, and dozens of castle sieges. During those turbulent years the crown became a political football and changed hands five times before Henry Tudor, Earl of Richmond overthrew Richard III in 1485. Henry Tudor, or Henry VII as he was styled thereafter, was the residual heir of the Lancastrian branch of the Plantagenet dynasty, which had ruled England since the twelfth century.

During the Wars of the Roses the Lancastrians' bitterest enemies were the Yorkist branch of that same Plantagenet dynasty, who used many emblems, including a white rose they often embroidered on their uniforms. But the Lancastrians rarely if ever used the red rose that has long been attributed to them. Nevertheless, after his capture of the throne in 1485, Henry VII believed his Lancastrian forebears had occasionally used a red rose; and once he married Elizabeth of York in January of 1486 as a way of ending the feud within the royal family, he merged that red rose with the Yorkist white rose to create the famous Tudor red rose with a white center. Much later, during the eighteenth and early nineteenth centuries, writers like David Hume and Sir Walter Scott popularized that idea, and the term "the Wars of the Roses" gradually came into use as a suitable name for the conflict.

In order to understand the causes of the Wars of the Roses, which still occupy a hallowed place in English history, we must first consider the various factors that worked to inhibit uprisings against the occupant of the throne. Then we will be in a good position to trace the complex developments, foreign and domestic alike, that triggered the prolonged conflict that claimed the first of its thousands of victims in a village some twenty miles north of London in May of 1455.

Rebellions against England's late medieval rulers seldom occurred without a decade or more of chronic misgovernment. Extremely conservative by nature, the people of the centuries after King John's

---

* The notes for this chapter begin on page 155.

time were reluctant to question royal commands because of their belief that an anointed ruler was God's vicegerent for the realm. Whenever policy failures became so blatant they could no longer be ignored, it was natural to blame them on evil or incompetent advisers, who could be replaced, whereas the King held the scepter for life. Almost all religious leaders preached such views, maintaining that opposition to royal actions was sinful under ordinary circumstances. Only if a ruler alienated the Church were clerics likely to advocate resistance, and even then there was no guarantee that the people would respond.[1] Because Parliament did not come of age until the end of the Tudor period and could not even assemble without the ruler's authorization, there was no agency in the realm that could press for the overthrow of a reigning monarch. All the advantages rested with the occupant of the throne because he controlled all the main political and administrative officials, the judges of the central courts, and such local dignitaries as the sheriffs and the justices of the peace. Whenever the monarch was strong and capable, there was little chance that the winds of rebellion would blow. But if the ruler was weak and vacillating--if he was irresolute or unduly merciful to his enemies--then the forces of opposition might gather and gain such strength that the hapless sovereign who failed to control them would be engulfed in the end.

During the mid fifteenth century the last of England's three Lancastrian rulers, Henry VI (1421-1461), was just such a weak and inept monarch.[2] Although Henry VI's character failings were minor compared to King John's, they were significant nonetheless. Henry was too quick to forgive those who challenged his government, while his blundering foreign policy, devised with the help of unpopular ministers, cost him a steady loss of support. Even worse, he refused to live within a yearly budget and failed to supervise his financial agents, who engaged in graft on a massive scale whenever left to their own devices. As a consequence the crown's financial position was undermined and Henry's government came perilously close to bankruptcy. All in all, his incompetent rule was the principal cause of the eventual Yorkist attack on his throne.

Born in December 1421 and elevated to the throne only eight months later by his father's untimely death, Henry VI did not participate in affairs of state until 1436, when he was declared of age.[3] Unfortunately Henry VI had none of the regal bearing or great political skill of his revered father. Except on important ceremonial occasions, he dressed in simple peasant clothes, which aroused wonder as did his total lack of interest in "manly pursuits" like hunting and hawking and his often somewhat baffled expression. Even worse, many of his most important appointments in Church and State led to unforeseen problems. For example, in 1437 he arranged for the great bishopric of Durham to go to Robert Neville, a younger son of the powerful Earl of Westmorland, which threatened the delicate political balance in the northeast between the Nevilles and the Percies, arguably the country's two most ambitious and determined families. During the same year he made a lifetime grant of the stewardship of the Duchy of Cornwall to Sir William Bonville, which he revoked and reassigned only four years later to Bonville's bitter rival, Thomas Courtenay, Earl of Devon. Thereafter those two men were fiercer enemies than ever, and their hostility led to periodic violence that brought the southwest to the brink of chaos. Problems of that sort were compounded by Henry VI's reluctance to use the courts to restrain local disputes, which festered until they could no longer be contained by a judicial system that can only be compared to a skiff bobbing along in the path of a hurricane.

During the 1440s Henry's chief interest was in educational matters, and he deserves to be remembered for his two great academic foundations, Eton and King's College, Cambridge, which he endowed with estates worth £3,400 per year. During that same decade he also became a generous patron of New College, Oxford and of two struggling Cambridge institutions, Godshouse and St. Bernard's College, which eventually became known as Christ's College and The Queens' College, respectively. Those ambitious undertakings, while laudable in themselves, put a heavy strain on the royal finances at a time when Henry was unwilling to limit the size of his household. Before 1436 the royal household had usually consisted of 250-300 servants and cost some £10,000 a year to maintain. But because Henry seldom rejected the pleas of suitors for office, the household expanded to over 800 individuals by 1450, when it required £17,000 per year for its support, and that at a time when the crown's annual revenues were less than £50,000 and its debts in the neighborhood of £373,000.

For several other reasons the English crown was on the verge of bankruptcy by 1450. The severe trade depression that had begun about 1440 and the resulting fall in the customs receipts was a major cause of that unhappy situation. But even more important was the heavy cost of the Hundred Years War, which took a disastrous turn for England after the death of John Duke of Bedford, England's finest general, and the subsequent collapse of the Anglo-Burgundian alliance of 1419-1435. Within several years the tide of battle shifted decisively in the direction of Charles VII of France, who was determined to rid his realm of English troops once and for all. A shrewd judge of military talent, Charles developed effective fighting forces that enjoyed repeated success, although his generals never forgot Henry V's great triumphs and concentrated on winning minor skirmishes rather than pitched battles in the field. Large stretches of French territory that had been under England's sway before 1435 were reconquered, and it became increasingly likely that Henry's armies would be driven into the sea.

Because of the darkening situation abroad and the growing financial problems at home, bitter discord developed within Henry's government about the proper course to follow. Hawkish Councillors like the Archbishop of Canterbury, Henry Chichele, and his uncle and heir apparent, Humphrey Duke of Gloucester, wanted to continue the war indefinitely, regardless of the cost. Yet several other magnates, including William de la Pole, Marquess of Suffolk, agreed with Henry that it was time for England to cut its losses and seek a negotiated peace. Once Archbishop Chichele died in 1443 and the King dismissed Duke Humphrey from the Council the next year, it was possible to make overtures to France for a cessation of hostilities. Because the French treasury was also nearing exhaustion, Charles VII welcomed the idea of a truce and formal peace talks began. By the Truce of Tours of April 1444, all fighting was to end for at least two years; and Charles's niece, Margaret of Anjou, was to cross the Channel and become Henry's wife, in the hope their union would promote a lasting peace. The fact that Henry accepted Margaret of Anjou without a dowry of any kind and even paid her attendants' travel expenses is clear proof of how desperately he wanted a cessation of hostilities at that juncture.[4]

Although not part of the official agreement, a secret promise was given by Suffolk that English forces would soon evacuate the county of Maine as a further way of appeasing Charles VII. That promise, which Suffolk would never have made without royal authorization, was a dubious undertaking because Maine had a long border with Normandy, the only other province in northern France still in England's possession. Should Henry's forces withdraw from Maine and French troops occupy its fortresses, Charles VII would be in a position to drive the English out of northern France once and for all.

After Henry's marriage to Margaret of Anjou in April of 1445, the English monarch felt morally bound--and indeed seems to have been under strong pressure from his wife--to honor Suffolk's promise to evacuate Maine. Yet most of his Councillors objected to such an important concession because England was not slated to receive a comparable advantage in return. Outside the royal Council the King's uncle, Humphrey, made repeated criticisms of the impending surrender. But he died under mysterious circumstances in February 1447, which sparked nasty rumors that a member of the King's entourage had murdered him.

Meanwhile Henry had lobbied his reluctant Councillors and won enough support to proceed with the surrender of Maine. In July 1447 the King directed his chief commander in France, Edmund Beaufort, Marquess of Dorset, to take the first steps toward an English withdrawal from the county. But Dorset's lieutenants refused to carry out such an unsavory order, causing an awkward delay to ensue. Within several months the French crown lost all patience, and in February 1448 Charles VII directed his army to surround Le Mans, the capital and leading town of Maine. With that development an English withdrawal began at last, and a month later the whole county was back in French hands. Although that turn of events was a serious blow to English power on the continent, Henry considered his foreign policy an unqualified success and rewarded his chief adviser, Suffolk, with a dukedom. In addition he created his cousin, Dorset, second Duke of Somerset, the title his older brother John had held until he took his own life in 1444.

If Henry was satisfied with the results of his foreign policy, his old ally, Francis I of Brittany, was not. Although Duke Francis was a nominal vassal of the French crown, he had long enjoyed virtual autonomy by using English support as a counterweight to keep the French from meddling in his affairs. But with the English departure from Maine and the French poised to drive them out of Normandy, Francis sensed that the English government was unwilling to fight. As a consequence he had little option but to seek the good will of Charles VII, whose strength was now considerably greater than before. This important shift in Breton policy enraged the Duke's brother Gilles, a strong Anglophile and confirmed troublemaker. In England Henry VI was annoyed by Gilles's imprisonment since 1446, which he protested by allowing mercenaries in his pay to attack the Breton fortress of Fougères. Once Fougères opened its gates on 24 March 1449, Francis nudged even closer to Charles VII and pledged to assist French attacks on English garrisons in Normandy. Because Charles's treasury had just been replenished by the great financier Jacques Coeur, the French crown was in a position to renounce the Truce of Tours of 1444 and begin a new campaign to oust English forces from northern France for good.

On 31 July 1449, Charles VII declared war and launched a new round of hostilities. Within a week four French columns crossed the border into upper Normandy; and from his headquarters at Pont de l'Arche, Charles himself directed the siege of Rouen, the provincial capital. Never tempted to lead the troops himself, Henry assigned the defense of Rouen to the new Duke of Somerset, a mediocre general at best.[5] Somerset received additional troops from England but not enough to withstand a determined assault. On 29 October Rouen surrendered, and Charles VII rode in from the south and accepted the keys to the castle's main gate, which amounted to a declaration of sovereignty over the eastern half of the province. Although Somerset and his wife were allowed to leave under safe-conducts, scores of Englishmen, including John Talbot, the respected Earl of Shrewsbury, were left behind as hostages. On the eve of his departure from Rouen, Somerset committed the English government to pay the enormous sum of 50,000 gold *salus* (approximately £73,000) for the hostages' release within a year's time.

Although the fall of Rouen was a serious blow to English prestige, a more significant defeat occurred nine weeks later when Harfleur accepted a French garrison. Located at the mouth of the River Seine, Harfleur was the most convenient port from which to launch a naval attack on southern England. Consequently in January of 1450 there was an outburst of panic among the inhabitants of Kent, Sussex, the Isle of Wight, and other coastal counties. Not since the dark days of the 1370s had there been such imminent danger of a French invasion. In order to coordinate defensive efforts and equip a large force to assist the beleaguered garrison at Cherbourg, Henry sent a trusted official, Adam Moleyns, Bishop of Chichester and Lord Privy Seal, to the southern coast on 9 January 1450. On arriving at Portsmouth Bishop Moleyns encountered an angry regiment that had just returned from France and taken control of the town. When they recognized Moleyns as a leading member of the royal Council, they fell on him and hacked him to pieces. However, shortly before he took his last breath, the Bishop denounced Suffolk as the main cause of all the realm's current problems.

Partly because of Moleyns' bitter denunciations, which were soon widely known, Suffolk came under furious attack in the House of Commons when a new Parliament opened on 22 January. For a week the clamor against the chief minister remained at a fever pitch, causing the King to agree to his imprisonment in the Tower. But at the same time Henry took steps to strengthen Suffolk's position by allowing his son and heir apparent, John de la Pole, to marry an important royal cousin, Lady Margaret Beaufort.[6]

Born in 1443, Lady Margaret was the only child of John Beaufort, first Duke of Somerset (d. 1444), from whom she had inherited lands worth approximately £1,000 per year. Even more important, Lady Margaret was a great-great grandchild of King Edward III (d. 1377), as was her second cousin, Henry VI. Thus Lady Margaret had a strong claim to the throne,[7] and for that reason Henry VI had assigned her wardship and marriage to Suffolk in 1444, several months after her father's suicide.

Six years later, when Suffolk came under bitter attack in the Commons, the monarch agreed to the marriage of Suffolk's son and intended heir to his seven-year-old cousin, hoping their marriage would stress his continued faith in the Duke and end the outcry against him. But the Commons had other ideas and interpreted the marriage as evidence of Suffolk's overweening ambition and a secret plan to secure the throne for his grandchildren. By 1450 the King had been married for five years, but his wife, Margaret of Anjou, had failed to become pregnant. Most people therefore assumed that the royal couple would never have children of their own and, as a result, Henry VI would eventually be succeeded by one of his many cousins. Because Henry had always been partial to his Beaufort relatives, most politically-minded observers believed he wanted the throne to revert on his death to Lady Margaret. But in that conservative age, Lady Margaret would be little more than a figurehead with the actual work of governing the realm being handled by her husband or, if he was still alive, by her father-in-law, the hated Duke of Suffolk.

Once the Commons learned of the marriage between Lady Margaret and John de la Pole, the Members were overcome by a paroxysm of bitterness that made their earlier attack on the chief minister seemed mild by comparison. Normally silent men added their voices to the uproar and the crown lost all control of the proceedings. But unfortunately for the infuriated Members, their case against Suffolk rested on weak legal grounds because there was no evidence that he had committed a crime of any sort. His chief faults were mediocrity and unwavering support of policies that usually backfired, for which there was no constitutional remedy provided he retained the King's confidence. As a result, the Commons had to base their attack on frivolous charges, some twenty-six in all, that were certified to the Speaker after several rancorous weeks of debate.

When Suffolk sought to defend himself in the Parliament Chamber on 13 March, he added fuel to the flames by making a defiant speech and declaring his complete innocence of all wrong-doing. The Members viewed this as a new sign of his intransigence; and within four days the mood in London became so ugly that Henry placed him under his special protection and directed him to leave the Tower for the safety of Eastthorp, his country house in Suffolk. On the first leg of their journey to Eastthorp, the Duke's party was pursued by a howling band of men who attacked and mortally wounded several of his grooms and servants.

Meanwhile Charles VII had decided against an invasion of England for the moment in order to focus on objectives closer at hand. On 15

April Charles's leading generals, Clermont and Richemont, won an overwhelming victory over the Duke of Somerset's forces at Formigny in lower Normandy, where more than 4,000 Englishmen died on the field. It was the worst defeat suffered by English arms since 1314, when the Scots annihilated Edward II's forces at Bannockburn. Shortly before the French triumph at Formigny, Charles VII sent reinforcements to assist the Count of Foix, his principal commander in Gascony. Because Henry's chief lieutenant in that region, Sir William Bonville, was more interested in enriching himself than in confronting the enemy, the Count of Foix faced only token opposition and soon subdued the territory around Bayonne, the second city of the district.

The military reversals abroad caused Henry to fear even more for his minister's life and to instruct him to leave the realm as a way of avoiding the popular fury. Hoping to spend the next few years in exile, Suffolk secured a safe-conduct from Philip the Good of Burgundy, a confirmed Anglophile for several decades. But while trying to cross the Channel, Suffolk's ship was intercepted by a royal warship, the *Nicholas of the Tower*. Recognized by its rowdy crew, Suffolk was transferred to the deck of the *Nicholas* and given a mock trial on 30 April. Declared guilty of high treason, he was beheaded and his body tossed overboard. Two days later his headless corpse washed up on a beach near Dover, and within another month the grieving King had it buried with full honors at Wingfield College in Suffolk.

For the next two months the counties of southern and eastern England were in an uproar, and the richest sections of the realm witnessed repeated acts of brutality. Bitter protests occurred in Sussex, Surrey, Kent, Hampshire, and adjacent counties. An early victim of the violence was William Ayscough, Bishop of Salisbury, who was killed by a Wiltshire mob in the village of Edington in June of 1450. Bishop Ayscough was rumored to have plotted the death of Humphrey of Gloucester in 1447, who was now generally remembered as "the good Duke"; but the Bishop's greatest offense was to have officiated at the wedding of Henry VI and Margaret of Anjou in 1445. On encountering Bishop Ayscough five years later, the mob berated him for his misdeeds before tearing him limb from limb.

Even greater turbulence erupted in Kent, the county that had provided so many rebels for the Peasants' Revolt of 1381. Again a motley band of laborers and artisans gathered in the central sections of Kent; and under the leadership of Jack Cade, an adventurer who had just returned from the continent, they marched on the capital during the last week of June. In panic the King and Queen fled Westminster Palace for the security of Kenilworth Castle in Warwickshire. As a consequence

Cade's forces continued their advance almost unimpeded. After killing William Crowemer, the hated sheriff of Kent, the insurgents reached the southern end of London Bridge, where government forces failed to block their entry into the city. Welcomed by the lower and middle classes, the rebels occupied the Guildhall and stormed the Tower, where they captured the odious Lord Treasurer, Lord Saye and Sele, whose life they quickly ended. They also released hundreds of prisoners from the Marshalsea and King's Bench prisons. With their ranks strengthened, Cade's men inflicted heavy damage on the capital's richer citizens, torturing several aldermen and ransacking dozens of mansions. Among the large dwellings pillaged was the house of Philip Malpas, where fine furniture and tapestries, silver vessels, and other valuables owned by Richard of York, the King's viceroy in Ireland, were either carted off or destroyed.

Significantly, while the rebellion was at its height, many people began to feel that a change of dynasty was both imminent and essential. In July 1450 two Sussex farmers were taken into custody by the constables at Brightling Fair for declaring to a large and enthusiastic crowd that "'the king was a natural fool ... and that another king must be ordained to rule the land.'"[8] Probably because of that incident the ambitious Jack Cade led his most ardent followers from London into Suffolk and assumed the name John Mortimer, thereby suggesting that Henry VI should be replaced by an adult male of the Mortimer line. After all, the Mortimers had been the legal heirs of Richard II in 1399, when Henry of Lancaster overthrew his half-crazed cousin and claimed the throne as Henry IV.

During the Lancastrian Revolution of 1399, the superior Mortimer claim had been ignored because of Henry IV's great popularity at the time and the youthful age of the only surviving male of the Mortimer line, Edmund Earl of March (1391-1425). Although the Earl of March eventually died childless, his sister Anne, the wife of Richard Earl of Cambridge, gave birth to a son in 1411, that same Richard of York who was away governing Ireland in 1450. That Richard of York, whose actions would eventually propel England into the Wars of the Roses, had inherited the Dukedom of York in 1415, when his uncle Edward died at Agincourt while fighting alongside Henry V. The most important of all the medieval Dukes of York, Richard was further enriched in 1425, when he inherited the estates of his childless cousin, Edmund of March.

As a consequence of his great dual inheritance, Richard of York was the richest landowner of the era, with lands worth £7,000 a year. Furthermore, after the sudden death of Humphrey of Gloucester in 1447, many Englishmen assumed that he would inherit the throne one day.

That expectation grew stronger as the years passed by because Henry VI seemed incapable of fathering a son by Margaret of Anjou, which meant the House of Lancaster would probably become extinct within another generation. In Ireland, where he spent most of the 1440s, Duke Richard was unaware of how extremely unpopular the current regime had become. But in England men high in his service were impressed by the violence that occurred during the summer of 1450 and by Jack Cade's assumption of the name John Mortimer. Conversations about the possibility of replacing Henry with Richard seem to have taken place in some circles, particularly among politically-informed men like William Oldhall, the Duke's dependable steward for many years. In February of 1453 a grand jury at Ipswich indicted Oldhall and several associates for conspiring to elevate Richard to the throne in 1450. If that indictment was an honest and not a malicious one, the idea of an eventual Yorkist assault on Henry VI's throne took root during the Cade rebellion even if it was not yet a conscious idea in Richard's mind.

Because the Cade rebellion had no practical goals and triggered an orgy of senseless violence, thereby alienating the propertied classes, it soon played itself out. During the second week of July the merchant oligarchy of London regained control of the city. As for the rebel leader, he was captured on 12 July by the new sheriff of Kent, Alexander Iden, but died from his battle wounds before being brought to trial. However, the bleak military situation across the Channel, which had triggered the rebellion in the first place, remained unchanged and caused violence to continue for several more months. This was especially true after Cherbourg's surrender on 12 August. Situated at the tip of the Contentin peninsula, Cherbourg was the last remaining fortress in Normandy held by an English garrison; and once it passed into French hands, the war in northern France came to an end, to the fury of most Englishmen, who expressed their fury in renewed acts of violence.[9]

Yet an unexpected benefit accrued from the fall of Cherbourg--the speedy return to England of Edmund Beaufort, Duke of Somerset. Despite his mediocrity as a general, Somerset was not without political and administrative abilities. Fifteen years older than the King, he possessed a wealth of practical experience that Henry VI would never attain; and during the autumn of 1450 he was instrumental in restoring law and order throughout the realm. Partly because of that invaluable service, he won the King's trust and favor to an exceptional degree.

There was a second reason for Somerset's emergence as the King's chief minister during September 1450. Despite Henry's uneasy relationship with most men, he never feared Somerset's domination.

Indeed, Somerset was dependent on the royal will to an exceptional degree owing to his limited wealth. In 1444 most of the estates of the Beaufort family had passed to his niece, Lady Margaret, whereas Somerset himself acquired lands worth only £300 a year.[10] Because Somerset lacked the means to live on the scale expected of a great nobleman, he felt compelled to ingratiate himself with the royal couple, whose favor he courted in his urbane manner. Because of his obvious desire to please and be of service, he quickly won the confidence of Margaret of Anjou, who granted him an annuity of 100 marks out of her yearly revenues. As for the King, he awarded Somerset a number of offices, including the valuable Captaincy of Calais. The Duke also received more than a dozen estates, including the great lordship of Glamorgan in Wales, which, with his many political offices and the Queen's pension, gave him an annual income of £2,000. However, his retention of all that needed income was completely dependent on the royal couple's good opinion, which he could ill afford to lose.

By contrast Somerset's arch rival, Richard of York, who was five years younger and without Somerset's courtly manner, was the richest peer in England, with landed estates worth £7,000 a year. Thus Richard enjoyed a princely income, which gave him a degree of independence Somerset could barely envisage. Moreover, Richard had powerful family connections that his older rival lacked. In 1428 or 1429 Richard had married Cecily Neville, the twenty-second and youngest child of Ralph of Raby, the influential Earl of Westmorland. As a consequence Richard became the brother-in-law of Westmorland's capable sons, Richard Earl of Salisbury and William Lord Fauconberg as well as the uncle of Salisbury's forceful and determined son, Richard Earl of Warwick.[11] Although the Nevilles faced bitter opposition in northern England from the Percies, whose equally ambitious leader was the Earl of Northumberland, the support of the extensive Neville connection would be of enormous value to Richard when he ultimately contested Henry VI's possession of the throne. Although the Earl of Salisbury clung to a neutral stance for several years, Warwick was more inclined to support Richard against Somerset and the Lancastrians. The grasping Warwick was determined to seize the Welsh lordship of Glamorgan from Somerset, who had received it from Henry several years before.

During the early 1450s Richard gave little if any thought to the idea of claiming the throne for himself. On leaving Ireland for London during the autumn of 1450, he expected only to be named to the post of chief minister. To his dismay he found Somerset, a man he detested, already entrenched in that office and the King unwilling to consider a change of advisers. Henry disliked Richard's brusqueness, his frequent references to his double descent from Edward III, and his frequent sneers at Somerset as a "spectacularly incompetent commander" when his own military record was little better. As a result Henry refused to place any trust in Richard and in fact developed an intense dislike of him.[12] That Henry sought to keep Richard at arm's length was applauded by Queen Margaret, who considered him the most odious Englishman of her acquaintance.

Doubtless the royal couple's attitude toward Richard was influenced by a motion made by Thomas Young during the Parliament of 1451. One of the Duke's principal advisers and an M.P. for Bristol, Young urged the House of Commons to recognize his master as heir apparent to the throne, a suggestion that caused the blundering lawyer to be clapped in the Tower, where he cooled his heels for several months.

With his political hopes thwarted at every turn, Richard formed an alliance with another dissatisfied magnate, the Earl of Devon, who wanted York's assistance against his archenemy, Sir William Bonville.[13] Together the two peers raised an army of 4,000 men and made threatening gestures toward the court in March of 1452. When the King wavered at the prospect of violence, Richard assumed that Henry was finally willing to discharge Somerset and appoint him chief minister in his place. However, when Richard appeared for an interview with the King at Dartford, he found his rival standing jubilantly at Henry's right hand. Thereupon Richard was arrested for misprison of treason and sent back to the capital under heavy guard.[14] A stronger and more resolute monarch than Henry would have had Richard executed or exiled for life at that point, thereby avoiding the violence of the next two decades. But Henry always shrank from extreme courses; and after holding Richard under house arrest for several weeks, he released him with only a mild rebuke. On his part, Richard was furious about being outmaneuvered again, and his hatred of Somerset became even greater than before.

Meanwhile, because of all the tension and divisiveness in England, Charles VII was facing only token opposition in Gascony, where England's position was increasingly precarious. On 23 June 1451 the large city of Bordeaux surrendered to a French army, and a few days later Charles made a triumphal entry with 10,000 men at his back. Two months after the second city of the province, Bayonne, opened its gates and admitted a French force as well.

After the summer of 1451 the English had only two reasons to hope for an eventual recovery of its position in southwestern France. First, the people of Gascony continued to have English sympathies because rule from Paris was likely to be harsher than the lax control of a distant government across the water. And second, within a month of Bayonne's capitulation, a series of anti-French riots broke out in Ghent and other cities in the Low Countries, over which the French crown had long claimed a vague overlordship. Those riots prompted Charles to rush troops from Gascony to the rebellious cities several hundred miles to the north. With that massive shift of military power, Henry and Somerset were able to contemplate an English return to Gascony, which might bolster their popularity and enable them to neutralize the threat posed by Richard of York once and for all.

Shortly after Richard was escorted from Dartford to London in March of 1452, the King appointed John Talbot, the respected Earl of Shrewsbury, to lead an expeditionary force to Gascony. Almost seventy years old, Shrewsbury was England's most distinguished general, with an outstanding record of military service extending back almost half a century. Most recently he had been Somerset's chief lieutenant during the siege of Rouen. After that city fell he was held captive until July 1450, when he was released and made a pilgrimage to Rome. On his eventual return to England, he expected to spend his remaining days on his estates in Gloucestershire. But during the spring of 1452 he was summoned to Westminster and learned of his appointment to go and reestablish England's sway over Gascony.

Because Henry and Somerset needed a resounding victory to rebuild their image and hold Richard of York at bay, they proceeded slowly and deliberately with their plan. Not until 2 September did Shrewsbury set sail with a fleet of twenty-four ships. When the English flotilla entered the Gironde River on 17 October, the people of Bordeaux rose in rebellion and expelled their new French masters. Six days later Shrewsbury and his men rode in to a joyful welcome. After the mayor granted him the keys to the city, Shrewsbury appointed his own grandson, Thomas Talbot, to be the new English governor. During the next few months Shrewsbury made repeated forays into the countryside and reestablished England's sway over the region between the Garonne River and the slopes of the Pyrenees Mountains.

By the early months of 1453 Henry and Somerset were pleased by their handiwork and assumed that their troubles were finally over. As a consequence this seemed an ideal time to clarify the succession to the throne as a way of undercutting Richard of York's position even more. In private they had the recent marriage of Lady Margaret Beaufort to the Duke of Suffolk's son annulled while arranging for Lady Margaret to marry the King's half-brother, Edmund Tudor, Earl of Richmond.[15] Although there is no conclusive proof, it appears that Henry had decided that his eventual heir should be his half-brother, who had no claim to the throne but could easily be married to a woman who did. If those were Henry's thoughts at that juncture, he had also decided that Richard's claim should be ignored altogether, which can only have increased that magnate's dissatisfaction to even higher levels.

Unfortunately for Henry and his minister, the French crown had solved its problems in the Low Countries by March of 1453. Thus Charles VII was able to redirect his attention to Gascony and concentrate on clearing that province of English troops once more. Within a month he ordered three armies to converge on Bordeaux from slightly different directions. The first army to enter the Bordelais consisted of 7,000 men and 300 cannons and was led by the experienced Jean Bureau. At the end of June 1453 Bureau captured the village of Chalais and beheaded its mayor and aldermen as traitors to the French crown. From Chalais Bureau advanced toward Chastillon, a walled town thirty miles east of Bordeaux, which he was approaching by 10 July. The frantic mayor of Chastillon, an English collaborator for many years, rode in haste to Bordeaux and pleaded for Shrewsbury's assistance. Although the Earl had planned to make a stand at Libourne, a village ten miles closer to Bordeaux, he was swayed by the mayor's argument that the French could be destroyed at Chastillon by being driven into the Dordogne River. On 16 July Shrewsbury rode out of Bordeaux with 4,500 men but no artillery, which meant his army would face hopeless odds should a pitched battle occur.

The next day the last real battle of the Hundred Years War occurred in the fields near Chastillon. With great bravado--he donned no armor for the attack--Shrewsbury led a headlong charge against the French emplacements, allowing Bureaux's cannons to open fire with devastating effect. After an hour of brutal slaughter, the fighting came to an end. Shrewsbury and 3,500 of his men lay dead, whereas the French lost only a tenth as many. One of the truly decisive encounters of the late middle ages, the battle of Chastillon brought an end to English power in Gascony and caused its few remaining troops to sail for home at once. No more fighting occurred, although the two countries never concluded a peace treaty owing to England's reluctance to admit the Hundred Years War was finally over.

News of the devastating defeat at Chastillon and of the Earl of Shrewsbury's death there weighed heavily on the King's mind. Always sensitive and prone to agonizing self-doubt, Henry concluded that he had sent the Earl, a military hero to most of the English people, to his death. Moreover, the King had been hoping for a resounding victory that would strengthen his hand against Richard of York. Instead a disaster of immense proportions had occurred, causing Henry to become deeply depressed and to recall the violent attacks of 1450 on the Duke of Suffolk, Bishops Moleyns and Ayscough, and several other prominent officials. Under the heavy pressure Henry's mind gave way during the first week of August while he was in residence at Clarendon, a royal hunting lodge near Salisbury. Until his partial recovery eighteen months later, Henry suffered from a heightened form of what would probably be diagnosed today as post traumatic stress disorder.[16] Permanently withdrawn and unable to communicate with his servants in any way, Henry gave no sign of recognizing anyone, not even his wife. Yet he never became violent (as his French grandfather, Charles VI, had often done during his periodic bouts of insanity), perhaps because of his concurrent physical problems. Wracked by agonizing pain, Henry found it difficult to move and was unable to hobble from room to room without assistance from grooms who guarded his chamber around the clock. Unable to feed or clothe himself, he was eventually taken from Clarendon to Windsor, where the Queen and Somerset felt they could protect him from Duke Richard and his faction.

On the eve of Henry's collapse, Queen Margaret was seven months' pregnant, and her husband was eagerly awaiting the birth of their first child.[17] Doubtless the Queen was horrified by Henry's collapse, which put the House of Lancaster in greater danger than ever. But Margaret was a determined and resourceful person, and on 13 October she gave birth to a healthy son, whom she quickly named Edward in honor of Edward the Confessor. After Prince Edward's birth Margaret's overriding goal was to protect his right to the throne. A woman of strong maternal instincts, she was willing to challenge anyone, even the powerful Duke of York, in order to preserve her son's inheritance; and because of her husband's limited abilities, even after his partial recovery in December of 1454, she emerged as the real head of the Lancastrian faction.

As for Richard of York, he was more anxious than ever to break Somerset's hold over the government. Earlier in 1453, as already noted, Somerset's niece, Lady Margaret Beaufort, had been married to Edmund Earl of Richmond, the oldest of the King's half-brothers. Because of Lady Margaret's descent from Edward III, Richard of York knew that his enemies were conspiring to weaken his claim to the throne. Moreover, after Prince Edward's birth on 13 October, it was obvious that Somerset would support his claim in preference to Richard's, which had thus fallen another notch on the growing list of contenders. If Richard was to have any chance of capturing the throne for himself and his descendants, he must overthrow his great enemy and assume control of the government. Then, should the King die at a relatively early age, he would be in a position to adopt whatever courses he deemed necessary in his and his sons' self-interest.

Accordingly Duke Richard pressed during the autumn of 1453 to be named Lord Protector for the remainder of the King's illness. That demand threw the Council into a quandary because it had no desire to offend such a powerful magnate, although Margaret and Somerset denounced Richard's demand to be the government's temporary head. After several weeks of worried deliberations, the Council temporized by deciding against the appointment of a Lord Protector for the time being and ordering Somerset's detention in the Tower. The Council hoped that Richard would be appeased by such a move and a greater voice in public affairs. However, such a makeshift arrangement failed to satisfy him, nor was it acceptable to the Queen, whose hatred of Richard was heightened by her favorite's arrest. Early in 1454 Margaret proposed the appointment of herself as regent with power over all governmental matters. Although French regencies had often been headed by women, there was no precedent for a female regent in England, and the Council dismissed her suggestion out of hand. However, it attempted to placate her by allowing her infant son to be invested with the titles of Prince of Wales and Earl of Chester.

For several more months events continued on that tense and volatile course, without any satisfactory arrangements being made for the government during Henry's illness. But when John Cardinal Kempe died on 22 March 1454, the period of temporizing came to an end because his two great offices, Archbishop of Canterbury and Lord Chancellor, could not remain vacant indefinitely. The Council had to appoint a Lord Protector with power to fill them; and because of Richard of York's lineage as England's senior peer, there was no alternative to his selection. Yet the worried Councillors placed clear limits on his authority, which was to expire as soon as Henry VI recovered his senses or Prince Edward came of age. This suggests that most of the Councillors were nervous about the situation, while Richard had little scope for maneuver and intrigue because of weak support from his fellow magnates.

Shortly after becoming Lord Protector on 27 March, Richard granted the great office of Lord Chancellor to his brother-in-law, the Earl of Salisbury; and within several more days he secured the translation of another kinsman by marriage, Thomas Bourchier, from Ely diocese to the great archiepiscopal see of Canterbury. About the same time he himself assumed the valuable Captaincy of Calais, which Somerset had held since 1450.

During the next nine months, in an attempt to build greater support, Richard sought to reform the royal finances and bolster the crown's financial position. There was little he could do to increase the receipts from the customs duties because the trade depression that had begun about 1440 still had several years to run; and despite being the greatest landowner of the period, Richard had a curious lack of interest in more systematic methods of estate management, which would have led to an automatic increase of the rents from the crown lands. In his view the best opportunity lay in a retrenchment campaign that would cut the size of the royal household and lower its cost. In that somewhat limited approach he enjoyed notable success. Within six months he reduced the household from slightly more than 800 servants to 599; and in the process he decreased its yearly budget from approximately £17,000 to £11,000. The resulting saving of £6,000 a year was his greatest administrative accomplishment, although more radical courses would be necessary if the royal budget was to be balanced again in the near future.

Richard's other main concern was to strengthen the fortifications of Calais, which the English retained for more than a century after their great defeat at Chastillon. Like most of his contemporaries Richard was convinced that Charles VII would eventually try to seize the port, England's only remaining possession on the continent. Accordingly, Richard launched a farsighted program during the summer of 1454 to strengthen Calais' fortifications. Possibly because of the improvements he effected, the French were unable to capture the port until 1558; and within a year the troops billeted there became overwhelmingly Yorkist in sympathy, a fact that served Richard and his faction well once their simmering quarrel with the Lancastrians burst into the open and they needed a safe haven where they could withdraw and rebuild their strength after a major defeat on the battlefield.

Largely because of his other duties, Richard failed to take steps to suppress local feuds, which had accelerated during the last twenty years. By the mid fifteenth century almost every English county was wracked by bitter quarrels between its leading families. In the southwest, as already noted, the Courtenays and the Bonvilles were pitted against each other; while in Gloucestershire and Lancashire the Talbots and the Stanleys had murderous rivalries with the Berkeleys and the Harringtons, respectively. In Lincolnshire Sir William Tailboys was involved in an ugly campaign to smear his chief rival, Lord Cromwell; and in much the same way the Pastons and the Moleyns of East Anglia were locked in a violent struggle for local influence. Yet the most dangerous rivalry of all was the Neville-Percy feud in northern England. Those two families had long fought over estates like the valuable manor of Wressle in the East Riding of Yorkshire. Wressle had once been a prized possession of the Earl of Northumberland, although by the early 1450s it had passed into the hands of Thomas Neville, a younger son of the Earl of Salisbury, whom the Percies despised. On 24 August 1453 a train of Neville followers was attacked at Heworth by a thousand Percy retainers as they were returning home from Tattershall Castle, where Thomas Neville had been married to Lord Cromwell's niece, Maud Willoughby. A fierce battle ensued and both sides suffered heavy casualties. Fifteen months later there was another pitched battle between the Nevilles and the Percies at Stamford Bridge, seven miles east of York. Those two encounters served as a curtain raiser of sorts for the first battle of the Wars of the Roses in May of 1455.

Although Duke Richard had little interest in local matters, he was unable to ignore the escalating feud between the Nevilles and the Percies, which was threatening to spread from Yorkshire into the northern midlands, owing to the Nevilles' closer ties with Lord Cromwell. During the spring of 1454 the Protector sent a commission of oyer and terminer into northern England to punish those responsible for the violence at Heworth the previous summer. That commission was led by Richard's nephew, the Earl of Warwick, who soon indicted 700 Percy retainers but not a single Neville supporter. Although that action may have been legally correct, it fostered the impression that Duke Richard and his followers had no intention of enforcing the country's laws fairly and impartially. In fact, most people concluded that the Yorkists had no desire to end local rivalries but only to exploit them for their own political ends. That view was strengthened by Richard's arbitrary imprisonment of two men with whom he had long had bitter quarrels, William Thorpe, a rich lawyer and former Speaker of the House of Commons, and Raymond Boulers, the respected Abbot of Gloucester.

In December of 1454 Richard's term as Lord Protector came to an end when Henry VI regained his senses and resumed control of the government. Although the King's recovery was only a partial one and his mind remained clouded, it had been clearly stated at the outset that Richard's authority would cease whenever the monarch was himself again. The Duke therefore had no choice but to step aside, and in January of 1455 he withdrew to his great northern fortress, Sandal Castle in Yorkshire, while the Queen resumed her customary place at her husband's side. With support from Archbishop Bourchier and Humphrey Stafford, the rich and influential Duke of Buckingham, Margaret pressed for Somerset's release from the Tower. Knowing how angry Richard would be if his arch rival was set free, Henry VI hesitated for several weeks. But on 26 January he finally consented to Somerset's release after the latter swore to refrain from all political activity and to remain at least fifteen miles beyond the verge of the court.

Still furious about his arbitrary detention in the Tower, Somerset had no intention of abiding by the conditions of his release. Within a week he formed an alliance with one of Richard's most vocal critics, James Ormonde, Earl of Wiltshire, and set out to recover his former influence. As weak and malleable as ever, Henry VI succumbed to Somerset's polished charm and granted all his requests. On 6 March the Duke was reappointed captain of Calais, the position Richard had wrested from him the previous year. Offended by that impolitic action, Richard's brother-in-law, the Earl of Salisbury, immediately resigned the Lord Chancellorship, which was granted the following week to Archbishop Bourchier. On 15 March another important administrative change occurred when one of Richard's leading followers, the Earl of Worcester, was replaced as Lord Treasurer by the Earl of Wiltshire, who was betrothed to marry Somerset's daughter Catherine. Thus in little over a month Somerset recovered his former influence, and by mid April he was again in a position to challenge the Yorkists' vital interests. Although the King tried to limit the political damage by appointing Buckingham and several other peers to mediate the deadly rivalry between the two Dukes, that well-intended move came too late and bore no fruit. Somerset continued blindly on his course, hoping to destroy the Yorkists once and for all.

In late April Somerset arranged for the Earl of Salisbury to be ousted from a valuable sinecure, the governorship of the castle and town of Portchester in Hampshire; and he also secured Richard's dismissal from the post of controller and receiver of the royal tin mines in Cornwall and Devonshire, a source of much income for him. Shortly after those provocative moves, Somerset summoned a Great Council to meet at Leicester on 23 May. Although it cannot be proved, the likely purpose of that Great Council was to find additional ways to humble the Yorkists and render them completely powerless.[18]

Once news of the Great Council spread, Duke Richard decided it must not be allowed to meet. Despite the danger of provoking a violent altercation, Somerset must be prevented from using it or any other means to weaken and humble the Yorkists further. Indeed, Somerset deserved to be severely punished for his recent actions, which were both inflammatory and self-serving. With strong backing from the Nevilles, Richard set out from Sandal Castle in order to intercept the royal train before it reached Leicester.

On learning that Richard was on his way south with an armed force, the Lancastrians stopped at the village of St. Albans, hoping reinforcements would reach them before the Yorkists could launch an attack. A last-minute effort to arrange a peaceful settlement was made at the urging of Buckingham, an honorable man with no personal stake in the outcome. But Buckingham's attempt to prevent a pitched battle failed owing to the Yorkists' determination to destroy Somerset once and for all.

On the morning of 22 May, the encounter now remembered as the first battle of St. Albans occurred, with some 3,000 well equipped Yorkists pitted against 2,000 poorly armed Lancastrians. Although often described as "a short scuffle in a street," the battle lasted for two hours and produced heavy casualties, as many as two hundred men according to one account, although perhaps as few as eighty according to other estimates.

The action began about 11:00 A.M., when the Yorkists fired a stream of arrows against their enemies, who were huddled behind barricades in St. Peter's Street, the town's only thoroughfare. Somerset and his supporters held their ground for almost two hours, until 600 Yorkists led by Warwick found a passage through a small garden and opened a wedge into St. Peter's Street and the town's principal square. Then the tide shifted in favor of the attackers, who drove Somerset into the Castle Inn, halfway between the parish church and the large monastery that had been built on the site where Britain's first Christian martyr had been put to death over twelve centuries before. As the Yorkists were about to batter down the inn's main door, Somerset emerged and fought valiantly for his life, ending the lives of four Yorkists before his own skull was split with a poleaxe.

During the fighting Somerset's eldest son, Edmund, was wounded so badly that his body had to be carted off, while Buckingham's eldest son, Lord Stafford, suffered a deep wound that never healed and probably contributed to his death several years later. Standing forlornly on the sidelines, Henry VI suffered a minor injury on the neck and retreated inside a tanner's cottage, where the victorious Yorkists found him after the fighting ended and renewed their allegiance to him. Buckingham also became a captive, but the Earl of Wiltshire fled inside the walls of the monastery. Hated by the Yorkists almost as much as Somerset had been, Wiltshire tossed his battle armor into a ditch before disguising himself in a monk's cowl. Then he stole a horse from the stables and galloped away to safety. Two other Lancastrian commanders, the Earl of Northumberland and Lord Clifford, were not so lucky and perished on the field that morning.

As news of the violence at St. Albans spread, most Englishmen were horrified and drew back from the abyss. Consequently another pitched battle did not occur until 1459. But although several years went by without more fighting and the Yorkist faction gave nominal support to Henry VI, the bitter tensions that had erupted at St. Albans did not subside. Richard of York was as watchful as ever of the interests of his branch of the royal family; while the deliberate killing of the second Duke of Somerset infuriated his eldest son, Edmund Beaufort the Younger, who was soon recognized as the third Duke of Somerset of that line. The new head of the Beaufort family was a more successful general than his father had been and arguably the best commander in the Lancastrian camp since John of Bedford's death in 1435. Because he was determined to avenge his father's murder at St. Albans and the serious wounds he himself had received there, a blood feud between the Beauforts and the Yorkists began at once. That blood feud led to a number of plots and attempted murders between 1455 and 1459, which not only disrupted the peace of the realm but also made a speedy return to open warfare all but inevitable.

Only one other point about the first battle of St. Albans and its causes needs to be made here. Doubtless the Yorkists were not out to overthrow Henry VI that day; but had they retained control of his person thereafter, he would have ruled only on their sufferance and as their puppet. Thus, whenever he died, whether from poison, an assassin's blow, or natural causes, his son, Prince Edward, would have had little chance of obtaining his rightful inheritance or even of growing to manhood. Although Richard of York did not openly claim the throne for himself until 1460, it is clear that by 1453 if not sooner, the succession issue weighed heavily on his mind, and he seems to have had no intention of respecting Prince Edward's claim to to the throne. Certainly Queen Margaret considered him the greatest threat to her son's position--and life--from the day he was born.

For Further Reading

Charles B. Ross, *The Wars of the Roses*. London, 1976. An excellent brief account by a great scholar. Lavishly illustrated.

David R. Cook, *Lancastrians and Yorkists: The Wars of the Roses*. London, 1984. Another brief account with a selection of documents.

John Gillingham, *The Wars of the Roses: Peace and Conflict in Fifteenth-Century England.* London, 1981. A balanced account of medium length.

Anthony Goodman, *The Wars of the Roses: Military Activity and English Society, 1452-1497.* London, 1981. For those with a deep interest in the military aspects of the conflict.

A. J. Pollard, *The Wars of the Roses.* New York, 1988. A brief work that assesses much of the recent historiography. Valuable for those with some previous knowledge of the period.

Desmond Seward, *The Wars of the Roses: Through the Lives of Five Men and Women of the Fifteenth Century.* New York, 1996. Focuses on five key individuals (Lord Hastings, the Earl of Oxford, Lady Margaret Beaufort, John Morton, and Jane Shore). Successfully describes the chaotic nature of that turbulent period.

J. R. Lander, *Conflict and Stability in Fifteenth-Century England*, 3rd ed., London, 1977. A short, popular work for general readers.

J. R. Lander, *Government and Continuity: England, 1450-1509.* Cambridge, Mass., 1980. An excellent work that puts the events of the 1450s and later decades in broad perspective.

S. B. Chrimes, *Lancastrians, Yorkists, and Henry VII,* 2nd ed. New York, 1966. A useful survey of the years 1450-1509.

A. J. Pollard, "The Characteristics of the Fifteenth-Century North," in John C. Appleby and Paul Dalton, eds., *Government, Religion and Society in Northern England 1000-1700.* Stroud, Gloucestershire, 1997. Argues that the northern counties, with the possible exception of the zone within thirty miles of the Scottish border, were no more violent or "feudal" than the rest of England.

Robin L. Storey, *The End of the House of Lancaster.* New York, 1967. An important work that argues that the Wars of the Roses grew out of a steady escalation of local feuds and rivalries. But marred by a failure to acknowledge that Henry VI's disastrous foreign policy played an important role in the coming of the conflict.

David McCulloch and E. D. Jones, "Lancastrian Politics, the French

War, and the Rise of the Popular Element." *Speculum*, vol. 58 (1983). A useful corrective to Storey's view that foreign-policy disasters played no part in the origins of the conflict.

John Talbot, *The English Achilles: An Account of the Life and Campaigns of John Talbot, 1st Earl of Shrewsbury*. London, 1981. A valuable account of the military and foreign-policy defeats of the era.

Ralph A. Griffiths, *The Reign of Henry VI: The Exercise of Royal Authority, 1422-1461*. Berkeley and Los Angeles, 1983. A work of outstanding scholarship, with a fine balance between domestic and diplomatic developments. Yet because of its massive detail and great length (almost 900 pages), too difficult for students and general readers. Intended for specialists.

B. P. Wolffe, *Henry VI*. London, 1981. An excellent, albeit extremely hostile, biography of the King. Considerably shorter than the work by Griffiths above. More suitable for students and general readers.

B. P. Wolffe, "The Personal Rule of Henry VI," in S. B. Chrimes and others, eds., *Fifteenth-Century England*. Manchester, 1972. A useful sketch of Henry's political role before his breakdown in 1453.

M. R. James, ed., *Henry the Sixth: A Reprint of John Blacman's Memoir*. Cambridge, 1919. A modern edition of a contemporary account of Henry VI's personality and actions. Written after the King's death by a cleric who saw him only sporadically and probably had no understanding of what he was like before his breakdown in 1453. A work whose accuracy has been bitterly attacked by B. P. Wolffe.

Roger Lovatt, "'A Collector of Apocryphal Anecdotes': John Blacman Revisited," in A. J. Pollard, ed., *Property and Politics in Later Medieval English History*. Gloucester, 1984. A partial vindication of Blacman's work.

P. A. Johnson, *Duke Richard of York 1411-1460*. Oxford, 1988. Based on extensive research, but rather dry because of excessive footnoting and the author's refusal to speculate about Richard's motives.

Ralph A. Griffiths, "Duke Richard of York's intentions in 1450 and the origins of the Wars of the Roses." *Journal of Medieval History*, vol.

1 (1975). A valuable article, like all of Griffiths' work.

Joel T. Rosenthal, "Richard, Duke of York: A Fifteenth-Century Layman and the Church." *Catholic Historical Review,* vol. 50 (1964).

J. M. W. Bean, "The Financial Position of Richard, Duke of York," in John Gillingham and J. C. Holt, eds., *War and Government in the Middle Ages*. Cambridge, 1984.

I. M. W. Harvey, *Jack Cade's Rebellion of 1450.* Oxford, 1991. An important study of the uprising that served as a curtain-raiser of sorts for the Wars of the Roses, which broke out five years later.

Ralph A. Griffiths, "Local Rivalries and National Politics: The Percies, the Nevilles, and the Duke of Exeter, 1452-1455." *Speculum*, vol. 43 (1968).

C. A. J. Armstrong, "Politics and the Battle of St. Albans." *Bulletin of the Institute of Historical Research*, vol. 33 (1966). An unusually important article.

J. R. Lander, *The Wars of the Roses*. New York, 1966. Selections from the chronicles and other contemporary sources in a chronological format. Especially useful to readers who want to get a "feel" for the period.

John S. Davies, ed., *An English Chronicle of the Reigns of Richard II, Henry IV, Henry V, and Henry VI, written before the Year 1471*. Camden Society, 1st series, vol. 64 (1856).

Cecil Monro, ed., *Letters of Queen Margaret of Anjou and Bishop Beckington and Others.* Camden Society, 1st series, vol. 86 (1863).

James O. Halliwell-Phillipps, ed., *Letters of the Kings of England*, 2 vols. London, 1848.

Sir Henry Ellis, ed. , *Original Letters, illustrative of English History*, 2nd series, 4 vols. London, 1827; repr. 1970.

For other works on the Wars of the Roses, see the suggested readings between the text and notes of each of

the next three chapters.

Notes for *The Wars of the Roses, I*

[1] As noted in Chapter II of this book, almost all of King John's barons remained loyal after his excommunication by Innocent III in 1209 because he shifted the burden of taxation from their estates to the lands of the Church, a politic move that rich laymen applauded.

[2] Although a member of the Plantagenet dynasty, Henry VI is remembered as a Lancastrian King because his grandfather, Henry IV, had been Duke of Lancaster in 1399 when he overthrew Richard II and took the throne for himself. Subsequently the Duchy of Lancaster passed along with the throne to Henry IV's eldest son, the illustrious Henry V (1413-1422), and then to Henry V's hapless son and successor, Henry VI (1422-1461 and 1470-1471).

[3] However, he was crowned in 1429, seven years before he began to take an active part in the affairs of government.

[4] Perhaps it should be noted that Henry settled lands worth £4,000 a year on Margaret once she arrived in England. This put an additional strain on the royal revenues at a desperate juncture.

[5] In fairness to Somerset, it should be noted that in 1439-1440 he had been responsible for England's last major successes on the continent--the recapture of Harfleur and the relief of Avranches from a French siege. Thus he was not the "spectacularly incompetent general," that the Duke of York and his other political enemies later claimed him to be.

[6] That marriage took place at some point between 28 January and 7 February 1450. On that matter and other points relating to Lady Margaret's early life, see Michael K. Jones and Malcolm G. Underwood, *The King's Mother: Lady Margaret Beaufort, Countess of Richmond and Derby* (Cambridge, 1992), and especially pp. 25, 36-7.

[7] Although the first members of the Beaufort family, whose name was

derived from the French castle where they had been born two generations before, came into the world before their parents, John of Gaunt and Katherine Swynford, were legally married, they had been legitimated by a parliamentary act passed during the reign of their half-brother Henry IV. In that act there had been a clause exempting them from the royal succession, which could be repealed at any time, as Henry VI and others of his generation well knew. Indeed, by the mid fifteenth century most Englishmen gave little if any thought to that clause and assumed it bore no weight.

[8] Quoted in Desmond Seward, *The Wars of the Roses* (New York, 1996), p. 26.

[9] In September 1450 another unpopular royal minister, William Tresham, Chancellor of the Duchy of Lancaster, was murdered.

[10] The first Duke of Somerset seems to have left estates worth £1,600 a year, of which lands worth approximately £1,000 went to his infant daughter Lady Margaret, as already noted, while the remaining lands were divided equally between his widow, Margaret Beauchamp of Bletsoe, who in 1447 became the wife of Lionel Lord Welles, and his younger brother Edmund, who was created second Duke of Somerset the following year.

[11] The younger Richard Neville, who had been born in 1428, was betrothed at a young age to Anne Beauchamp, whose father, Richard Earl of Warwick, had died in 1439, leaving her an inheritance worth approximately £3,900 a year. As a result of his eventual marriage to Anne Beauchamp, the younger Richard Neville became one of the wealthiest landowners of the era and in July 1449 received his late father-in-law's title.

[12] Henry VI's deep dislike of Richard seems to have dated from 1450 or 1451. In 1456 Henry wrote to James II of Scotland that "ever since the time Jack Cade or Mortimer raised insurrection, everything has been in turmoil willed by the Duke of York of Mortimer descent." On this important point, see I. M. W. Harvey, *Jack Cade's Rebellion of 1450* (Oxford, 1991), p. 147.

[13] Unfortunately for the Earl of Devon, Richard seems to have distrusted him and eventually threw his support to Lord Bonville, causing Devon

to be a staunch Lancastrian once the Wars of the Roses began in 1455.

[14] During the middle ages the act of raising troops against the King was considered a treasonable offense, whether those troops were actually used or not.

[15] Shortly After Henry V's death in 1422, his widow, Katherine of Valois, the mother of Henry VI, married Owen Tudor, one of her household officials. By her second husband, Katherine subsequently had several children, including Edmund Tudor, Earl of Richmond and Jasper Tudor, Earl of Pembroke. Katherine died in obscurity in 1437.

[16] Most historians assume that Henry VI suffered from a heightened form of schizophrenia, similar to the mental condition that incapacitated his French grandfather, Charles VI (d. 1422). But Henry VI was thirty-three at the time of his breakdown in 1453, and a person who suffers from schizophrenia almost always shows symptoms of that condition by the age of sixteen. As a consequence Henry VI's collapse brings to mind Shakespeare's contention that cowards die a thousand times but heroes only once.

[17] Five months earlier Henry had granted an annuity of £40 to the lucky groom who informed him that Margaret was finally pregnant.

[18] A Great Council was less than a Parliament but considerably more than a routine meeting of the King's Council. Usually a Great Council consisted of specially chosen peers and commoners along with a representative group of great ecclesiastics, especially those who were felt to be politically dependable. Apparently Somerset felt more comfortable about holding a Great Council in Leicester than in London, where he had slight popular support.

The Wars of the Roses, II*

Once the first battle of St. Albans ended, the victorious Yorkists sacked the town and carted off whatever wine, money, plate, and other valuables they found in the houses and shops of its hapless inhabitants. Meanwhile Richard of York and the Earls of Salisbury and Warwick appeared before Henry VI in the tanner's cottage where he had sought safety during the battle. They knelt before him and swore they meant him no harm before formally renewing their oath of allegiance. After he thanked them for their continued friendship and service, they escorted him to the nearby monastery, where the Abbot, John Whethamstede, gave them dinner and lodging for the night. The next morning the Yorkists accompanied Henry and the remnants of his train back to London and the Great Council Somerset had planned to use against them was cancelled.

The summer of 1455 passed uneventfully, with Richard again the *de facto* head of government and both sides trying to put a good face on a bad situation. A short parliamentary session occurred, with Sir John Wenlock, the Queen's former Chamberlain who had recently defected to the Yorkists, serving as Speaker of the House of Commons. That Parliament passed an Act absolving Richard and his followers of all responsibility for the violence that had occurred at St. Albans, which was attributed rather to the evil designs of the late Duke of Somerset and his faction. But Parliament also passed a measure recognizing the King's son Edward as Prince of Wales and Earl of Chester, probably because there was still considerable support for the House of Lancaster and the Yorkists felt compelled to reassure the general public about their peaceful intentions.

The seeming harmony of those months ended when the King suffered a second, albeit relatively minor, breakdown during the final days of September. Simultaneously there was a resurgence of violence between the Courtenays and the Bonvilles in the West Country, which culminated in the murder of a leading Bonville supporter, Nicholas Radford, a respected official of Exeter. Because Henry VI's condition precluded any royal intervention, Duke Richard was named Lord Protector again on 19 November with powers almost identical to those he had enjoyed during his first Protectorate. However, because Richard was

---

* The notes for this chapter begin on page 183.

reluctant to start proceedings against a magnate as powerful as the Earl of Devon, he did nothing to punish Thomas Courtenay for his attack on Radford,whom an intimidated jury ruled had committed suicide. That blatant miscarriage of justice was deplored by the Duke of Buckingham and other independents on the Council. So as soon as the King's health improved in February 1456, they urged him to appear in the Parliament Chamber and resume control of the government.

Even after the second Protectorate ended, the Queen remained deeply suspicious of Richard's intentions. In the early spring she and Prince Edward left the capital for the midlands, where among her dower lands were the valuable honours of Tutbury, High Peak, Kenilworth, and Leicester. Several months later the King travelled north and joined his family there. Although Henry probably objected, Margaret mobilized an army with help from the new Duke of Somerset and Sir Edmund Hampden, an official of her Privy Chamber. She also had unwavering support from the Earl of Wiltshire, Viscount Beaumont, and Henry Holland, the fiery Duke of Exeter. But her most trusted adviser during those years was probably John Morton, a cleric from Dorset who was archdeacon of Norwich as well as rector of Bloxworth in his home county. Morton held a doctorate in civil and canon law from Oxford, and Margaret arranged for him to be appointed Chancellor of Prince Edward's household, in which capacity he lived almost continuously at Kenilworth and often met privately with the Queen.

Because Morton convinced her of the need for better artillery, an enterprising London merchant, John Judde, was appointed Master of the Ordnance in December of 1456. Within a short time Judde delivered twenty-six serpentines to Kenilworth, with similar deliveries of serpentines and heavy bombards following during the next several years. The Lancastrian stress on better weaponry soon paid handsome dividends and enabled them to win several battles against the Yorkists when fighting broke out again in 1459.[1]

Despite the court's absence from London during the latter part of 1456, the Lancastrians retained their influence in the capital, where moderates like Buckingham guided the Council's work. Consequently Margaret was able to secure Archbishop Bourchier's ouster from the Lord Chancellorship because of his close family ties with the Yorkists. As the next holder of the Great Seal, Margaret secured the appointment of William Waynflete, Bishop of Winchester, a much more pliant man because of his preoccupation with his large new Oxford foundation, Magdalen College. Margaret was also successful in securing the election of another follower, Lawrence Boothe, to the wealthy bishopric of Durham in the extreme northeast.

Margaret was far from victorious in all matters, however. Indeed, she suffered a major defeat in 1456 when she sought the bishopric of Exeter for one of her chaplains, John Halse. Since Bishop Lacey's death in 1455, Margaret had attempted to secure that office for Halse, and at first it appeared that her efforts would succeed. But before the cathedral chapter certified his election to the King, the Yorkist lords intervened and forced him to withdraw his candidacy. Thereupon they secured the post for George Neville, a younger brother of the Earl of Warwick and one of Richard of York's many nephews. Although an able scholar and the nominal Chancellor of Oxford University since 1453, George Neville was ineligible for his new office by canon law, being several months short of his twenty-fifth birthday in 1456.

Of even greater significance, the Council discharged Margaret's trusted follower, the Duke of Exeter, from the great office of Lord Admiral in October of 1457. A corrupt and hated man, Exeter had done nothing to rid the Channel of pirates, and the merchants of London and other southern ports were clamoring for the appointment of an Admiral who would perform his duties conscientiously. As a consequence Exeter was ordered to step aside, and his great office was bestowed on Warwick. Luckily for the Yorkists, Warwick took his duties seriously and used his own commercial fleet of a dozen vessels to patrol the Channel and suppress piracy. London's richer merchants were delighted, and their political sympathies veered toward the Yorkists for the first time.

Even before Warwick succeeded Exeter as Lord Admiral, several assassination plots were fomented by the new Duke of Somerset and other embittered Lancastrians. For too long, they held, the initiative had lain with the other side. It was time for stronger courses that would force the Yorkists to their knees and cripple their ability to disrupt the peace of the realm. On 5 November 1456, Somerset and Exeter, with help from the new Earl of Shrewsbury, lay in wait for the Earl of Warwick as he was travelling through the midlands to London. To their dismay, Warwick fought his way out of that ambush and escaped to safety. Disappointed but not deterred, Somerset continued to seek revenge for his father's death and his own painful injuries at St. Albans in 1455. In December of 1456 he lay in wait for Richard of York near Coventry, but success eluded him once again.

During those same months a violent feud began in South Wales between Gruffyd ap Nicholas, an ardent Lancastrian, and Sir William Herbert, whose sympathies lay with the Yorkists. After Gruffyd arranged the murder of one of Herbert's cousins, Sir William mobilized his tenants and pursued Gruffyd's henchmen across the border into Herefordshire. There he arrested the mayor of Hereford and so intimidated the justices of the peace that six of his enemy's retainers were condemned and quickly beheaded. That act of private vengeance prompted Gruffyd to respond in kind, and by the spring of 1457 South Wales was on the verge of anarchy.

In Warwickshire and adjoining counties there was almost as much disorder during the spring and summer of 1457. Indeed, before the end of July the King appointed special posses in fifteen counties of the midlands and the north in a frantic but unsuccessful attempt to maintain peace in that region.

Because of all the violence in England and Wales, the French crown decided to strike a blow for the recovery of Calais. Yet the fortifications of that port, where Warwick was now captain of the garrison, were so strong that it might cost thousands of lives to take the town by storm. For that reason and because of the English government's obvious weakness at home, it seemed better strategy to the French to seize a poorly defended English port and use it as a bargaining chip for the recovery of Calais. During the summer of 1457 Charles VII organized a force of 1,800 men under the command of Pierre de Brézé, whom a contemporary writer characterized as "the best warrior of all that time." On 28 August Brézé and a large squadron sailed across the Channel and plundered the port of Sandwich. However, within several days a rich landowner of the district, Sir Thomas Kyriel, arrived with troops and drove the French away, killing hundreds of their men in the process.

Probably because of the shock of that attack, the violence in England died down momentarily. But it began anew the following November, when Warwick appeared in London on legal business and Somerset and his friends made another attempt to assassinate him. Within a month the Yorkists gained revenge for that assault by murdering one of the Queen's attorneys during a bitter altercation in Fleet Street.

Meanwhile Henry VI was alarmed by the violence and was spending long hours in prayer each day. This is probably why John Blacman, a Carthusian monk who was deeply impressed by the King's piety, portrayed him as a saintly man, too high-minded for the duties of his great office. In actuality weakness and indecision were the King's chief characteristics, although he eventually tried to reconcile his feuding subjects before it was too late. In February of 1458 he devised a plan to provide financial compensation to Lancastrians who had lost relatives at St. Albans. Because of strong royal pressure the Earl of Warwick reluctantly paid 1,000 marks to the heirs of Lord Clifford, while Richard of York agreed to the transfer of Exchequer tallies worth 5,000 marks to the Duke of Somerset and his widowed mother.

While making those complex arrangements, Henry scheduled a national day of reconciliation for the latter part of March. If his feuding magnates came together on that occasion, he reasoned, it might be possible to make amends for past insults and bring dangerous quarrels to an end. Given everything that had happened during recent years, such a proposal had no more chance of succeeding than an attempt to square a circle. But Henry was determined to persevere, and he summoned all of his leading magnates to attend a Great Council at Westminster on 24 March 1458. That famous event, Henry's last real effort to influence events, was soon characterized by cynical contemporaries as "the King's love-day."

That Henry's "love-day" would probably fail was apparent as soon as his leading subjects arrived in London with hundreds of heavily armed retainers, which demonstrated the continuing hatred between the two factions. On 21 March Richard of York appeared in the capital with 400 supporters and took up residence in Baynard's Castle. A day or two later the Earl of Salisbury rode in with 500 men, whom he lodged at Cold Harbour, his mansion on the northern bank of the Thames. By that juncture the Earl of Warwick was also in the city with at least 600 men, for whom he procured rooms at the Grey Friars' convent. Meanwhile such Lancastrian magnates as the Dukes of Somerset and Exeter and the Earl of Northumberland had arrived on the scene with a combined force of approximately 2,300 men. They wisely stayed in scattered inns outside the city walls as a way of avoiding accidental acts of violence that might trigger a major battle.

On the morning of 24 March all those hostile and deeply suspicious men gathered at Westminster and sealed indentures for the financial compensation Henry VI had negotiated so laboriously. Once that largely symbolic act was completed, a procession through the streets to St. Paul's Cathedral began, during which Somerset marched alongside the Earl of Salisbury, whose son Warwick he had sought to assassinate on several occasions; while Warwick himself walked in tandem with the Duke of Exeter, one of his bitterest enemies. According to a contemporary account, Richard of York comported himself that day as "a loving friend" of Queen Margaret, whose hand he held tightly in his the whole way "with great familiarity in all men's sight." As for the King, he was clad in his ceremonial robes of ermine and blue velvet with the crown of state perched squarely atop his head. Along the way he waved happily to the crowd in the naive belief that a new era of peace and harmony was about to begin.

After Henry's love-day of 1458 there was a steady descent back to the explosive situation of 1455 because the Lancastrians were aware of their growing strength and were determined to destroy the Yorkist faction for good. During the summer of 1458 another plot against Warwick's life came within an inch of succeeding. Although he left London at once and found a safe haven in the countryside, Warwick concluded that there was no longer any chance for a peaceful settlement with the Lancastrians, a conclusion the other Yorkist leaders resisted until the following spring.

On her part, Margaret of Anjou persuaded the Council in October of 1458 to interrogate Warwick about his conduct as captain of Calais and Lord Admiral. The Queen hoped to wrest those positions from him and grant them to one of her followers, which Warwick fully understood. He therefore ignored the Council's summons and sailed across the Channel to Calais, claiming that another conspiracy against his life was afoot, which may well have been true. Nevertheless, his willful disobedience caused moderates like Buckingham to veer sharply toward Margaret and her followers, who were heartened by the support of the great Stafford affinity. Within weeks the Queen and her faction began to plan almost openly for new hostilities.

By the early months of 1459 the Yorkists were well aware of Margaret's military preparations. They retaliated with inflammatory handbills that were widely distributed during February and early March. In their political propaganda the Yorkists accused the Queen of adultery with the Earl of Wiltshire, supposedly the handsomest peer of the age, and of securing Wiltshire's appointment to be Lord Treasurer so they could plunder the royal treasury at will. In addition the Yorkists asserted that Margaret was plotting her husband's abdication so she could elevate her son, a bastard waif in their eyes, to the throne.

Confronted by such nasty charges, Margaret concluded that an armed confrontation was in fact inevitable. In May of 1459 she gave orders for the purchase of 3,000 longbows for her burgeoning forces. About the same time she left London with her husband and their young son in tow. Within several days the royal family established itself at Coventry, the strongest walled town in the midlands.

By that juncture Richard and his main followers also believed that another another pitched battle was imminent. At Middleham Castle, in Yorkshire, the Earl of Salisbury had already mobilized a thousand retainers; while at Ludlow on the Welsh border, the Duke of York was in the process of doubling his levies. Across the Channel at Calais, the Earl of Warwick was taking steps to bind the garrison tightly to himself and the Yorkist cause. Should the impending campaign in England go against them, Warwick and his allies would need a haven where they could safely withdraw and rebuild their strength. Calais would serve that purpose nicely, provided the garrison did not defect to the Lancastrians once Warwick sailed back across the Channel and joined his father and uncle at Ludlow. Luckily, since becoming captain of the garrison in 1456, Warwick had made successful efforts to supply the men's material needs. Through his own privateering activities in the Channel, he raised enough money to keep the troops paid on time and all their food and clothing needs supplied. As a result the men felt deep gratitude to him, and during the summer of 1459 their morale was high.

In early September Warwick divided the Calais garrison into two parts, the larger under Sir James Blount and Sir Andrew Trollope, grizzled veterans of the French wars, and the smaller under the command of his uncle Lord Fauconberg, to whom he granted full authority while he was away. Then Warwick embarked with Blount, Trollope, and their troops for the coast of Kent, from which they used back lanes to reach Ludlow within two weeks.

Meanwhile the Earl of Salisbury had left Yorkshire for Ludlow, also hoping to merge his troops with Duke Richard's legions. Along the way Salisbury's men were strengthened by a regiment commanded by Sir William Stanley, a rich landowner in Cheshire and North Wales. Despite its considerable size, this advancing Yorkist force was ambushed on 23 September by a larger Lancastrian army at Blore Heath, about halfway between the Shropshire villages of Newcastle and Market Drayton. The attackers that day were 10,000 Lancastrians from Cheshire, whose commander, James Lord Audley, was an elderly man who had not seen military service since 1431. Determined to keep the Yorkists from reaching their destination, Lord Audley gave the signal to attack and launched a battle that ended four hours later with the Yorkists in possession of the field and the Lancastrians mourning their many dead. Audley himself had perished, while his chief lieutenant, Lord Dudley, was a prisoner. The next day the Yorkist troops were ambushed again near Market Drayton, where they suffered somewhat heavier losses. As a consequence Salisbury's army was considerably weaker when it reached Ludlow, where Warwick and his men had already appeared.

Within a week the Yorkists moved from Ludlow to Worcester, where they worshipped in the cathedral and swore an oath to respect Henry VI's authority. But word soon arrived that a sizable Lancastrian army was approaching from the northeast with the King himself in tow. As a consequence the Yorkists retreated back toward Ludlow, in the hope of finding a good spot for a pitched battle. At Ludford Bridge they stopped and built extensive earthenworks to defend their artillery, which they hoped would scatter the Lancastrians whenever they appeared on the scene.

After passing through Worcester the Lancastrian army under the Duke of Somerset advanced toward Ludford Bridge. Along the way it tripled in size owing to the arrival of over twenty Lancastrian peers, most of whom brought along scores of their own retainers. By the time this growing horde was within several miles of Ludford Bridge, it had the Yorkists outnumbered almost two to one. Moreover, the Lancastrians were equipped with considerably more serpentines and bombards, thanks to John Judde's deliveries since 1457. Thus in the event of a pitched battle, the Lancastrians were almost bound to win an impressive victory. On the Yorkist side Duke Richard had the support of only five peers--his own teenage sons, Edward Earl of March and Edmund Earl of Rutland; his brother-in-law the Earl of Salisbury and the latter's experienced son, Warwick; and the poorest of the kingdom's barons, Lord Clinton. Although the Yorkist lords occupied a defensible position at the western end of Ludford Bridge with several serpentines ready to fire on the advancing Lancastrians, they had no margin for error. Everything had to go perfectly for them if they were to have any chance of victory.

Unfortunately for the Yorkists, their opponents' guns had a longer and more accurate range, and a deadly bombardment at dusk on 12 October wrecked the Yorkist emplacements. Even worse, Blount, Trollope, and their regiments from Calais defected without warning to the Lancastrian side. Before sailing for England the two commanders had been told that Henry VI was dead so they would have no reservations about taking the field against a royal army. But when reports spread that Henry was still alive and was actually with Somerset's men on the other side of the river, the members of the Calais garrison felt betrayed and rushed to join the Lancastrians. Once that happened the Yorkists knew they had no chance of victory the next morning. If they remained on the spot to fight, they would face certain death, either during the battle itself or on an executioner's block later.

During the evening of 12-13 October the main Yorkist leaders fled under the cover of darkness. With his son Edmund of Rutland, Richard of York galloped to the Welsh coast, where he and his son sailed further west to Ireland. The other Yorkist leaders--the Earls of Salisbury, Warwick, and March--rode off to the southern coast, hoping to hire a vessel that would take them to Calais. Thus at dawn on 13 October, the Lancastrians discovered that their main opponents had fled and no battle was necessary, the Yorkist rank-and-file being glad to surrender without firing a shot. This celebrated non-event has become known to history as "the rout of Ludford." Unfortunately, it was followed by an assault on

Ludlow, where the town was plundered and many women "grievously defouled" by the Lancastrians.

As for the Yorkist leaders who fled southward, they secured help from a local squire, John Dinham, who gave them shelter in his manor house near Newton Abbot. After a week he purchased a fishing vessel for £73 that transported them to Calais, where they arrived on 2 November.

After the rout of Ludford the Yorkist faction was in disarray, seemingly defeated beyond hope of recovery. Margaret and her supporters had complete control of the government and were free to adopt whatever courses they deemed necessary. Within a short time the Queen summoned a Parliament to meet at Coventry in order to attaint the Yorkist lords and confiscate their estates. On 20 November 1459 a carefully chosen assembly of 260 members that the Yorkists later denounced as a "Parliament of Devils" opened under the leadership of Viscount Bourchier and the Earls of Wiltshire and Shrewsbury. Although the Bishop of Exeter, George Neville, tried to lessen the Lancastrians' thirst for vengeance, the Parliament of Devils passed a sweeping attainder bill against the Yorkist lords and twenty-one wealthy commoners. Drafted mainly by John Morton, and Sir John Fortescue, Chief Justice of the King's Bench, that Act confiscated hundreds of valuable estates. It also decreed the payment of heavy fines before the heirs of the attainted men could apply for pardons and eventual restitution.[2] Shortly before the Parliament of Devils disbanded on 20 December, thirty-two noblemen--over half the peerage of the era--and thirty-four leading clerics knelt before the King and renewed their allegiance to him and his son.

During the next few weeks Margaret and her adherents remained in the north and demobilized their forces. They would have been wiser to keep their retainers in readiness so that, once the Christmas festivities ended, they could march south and take control of London. During that period a government without effective control of the capital was unlikely to dominate the outlying sections for long because possession of London was truly the key to the rest of the kingdom. Although tiny by modern standards, London's population of less than 50,000 was between three and four times that of Bristol, Norwich, or York, the other largest towns of fifteenth-century England. Moreover, London was the hub of the internal transportation system; over half the foreign trade of the era passed through the port of London; the royal courts and chief government offices were all located there; and the leading merchants of the city were considerably richer than their counterparts elsewhere, making them the best source of emergency loans in the entire country.

Also of significance, the pulpit at Paul's Cross was the most important podium in the kingdom for the dissemination of news and political propaganda. That Margaret's faction failed to take control of London meant that the Yorkist lords had an unexpected opportunity to return from exile and make another bid to win the ultimate prize.

Across the Channel at Calais the Earl of Warwick grasped the situation at once. Courageous and resourceful, if prone to over-confidence, Warwick had just the right qualities to exploit an enemy's mistake. Moreover, he was extremely popular with the merchant shippers of London because of his campaign to rid the Channel of pirates; and in his own privateering activities on behalf of the Calais garrison, he had never allowed his vessels to attack English cargo ships.

The great support Warwick enjoyed in London and the southeast was also owing to the propaganda campaign he had directed during the spring of 1459. On that occasion he and his associates had spread nasty charges against Queen Margaret and the Earl of Wiltshire, who mounted a weak counter-attack at best. During the winter of 1459-1460 Warwick and his followers launched a new propaganda barrage in order to prepare the people of London and the adjacent counties for their return. This new outpouring of propaganda included the usual handbills but also such innovations as political ballads that asserted the moral superiority of the Yorkist cause. It even included genealogical rolls that purported to trace the lineage of Richard of York and his main followers back to the Kings of ancient Israel.[3]

After laying the groundwork for a new round of hostilities, Warwick sailed to southern Ireland during the spring of 1460 to confer with Richard of York. How long the two men consulted, and to what degree they developed a common strategy, is unclear. But they obviously agreed to return to England from their respective exiles in Calais and Ireland within six months; and it also seems likely that they collaborated on the campaign manifesto that was published at Calais shortly after Warwick's reappearance there in May.

That political declaration, one of the best examples of early English political propaganda, was essentially a long letter of grievance that set forth twelve major complaints against the Lancastrians. Considerable space was given to the many plots to assassinate the Yorkist leaders during recent years and it was also alleged that a member of the King's entourage had murdered Humphrey of Gloucester in 1447. Yet the two most important points related to the many defeats suffered by English arms in France between 1449 and 1453 owing to the "spectacular incompetence" of the second Duke of Somerset and to the hated system of purveyance, by which the royal household's food and drink needs were supplied as the expense of helpless grocers and brewers. Cleverly the manifesto made no reference to Queen Margaret or Prince Edward, for whom the framers were determined to create no backlash of sympathy; nor did they mention Henry VI, whose faults were so well known they needed no comment. However, the manifesto castigated Viscount Beaumont and the Earls of Wiltshire and Shrewsbury for their leadership of the Parliament of Devils and their introduction of punitive measures that violated sacred rights of property. All in all, the Yorkists' manifesto was an effective piece of propaganda that brought them greater public support.

On 21 June Warwick's uncle Lord Fauconberg sailed across the Channel and attacked the Lancastrian garrison at Sandwich. After several hours of fierce combat, all 300 Lancastrian defenders threw down their arms after which their captain was beheaded in an unnecessary act of vengeance. Five days later the Earls of Warwick, Salisbury, and March arrived with their retainers. From their beachhead on the Kentish coast, the Yorkist lords marched to London, which they entered to great acclaim on 2 July. After conferring with Archbishop Bourchier and various other dignitaries, they attended a *Te Deum* in St. Paul's Cathedral. Yet they made no attempt to capture the Lancastrian garrison in the Tower and its ineffectual commander, Lord Scales, a man of little common sense. Once the Yorkist troops moved off to the north to confront a Lancastrian army in the midlands, Lord Scales launched a bombardment of the capital itself. That cannonade caused havoc throughout the city, which developed stronger Yorkist sympathies as a result. Moreover, Lord Scales and his men were isolated in the Tower, from which there was no escape owing to the army of 2,000 men that the departing Yorkists had left to hold London until their return.

As the Earls of Warwick and March entered the midlands, they reaped the benefit of their recent propaganda. For the first time a substantial number of peers, some fifteen in all, joined them with 10,000 men. Scores of country gentlemen also appeared and offered additional assistance. By the time the Yorkist army reached Northampton, where the Lancastrians were encamped, it had doubled or even tripled in size, giving it a substantial advantage.

On 10 July 1460 a pitched battle occurred outside Northampton in the fields near Delapré Abbey. That encounter was over in half an hour owing to the unexpected defection of Lord Grey of Ruthin, captain of the Lancastrian vanguard. Despite the unusual brevity of the battle, approximately 300 men died that day, several dozen at the hands of Edward of March, who won his battle spurs on that occasion. The eldest and most capable of the Duke of York's sons, Edward was only eighteen years old in 1460, but he was already an exceptional man, standing almost 6' 4" tall in his stocking feet and possessing exceptional stamina and strength. His courage and fighting skills were an inspiration to those who fought under his banner; and for his great contributions that day he would soon receive a military command of his own.

By the time the battle of Northampton ended, several Lancastrian peers, including the Earl of Shrewsbury and Viscount Beaumont, lay dead on the field. Doubtless the most important casualty that day was the Duke of Buckingham, whose growing support of Queen Margaret during recent months had infuriated the Yorkists. Originally a moderate who had followed a middle course between the warring factions, Buckingham had made the mistake of accepting large tracts of Neville land confiscated by the Parliament of Devils; and for that offense the Yorkist lords eliminated him, just as they had eliminated the second Duke of Somerset five years before at St. Albans.

However, the most coveted prize of all eluded the Yorkists at Northampton. Prince Edward observed the first part of the battle from the sidelines with his mother. When it became obvious that Lord Grey's defection had doomed their cause, the Prince and his mother fled toward the northwest with several attendants. On entering Lancashire they were captured by thieves and robbed of all their possessions. After wandering around North Wales in a futile effort to join up with Jasper Tudor, they turned northward again and crossed the border into Scotland, where they received shelter from the youthful James III and his mother Mary of Guelders, the official regent. While Prince Edward and Margaret of Anjou were still in Scotland, Lancastrian troops gathered in Yorkshire in order to do battle on their behalf, as we shall soon see.

As for Henry VI, he was captured by the Yorkists once the fighting at Northampton ended. The Earls of Warwick and March treated him respectfully and reaffirmed their support of him once again before escorting him back to London. During that procession Warwick rode just ahead of the King with a naked sword of state upright in his hand. After entering the capital on 19 July, the Yorkist lords captured most of the Lancastrian garrison as it streamed out of the Tower and tried to flee the city. As for Lord Scales, he sought to escape down the Thames on a barge but was recognized and killed by a group of boatmen, who left his corpse in the churchyard of St. Mary Overy that night.

During the latter part of July the most important government offices changed hands once again. Viscount Bourchier, a brother of the Archbishop, succeeded the Earl of Wiltshire as Lord Treasurer; while Bishop Neville replaced Bishop Waynflete in the great office of Lord Chancellor. During those same weeks writs were sent out for a Parliament that would reverse the attainders decreed eight months earlier by the Parliament of Devils.

Meanwhile in southern Ireland, Richard of York had done almost nothing to prepare for his return to England. Even after learning of the Yorkists' victory at Northampton on 10 July, he showed no concern for haste; and not until 8 September did he and his son Edmund of Rutland land on the Cheshire coast with 500 followers. From Radcliffe they made a leisurely trip to the capital, which they finally entered on 10 October, three days after Parliament opened.

Historians have long debated Richard's reason for making such a slow journey to London, which bore all the hallmarks of a royal progress, a naked sword being borne ahead of him the whole way. The most plausible explanation is that Richard had finally decided to assert his claim to the throne as boldly and dramatically as possible. Yet he doubted that his Neville kinsmen would support him in such a risky move. In effect he hoped to keep his closest allies from declaring their opposition in advance, which he could easily do by postponing his arrival at Westminster until the new Parliament was in session. Once the two Houses were organized and a Speaker elected, he would appear and assert his claim to be the country's rightful ruler in such a way that everyone present, even his kinsmen and strongest backers, would be confronted with a *fait accompli*.

Whether that was his actual strategy, Richard was at Barnet, less than twenty miles away, when Parliament opened on 7 October. Henry VI and both Archbishops were present that morning, as were some forty peers and two hundred burgesses and knights of the shire. The preacher that day was Bishop Neville, the new Lord Chancellor, who called for greater unity and self-sacrifice in the face of a probable attack from the north, an obvious reference to Queen Margaret and the Prince, who were expected to strike across the border at any moment. During the next two days routine tasks were performed, including the election of John Green to be Speaker of the House of Commons and the appointment of the four customary panels to receive and make preliminary rulings on private petitions.

On 10 October Richard of York finally appeared in the Parliament Chamber to a blare of trumpets and with a naked sword still borne directly ahead of him, which made it obvious that he was now claiming to be England's rightful monarch. He approached the empty throne, placed his hand on its arm as if to say this was his proper place, and turned around to face his fellow peers, expecting them to burst into cheers and applause. Instead a hushed silence descended on the chamber, which was broken only when Archbishop Bourchier approached and asked if he wished to see the King. To the primate's pointed question Richard gave an angry retort: "I know of none who would not more fitly come to see me than I to him." Deeply embarrassed by the Members' reaction to his misstep, Richard stormed through a nearby doorway into the royal apartments and, according to one contemporary writer, "lodged there for no little time more like a King than a Duke."

With Richard's action on 10 October, a tense period lasting more than two weeks began. On 16 October the Duke appeared in the Parliament Chamber again with genealogical materials that purportedly demonstrated his hereditary claim to the throne. The Members naturally hoped to avoid a vote on such a dangerous matter and referred it to the judges and serjeants-at-law. But the judges and serjeants had no wish to become embroiled in such a sensitive question, and on 20 October they ruled that they were unable to decide the matter, thereby tossing it back into Parliament's lap. The average Member was unwilling to countenance the deposition of Henry VI, whose coronation in 1429 still cloaked him with a sacred aura, although virtually no one felt compelled to respect the rights of his son, Prince Edward. That small ray of hope opened the door to a compromise settlement, which was debated and tentatively adopted on 20 October although not ratified until a week later. By that celebrated Act of Accord, Henry VI would remain on the throne for the rest of his days, but on his death the crown would pass not to Prince Edward but to Duke Richard and the heirs of his body. In addition, the Duke was henceforth to be known by all the titles that had been granted several years earlier to the Prince.

Once the succession was legally vested in him, Richard announced that he intended to occupy the royal apartments at Westminster and brusquely directed Henry VI to obtain lodging with the Bishop of London, whose palace often accommodated royalty before the construction of St. James's Palace in the early sixteenth century. At the same time Richard bullied Henry into granting him estates worth 10,000 marks a year, thereby doubling his annual revenues at a stroke.

While those important developments were taking place in the capital, the northern Lancastrians were preparing for a new campaign. By the middle of November more than 12,000 men had been mobilized by such Lancastrian peers as the Dukes of Somerset and Exeter, the Earls of Devon and Northumberland, and Lords Latimer, Clifford, Dacre, Greystocke, and Roos. Because the Queen's supporters controlled most of the countryside between York and Hull, the Yorkist regime in the south could not feel safe until the Lancastrians were defeated or forcibly dispersed.

During the last week of November, Duke Richard appointed Warwick and the Duke of Norfolk to supervise affairs in the capital while he went north to confront his enemies. Additionally he instructed his eldest son, Edward of March, to travel to Ludlow and keep watch over the movements of Jasper Tudor, Earl of Pembroke in North Wales and the border counties. Several days later Richard set out for Yorkshire, accompanied by the Earls of Rutland and Salisbury and a force that increased along the way to at least 7,000 men. By 21 December the Yorkist troops had arrived at Richard's great northern fortress, Sandal Castle, where they spent a jittery Christmas season.

Meanwhile the Lancastrian forces under the Dukes of Somerset and Exeter had converged on Pontefract, a short distance from Sandal Castle and the nearby village of Wakefield, where many of the Yorkist troops had been billeted. With almost 15,000 men in their ranks, the Lancastrian commanders passed several days at Pontefract before marching toward Wakefield on 30 December. Richard's lieutenants begged him not to engage an army twice the size of his own. But he rejected that advice, probably because he had spent the previous summer safely in Ireland and felt compelled to demonstrate his military prowess. On 31 December he left his great walled fortress and launched a pitched battle. The outcome was an overwhelming victory for his enemies, who lost only 200 men as a result of their greater numbers and superior artillery. As for the Yorkists the battle of Wakefield was one of their worst defeats because they suffered almost 2,500 casualties, including Duke Richard himself. Also killed that day were Richard's second son, Edmund of Rutland, and one of the younger sons of the Earl of Salisbury, Sir Thomas Neville. Salisbury himself was captured shortly after the fighting ended by Lancastrian partisans who hoped to ransom him for a large sum of money. But when he was escorted in chains to Pontefract the next day, a group of Margaret's most rabid supporters gathered and insisted that he be executed at once.

Within a week news of the Yorkist débàcle reached Edward of March at Ludlow. Although Edward automatically inherited his father's titles and estates, there was nothing he could do at the moment to confront the Lancastrians in northern England. His hands were tied by a large Welsh army commanded by Jasper Tudor and the Earl of Wiltshire.

Little is known about the campaign that occurred in the border area during late January and the first few days of February 1461; but with help from Sir William Herbert and Sir William Hastings, the new Duke of York won a smashing victory in Herefordshire on 2 February.

During that encounter at Mortimer's Cross, in a meadow about six miles from Leominster, Edward forced the Earls of Pembroke and Wiltshire to flee the field and captured Pembroke's aged father, Owen Tudor, who was soon beheaded in the market place at Hereford. Because hundreds of Lancastrians perished at Mortimer's Cross, that battle clearly demonstrated that the new Duke of York was the best general on the Yorkist side. Indeed, he was in many ways a born leader of men and never lost a pitched battle, although his best biographer, Professor Ross, believes he often took dangerous chances that might have ended in disaster. Still, generals who never gamble seldom achieve real success.

A day or two before the battle of Mortimer's Cross, Queen Margaret and her son crossed the Scottish border into northern England. Elated by her followers' triumph at Wakefield and the deaths of Richard of York and the Earl of Salisbury, the Queen was confident that final victory lay within her grasp. She ordered a march on London, thinking she could regain control of Henry VI and thereby deprive the Yorkist government of all pretense of legitimacy. Margaret herself assumed command of the advancing army but was unable to maintain discipline because her forces had little option but to live off the land. As a consequence, when they passed through towns like Beverley, Grantham, Stamford, and Huntingdon, they looted and plundered, although they probably did less damage than their angry victims claimed. Whatever the case, tales of horror spread, and the people of the midlands and south turned their back on Margaret's cause once and for all.

News of the Lancastrian approach soon reached the Earl of Warwick and his associates in London. They mobilized their troops and set out for the midlands with Henry VI in tow, hoping that the King's presence would deter an attack on their smaller army. Warwick and his men proceeded as far as St. Albans, where they occupied a strong position shortly before another pitched battle occurred on 17 February.

The second battle of St. Albans was a long and bloody encounter that produced casualties of between 3,400 and 11,000 men, according to contemporary estimates. The higher figure is not completely implausible because, according to John Whethamstede, who observed the fighting from a tower of his monastery, the Lancastrian forces alone numbered 25,000 men that day. However, a somewhat later chronicler, William Gregory, maintained that Margaret's army consisted of only 5,000 men in all. Whatever the size of the opposing forces and the actual number of casualties, Warwick and the Yorkists suffered a major setback during the encounter. Warwick himself galloped away from the field in panic, while lesser commanders like Sir William Bonville, who had fought for years against the Earl of Devon, were captured and executed.

Once the battle ended, Margaret's troops plundered the town before setting out for London. The Lancastrians expected to receive an enthusiastic welcome from the city's inhabitants; but as they neared the city gates, the mayor and aldermen bolted them securely in order to prevent their entry and probable harm to the citizens' property. Because their artillery was inadequate for a long siege, the Queen's forces fell back after several days and returned to Yorkshire. But before leaving the region for the north, they regained control of Henry VI, who was happy to accompany Margaret wherever she wanted to go.

After his crushing defeat at St. Albans, Warwick rode toward the west in search of his cousin Edward and his army. In fact Edward was already advancing toward London with 10,000 men, and on 22 February the two Yorkist leaders met somewhere in the Cotswolds. Warwick spurred his horse around, and together they made haste for the capital, which they entered four days later.

Because Henry VI was now in the north with Margaret and the Prince, all legal sanction for a Yorkist government had disappeared. Remembering how they had been attainted and all their estates confiscated by the Parliament of Devils, the Yorkist leaders naturally expected similar measures to be passed against them within several weeks. Thus, despite their momentary control of the capital, their legal and political situation was precarious, and they quickly concluded that a desperate situation required desperate measures. In fact it now seemed essential to depose Henry VI and proclaim a new King as the best way to circumvent their enemies' designs for them.

A careful campaign began at once to prepare the local people for Duke Edward's proclamation as England's rightful monarch. On Sunday, 1 March Bishop Neville addressed a crowd of 4,000 people in St. James' Fields. The Lord Chancellor described Henry VI's faults and the many reasons he was no longer entitled to occupy the throne. Then he explained his cousin's "superior claim" to the position and praised his virtues before asking if the people were ready to accept him as their ruler. They responded with loud cheers and repeated cries of "God save King Edward!" Within several hours Bishop Neville and several associates drew up a petition urging him to mount the throne at once. That petition was presented to him at Baynard's Castle later that same day.

The next morning a document outlining Edward's claim to the throne was circulated through the city streets in preparation for major events that were to follow. On Tuesday, 3 March a meeting that its leaders attempted to portray as a Great Council occurred at Baynard's Castle. In addition to Edward and his cousin Warwick, those in attendance that day included Archbishop Bourchier, the Bishops of Exeter and Salisbury, the Duke of Norfolk, Lords Ferrers and Fitzwalter, Sir William Herbert, and probably Sir William Hastings. Hardly an impressive group to promote such an important political and dynastic change, that group of less than a dozen men considered the dangers of their course but decided it would be even riskier to hold back. After ratifying the document that outlined Edward's lineage, which had been circulated through the streets the previous day, they ruled that his elevation to the throne should take place at once.

On Wednesday the 4th of March, royal heralds at Paul's Cross announced Edward IV's accession to the thrones of England, France, and Wales. Within an hour a procession to Westminster Palace began, and on entering the Great Hall Edward took an abbreviated form of the coronation oath before Archbishop Bourchier and Lord Chancellor Neville, after which he solemnly swore to enforce the laws of the realm and to rule as "a true and juste Kyng." Thereupon he put on "the cap of estate" (which almost equalled the crown in dignity) and took the scepter into his hand. Then he proceeded to the section of the Great Hall occupied by the Court of King's Bench and sat down on the marble seat always reserved for the monarch. After those important symbolic acts, Edward and scores of courtiers crossed the street to the Abbey, where they attended a *Te Deum*. After worshipping privately before the shrine of Edward the Confessor, the new King took a barge down river to the city and spent the night in the Bishop of London's palace.

During the next few days most of Edward's principal supporters returned to their estates to mobilize regiments for a new campaign against the Lancastrians. Edward himself remained in the capital for several days and negotiated a loan of £4,000 from the municipal corporation, which was happy to give him financial aid at this juncture. On 11 March the new ruler's uncle, Lord Fauconberg, set out for Yorkshire at the head of an advance column. Two days later Edward himself departed in the company of the Duke of Norfolk and many lesser followers. By slow stages they proceeded first to Cambridge, being joined along the way by additional troops. Because Margaret's army had lived off the land on its return to Yorkshire, scores of gentlemen appeared and offered their help. In addition at least a dozen peers arrived with several thousand retainers, which enabled the Yorkists to claim they now had the support of most of the nobility and gentry. By the time Edward and his troops reached Pontefract on 27 March, the Yorkist army had grown to almost 25,000 men, which made it almost as large as Margaret's legions.

On Saturday the 28th, several small skirmishes occurred. The next day--Palm Sunday--a bitter nine-hour engagement took place near the village of Towton during a blinding snow storm. Although most battles of that era were over in three hours because of the crushing weight of the troops' armor, the unusually large number of men arrayed at Towton required a much longer period just to bring all the combatants into the fray, which explains the unusual length of the battle. Just as Towton was the longest battle of the era, it produced the greatest number of casualties. One chronicler estimated the number of deaths at 36,777, while another maintained that at least 38,000 men died. Both those figures seem too high because there is little likelihood that the death rate exceeded thirty per cent, an extremely high casualty rate then or now. Assuming that approximately 55,000 men were engaged on the two sides, it seems unlikely that more than 16,500 soldiers perished, and one chronicler put the death toll as low as 9,000, which is not altogether implausible.

The Lancastrians might have won at Towton had the Earl of Northumberland closed in on Edward IV's cavalry shortly after Somerset and Sir Anthony Trollope forced it from the field by a clever maneuver. But Northumberland failed to exploit an unexpected opportunity, and Edward was able to rally his horsemen and return to the fray. In the end, as usually happened during that era, the outcome of the battle was determined by hand-to-hand combat between foot soldiers. With his superior height and strength, Edward wielded the sword and poleaxe with exceptional skill and provided an inspiring example to his men. On the Lancastrian side no single commander provided such an effective lead, and the Lancastrian line eventually crumbled under the weight of repeated Yorkist charges and the arrival in the early afternoon of Sir John Howard and fresh Yorkist regiments.

As the Queen's forces broke and ran, many of them were killed by their pursuers, although considerably more drowned in their heavy armor while trying to cross the River Ouse at Tadcaster. The previous day the Lancastrians themselves had broken the bridge over the Ouse, assuming they would win the battle and need to prevent a Yorkist flight. Although several dozen Lancastrians reached the sheltering walls of York, they were captured and executed within a week.

Edward IV's great victory at Towton shattered the Lancastrian army beyond hope of recovery. Many of Margaret's best commanders died on the field that day, including Sir Andrew Trollope and Lords Clifford, Dacre, Egremont, and Welles. The Earl of Northumberland also perished while the Earl of Devon was executed the next morning along with forty-two Lancastrian knights who had been captured. Only the Dukes of Somerset and Exeter made a successful escape to safety.

Because the Lancastrian losses were so much heavier than the Yorkists', Margaret fled across north again with her confused husband, Prince Edward, and Somerset. The Lancastrian party was soon within a dozen miles of Edinburgh, but James III and Mary of Guelders refused to give them assistance until Margaret directed the garrison at Berwick Castle to surrender that fortress to a Scottish regiment. That important castle remained in Scottish hands for the next two decades, until it was recaptured by Edward IV's younger brother, Richard of Gloucester, in 1482.

Once it was obvious that Lancastrian resistance in the north had collapsed, Edward IV made a leisurely progress through the region in an effort to build popular support. After a brief stay in York, he travelled further north to Durham and established cordial relations with Bishop Boothe, one of the Queen's strongest supporters during recent years.[4] Boothe felt it was pointless to continue his support of the Lancastrians and agreed to become Edward IV's confessor and almoner.

On 1 May Edward IV arrived at Newcastle and witnessed the execution of the Earl of Wiltshire, one of his family's greatest enemies. Then he journeyed south and reentered the capital, where he enjoyed a respite of peace and harmony for the first time in several years. On Friday, 26 June he created twenty-eight new Knights of the Bath as a way of rewarding men who had repeatedly risked their lives on his behalf. Two days later his formal coronation in the Abbey occurred with great pomp and fanfare. During the festivities that day Edward invested his brother George with the dukedom of Clarence, although he delayed the elevation of his youngest brother, Richard, to the dukedom of Gloucester until the following November.

Because there were still a dozen Lancastrian castles in Wales and the northeast to be subdued, the new regime was reluctant to demobilize its forces, as Margaret had foolishly done after the Rout of Ludford. Indeed, during the summer of 1461 there was additional hard fighting, especially in North Wales, a hotbed of Lancastrian activity under the leadership of Jasper Earl of Pembroke. To confront Jasper and his followers, Edward IV granted extensive power to Sir William Herbert, arguably the greatest Welshman of the age.

Sir William Herbert had fought on Edward's side at Mortimer's Cross and probably at Towton as well. Shortly before the coronation Edward raised him to the peerage as Baron Herbert of Raglan, Chepstow, and Gower; and in quick succession the King granted him such important posts as justiciar of South Wales, constable of Cardigan and Carmarthen castles, and steward of both Cardiganshire and Cantrefmawr. Thereafter the King considered him his "master-lock" (or "main man" in contemporary American terminology) for the principality; and during the summer of 1461 Edward directed him to put an end to the intrigues of Jasper Tudor and the Welsh Lancastrians. Lord Herbert discharged that task brilliantly, routing Jasper's troops within several months and capturing his chief stronghold, Pembroke Castle, on 30 September. Thereupon Jasper fled to the continent, where he lived in exile for the next nine years.

Meanwhile, in the northeastern counties of England itself, the task of recapturing the Lancastrian castles in that thinly populated district was entrusted to the Earl of Warwick and his younger brother, John Lord Montagu. They performed that dangerous assignment with workmanlike precision, and by the end of 1461 the Yorkists had taken control of Alnwick, Bamburgh, Dunstanburgh, and Warkworth Castles, to name only a few.

However, while the Yorkists were chipping away at Lancastrian power in the northeast, Margaret of Anjou was plotting to nullify their victories in the near future. Still a pensioner of the Scottish crown, she sent Somerset as a special envoy to Paris during the autumn of 1461. The new French King, Louis XI, was as eager as Charles VII had been to wrest Calais from England's grip, and Margaret was willing to surrender that important port to her countrymen in return for substantial French aid against Edward IV.

Somerset remained in France during the winter of 1461-1462 but failed to conclude an alliance with Louis XI, probably because the latter's advisers were still feeling their way and reluctant to adopt risky courses during the first year of a new reign. On Somerset's return to Edinburgh in 1462, Margaret decided to go to Paris and negotiate with Louis XI in person. In April she sailed to the continent with Prince Edward and Somerset, although she left her husband behind in Scotland. Once she arrived at the Louvre she met privately with Louis, whom she quickly persuaded to assist the fallen Lancastrians in return for the surrender of Calais. A treaty was concluded in which Louis agreed to provide Margaret with fifty-two ships and 1,000 men-at-arms under the command of Pierre de Brézé.

Margaret and her supporters sailed back across the Channel in late October of 1462, and on the 25th they landed near Bamburgh on the Northumbrian coast. Almost at once the constables of Bamburgh, Dunstanburgh, and Warkworth Castles declared for the Lancastrians, and within a week Somerset and Brézé took Alnwick Castle by storm. Once those strongholds were back in Lancastrian hands, Margaret rode north, hoping to obtain assistance from James III.

Meanwhile in London, Edward IV had mobilized an army and set out for the north in mid November. But because the King came down with a bad case of measles at Durham and had to remain in his bedchamber, it fell to the Earl of Warwick to recapture the errant castles once again. Luckily, Warkworth Castle opened its gates as soon as Warwick and the Yorkist army appeared on the horizon. As for the other castles, Warwick decided to starve them into submission rather than take them by storm at enormous cost to the royal forces. On 26 December the garrison of Bamburgh Castle surrendered, and the next day the garrison at Dunstanburgh followed suit. Because the Earl of Angus had arrived with a regiment to strengthen the garrison at Alnwick castle, it held out a few days longer. But by 6 January 1463, that important fortress was back in Yorkist hands also.

Shortly after the capture of Alnwick Castle, Edward IV and Warwick returned to London, accompanied by Somerset. By that juncture Somerset had quarreled with Margaret of Anjou about basic strategy, and Margaret had upbraided him for making exaggerated claims about his political influence during his embassy to Paris. Temporarily at least Somerset was interested in an accommodation with Edward IV, who was delighted and made every effort to secure his full support. Shortly after a new Parliament met on 10 March 1463, Somerset's attainder, part of a general measure passed in November 1461, was reversed and all his confiscated estates restored to him. In addition, Edward IV granted him a generous annuity of £222 as well as an equal sum in cash for his immediate needs. Clearly, Edward hoped to win the Lancastrian leader to his side, although he refused to grant him any real power so soon. As a consequence, Somerset grew dissatisfied again and was unable to refrain from more plotting, which soon cost him his life.

During the spring of 1463, while Edward was doing his best in the southeast to gain Somerset's support, the northern castles passed back into Lancastrian hands once again. To make matters worse, a Scottish invasion in June led to a prolonged siege of Norham Castle, on the River Tweed, one of the few northern fortresses still in Yorkist hands. To keep Norham from falling to his enemies, Edward IV sent Warwick back to the north; and with help from his brother Lord Montagu, Warwick was able to raise the siege within several weeks.

In late July 1463, shortly after forcing the Scots back across the border, Warwick made a desperate bid to seize Margaret of Anjou and Prince Edward, who were in northern England at the time. But Margaret and the Prince along with the Duke of Exeter, Sir John Fortescue, and John Morton were able to make their way to the coast and catch a ship bound for France.

On returning to Paris Margaret appealed again to Louis XI for assistance but he was unwilling to give any further help to a seemingly hopeless cause. In October 1463 he even concluded a peace treaty with Edward IV, and two months later the Scots followed his example. As a consequence Margaret had no option but to remain on the continent and obtained financial help from her elderly father, René of Anjou. He allowed her to live at his château of Koeur-la-Petite in Lorraine and provided 6,000 crowns a year for the support of a small Lancastrian court-in-exile there.

With all French aid cut off, the Lancastrians in northeastern England were isolated, and within a month most of their castles were back in Yorkist hands again. As the tide shifted more strongly in Edward IV's direction, Somerset reappeared on the scene and made a frantic bid to rally support for the Lancastrian cause. But it was too late, and on 15 May 1464 he and a small band of followers were overwhelmed at Hexham by Warwick's brother, Lord Montagu. Somerset himself was captured and beheaded as "a proven disturber of the peace," as were Sir Thomas Findherne and several other Lancastrian stalwarts.

Several weeks later the last remaining Lancastrian fortress in northern England, Bamburgh Castle, surrendered after a punishing bombardment by Warwick's artillery. At that point the whole region was essentially pacified, although Harlech Castle in North Wales held out until 1468. Thus with only one exception, the whole realm was ready to accept Edward IV as its rightful monarch, although Henry VI was still at large.

Sheltered for a time at Bamburgh Castle, Henry VI escaped from that great stone fortress shortly before its capitulation in June of 1464. For another year he wandered across the windswept countryside of northern England in the company of several grooms and priests, taking shelter with anyone who would offer it. During the summer of 1465 his whereabouts were discovered by a Yorkist supporter, Sir James Harrington of Hornby Castle, Lancashire; and within a week Harrington's troops captured him in a wood near Clitheroe, attended by only one groom and two priests. Harrington quickly took the former monarch to London, where he was paraded through the streets before being imprisoned in the Tower. Still less than forty-four years old, Henry was a completely broken man, and Edward IV saw no reason to have him executed. A generous and kind-hearted ruler by the standards of that age, Edward was willing to let the former ruler live on in a measure of comfort under his supervision in the capital. But Edward's decision to spare Henry's life contributed to another round of hostilities that began several years later and culminated in Henry's brief restoration to the throne and Edward's hasty flight to the continent for safety's sake. Those events will be the focus of the next chapter.

For Further Reading

In addition to the works listed between the text and the notes of the previous chapter, the following books and articles are recommended:

J. R. Lander, "Henry VI and the Duke of York's Second Protectorate," in *Crown and Nobility 1450-1509*. Montreal, 1976.

Philippe Erlanger, *Margaret of Anjou, Queen of England*. Paris, 1961.

Paul Murray Kendall, *Warwick the Kingmaker*. New York, 1957. A zestful life of that controversial figure.

Charles B. Ross, *Edward IV*. Berkeley and Los Angeles, 1974. A work of great quality. Replaces Cora L. Scofield's *Life and Reign of Edward IV*, 2 vols. London, 1923.

Mary Clive, *This Sun of York: A biography of Edward IV*. London, 1973. A less scholarly work than the biographies by Ross and Scofield. Intended for students and general readers.

Charles B. Ross, "Rumour, Propaganda and Popular Opinion during the Wars of the Roses," in Ralph A. Griffiths, ed., *Patronage: The Crown and the Provinces*. Gloucester, 1981. A valuable article.

Alison Allan, "Yorkist Propaganda: pedigree, prophecy and the 'British History' in the reign of Edward IV," in Charles Ross, ed., *Pedigree and Power in Later Medieval England*. Gloucester, 1979.

Alison Allan, "Royal Propaganda and the Proclamation of Edward IV." *Bulletin of the Institute of Historical Research* , vol. 69 (1986).

C. A. J. Armstrong, "The Inauguration of the Yorkist Kings and their Title to the Throne," in *England, France and Burgundy in the Fifteenth*

Century. London, 1983.

Colin Richmond, "The Nobility and the Wars of the Roses, 1459-1461." *Nottingham Medieval Studies*, vol. 21 (1977).

R. J. Knecht, "The Episcopate and the Wars of the Roses." *University of Birmingham Historical Journal*, vol. 6 (1957).

Ralph A. Griffiths, "Wales and the Marches," in S. B. Chrimes and others, eds., *Fifteenth-Century England.* Manchester, 1972.

Additional works on the Wars of the Roses are listed between the text and the notes of the next two chapters.

Notes for *The Wars of the Roses, II*

[1] Judde was hated by the Yorkists for supplying the Lancastrians not only with with cannons but also with sulphur and saltpetre, the main ingredients of gunpowder. In June 1460 he was killed near St. Albans while attempting to make another delivery to the Queen's camp.

[2] Among those attainted by the Parliament of Devils were Duke Richard and his sons the Earls of March and Rutland; the Earl of Salisbury and his son the Earl of Warwick; Sir John Neville and his brother Thomas; Sir Thomas Parr; Sir John Conyers; and Sir Thomas Harrington. The only woman attainted by that Parliament was Lady Alice, the wife of the Earl of Salisbury.

[3] Charles Ross, in *Patronage: The Crown and the Provinces in Later Medieval England*, ed. Ralph A. Griffiths (Atlantic Highlands, N. J., 1981), p. 23.

[4] Margaret's Chancellor since 1451, Lawrence Boothe was elected Bishop of Durham in August of 1457 because he had her strong backing at that juncture.

The Wars of the Roses, III*

By the time Henry VI was captured in 1465, the unity of the Yorkist faction was breaking down. This was largely owing to the underlying rivalry between Edward IV and his cousin Richard Neville, Earl of Warwick. During the previous decade Warwick had risked his life many times for the House of York, and as a consequence he expected preferential treatment from the crown. Indeed, Warwick was bent on receiving the greatest rewards of any Yorkist supporter, including a veto of sorts over policies he felt to be dangerous or unwise. Unfortunately for him, Edward IV never doubted his own ability to govern the realm and opposed even tacit recognition of his cousin's right to be co-ruler with him. Moreover, the two men seldom saw eye-to-eye in regard to goals and strategies, especially in the diplomatic realm, and by the end of the 1460s they were at complete loggerheads. But the more they drifted apart, the more optimistic the Lancastrians became about reopening the Wars of the Roses and recovering the throne for Henry VI or his son Prince Edward.

Until 1463 there was little sign of the friction that would engulf the Yorkists and lead to another round of fighting in six more years. During the aftermath of Edward's coronation on 28 June 1461, the King was extremely generous to Warwick, whom he appointed to the great ceremonial office of Lord Constable, a position almost hereditary in the line of the de Veres, Earls of Oxford. In addition Warwick received such important offices as Lord Admiral, Lord Warden of the Cinque Ports, Captain of Calais, constable of Dover Castle, steward of several lesser castles, chief steward of the Duchy of Lancaster, and warden of the eastern and western marches along the Scottish border. All those offices made Warwick the most powerful man in the realm aside from the King himself with duties similar to those of a modern Minister of Defense.

As for Warwick's younger brothers, the King conferred generous rewards on them too. George Neville continued in the great office of Lord Chancellor, and shortly after the twelfth Earl of Oxford's execution for treason in 1462, George became guardian of his teenage son with control over nineteen valuable manors. During those same years Warwick's other brother, John, received similar rewards. In 1461 Edward IV granted him the important barony of Montagu; and several months later that grateful young man received nine large

* The notes for this chapter begin on page 215.

manors forfeited by the Beaumont family as well as the profits of all the royal tin mines in Devonshire and Cornwall. During the summer of 1464, after routing the third Duke of Somerset and his forces at Hexham, John received the earldom of Northumberland and former Percy estates worth approximately £700 a year.

Of the many Nevilles who had fought on behalf of Edward's claim to to the throne, William Lord Fauconberg, probably received the most valuable rewards of all. Indeed, in 1461 Lord Fauconberg was created Earl of Kent and received some sixty manors that had been confiscated from various Lancastrian magnates.

If Warwick was jealous of the estates his kinsmen received, he had no reason to complain. Early in 1462 the King granted him the manors of Appleby and Brougham in Westmorland, which had been seized from the Cliffords because of their long support of the House of Lancaster; and subsequently Warwick obtained the Percy lordship of Topcliffe in the North Riding of Yorkshire as well as a dozen Percy estates in Craven. All those acquisitions consolidated Warwick's position as the richest subject in the realm with well over 100 manors scattered across twenty-one counties. From land and office together, his yearly income was almost £6,000, an enormous sum for that era. Yet he aspired to even greater wealth and was determined to gain possession of the lordship of Dunster, which consisted of scores of manors located in Devonshire, Dorset, and Somerset.

By virtue of his marriage to the great heiress Anne Beauchamp, whose father had died in 1439, Warwick was already an important landowner in South Wales. In fact, his wife's dowry included extensive properties in Glamorgan, Morgannwg, and Abergavenny, which were located within an easy ride of the principal estates of the lordship of Dunster. If Warwick could obtain that great conglomeration of lands, he would own valuable estates in southwestern England as well as in South Wales; and for some months he made veiled hints to the King in that regard. But Edward was unwilling for Warwick or any other peer to become an "over-mighty subject," strong enough to challenge the power of the central government. So in June of 1463 he assigned the lordship of Dunster to his leading Welsh supporter, William Lord Herbert.

As noted in the previous chapter, Sir William Herbert had fought alongside Edward IV at Mortimer's Cross and probably at Towton as well, for which service he was granted a barony just before the coronation. During the summer of 1461 Edward directed Lord Herbert to lead a campaign against Jasper Tudor, Earl of Pembroke, and the Welsh Lancastrians, and by 30 September Herbert had captured Jasper's chief stronghold, Pembroke Castle, causing him to flee to the continent. In gratitude Edward gave Herbert additional Welsh lands and granted him the wardship of two important Lancastrian peers: Henry Percy, son and heir apparent of the third Earl of Northumberland, who had died at Towton, and Henry Tudor, the four-year-old Earl of Richmond, who was Jasper Tudor's nephew and a possible claimant to the throne as Lady Margaret Beaufort's only child. Herbert took those two young noblemen into his family circle at Raglan Castle and planned to marry Henry Tudor to his daughter Maud once they both came of age.

After Jasper Tudor's flight to the continent, Wales was largely quiet, although Harlech Castle remained a Lancastrian stronghold until Lord Herbert captured it in 1468. In gratitude for Herbert's distinguished service, and to enable him to govern Wales more effectively on the government's behalf, Edward granted him the valuable lordship of Dunster in June of 1463, as already noted. But Warwick was deeply offended, although he refused to regard Dunster as irretrievably lost to himself and his two daughters, Isabel and Anne.

Shortly after granting the lordship of Dunster to Lord Herbert, Edward IV took another step that irritated Warwick almost as much: he stripped the latter of the great ceremonial office of Lord Constable, which he reassigned to a peer of much lower wealth and status, Sir Richard Woodville, Lord Rivers.

Despite Sir Richard Woodville's marriage in 1436 to Jacquetta of Luxembourg, the cultivated daughter of the Count of Saint-Pol in the Low Countries and the widow of Henry V's brother John Duke of Bedford (d. 1435), he was a man of little eminence until 1449, when he received a barony for his long service in France. Thereafter Lord Rivers was a fervent Lancastrian until the spring of 1461, when Edward IV won his great victories at Mortimer's Cross and Towton. A shrewd and accommodating man, Lord Rivers was willing to bend with the times, and he was one of the first Lancastrian peers to recognize Edward IV as England's rightful King. Gratified and deeply impressed, Edward appointed him to serve on the royal Council in 1463; and early the next year Edward visited him several times at Grafton Regis, his country house in Leicestershire.

During those visits to Grafton Regis, Edward was captivated by the charms of Lord Rivers' beautiful daughter, Elizabeth, one of the best educated women of the time although she was often rude and arrogant to those who did not share her bookish interests. Some five years older than the King, Elizabeth had already buried one husband, Sir John Grey, who had died while fighting against the Yorkists at St. Albans in February of 1461. By her first husband, Elizabeth had given birth to two sons, Thomas and Richard, who were still young boys in 1464.

Despite the Woodvilles' strong Lancastrian sympathies and the fact that he would be getting a ready-made family in the bargain, Edward IV decided to marry Elizabeth as quickly as possible; and to prepare for their wedding he appointed her father to the great ceremonial office of Lord Constable, which Warwick was obliged to resign.

As Edward looked forward to his union with Elizabeth, he began to consider the other ways his marriage might annoy Warwick, who as yet knew nothing about his matrimonial plans although he probably suspected something was afoot. Like most of his contemporaries Warwick regarded the huge Woodville clan--Elizabeth was one of thirteen children--as social climbers or *novi homines* as one writer of the age put it. Endowed with no real wealth, they were barely able to live on the scale expected of a prominent aristocratic family and certainly not in the manner of a fabulously wealthy magnate like Warwick, who dispensed hospitality to friends and relatives with great largesse. Even worse, Edward's plan to marry Elizabeth was directly contrary to Warwick's ideas about the woman his cousin should marry and the foreign policy England should follow during the next twenty or thirty years.

Although Edward hoped to reopen the Hundred Years one day and win military glory for himself as Henry V had done earlier in the century, Warwick refused to think in such old-fashioned terms. Indeed, he was convinced of the need to work with the French crown as a way of undercutting Margaret of Anjou and her son, who still hoped to recover their position in England.

From the time they established their court-in-exile in Lorraine in 1463, Margaret and Prince Edward felt they might secure substantial aid from Louis XI one day As long as that possibility existed, the Yorkist regime at Westminster could not relax its guard altogether. Accordingly, Warwick pressed for a dynastic alliance with the French crown in order to end the threat posed by Margaret and Prince Edward once and for all. Because Edward IV was still unmarried, Warwick urged him in the spring of 1464 to accept Louis' niece, Bona of Savoy, as his wife while bringing a final end to the Hundred Years War and neutralizing the threat posed by Margaret and her son. To Warwick that seemed a small price to pay for the consolidation of Yorkist power in England.

But Edward IV was fourteen years younger than Warwick and of a far more adventurous nature; and as such he was reluctant to give up his dream of continental victories like Agincourt. Moreover, he was completely smitten by the charms of Elizabeth Woodville, whom he was determined to marry, regardless of any harmful consequences that might result from their match. However, Edward insisted that the ceremony be conducted in utmost secrecy at Grafton Regis on Mayday of 1464, probably because he knew the public reaction would be hostile and he hoped to find a way to nullify Warwick's anger.

During the early summer of 1464, Warwick had no inkling that his cousin was already married to one of his own subjects and continued to press for marriage talks with France. Edward IV was embarrassed by that demand because he knew he had contracted his marriage impulsively and thereby deprived his government of a valuable bargaining chip. Unfortunately, Edward made the situation even worse by allowing Warwick to travel to Paris as a special envoy and open formal negotiations for a marriage alliance that was now manifestly impossible. Those talks proceeded more smoothly than Edward had expected, and Warwick soon returned to Westminster with the unwelcome news that Louis was serious about wanting a marriage treaty with England. Then Warwick left for the north to discharge his duties there, several castles along the Scottish border having fallen into Lancastrian hands once again.

While Warwick was away in the north, word leaked out that the King was already married; and during a Great Council at Reading in September, Edward finally admitted that fact, to his utter embarrassment and Warwick's furious disbelief. To the latter it was now painfully obvious that he had no special standing with the King, who had sent him on a bootless errand that made him look ridiculous in other men's eyes. Furthermore, Edward's marriage to Elizabeth Woodville meant that the chances of securing better relations with France were dead for the moment and the French Council of State might give substantial support to Margaret and and her son in the near future. That fact and reports that Prince Edward was being trained in the martial arts and often spoke of the need to wage war against his family's enemies and cut off their heads cannot have warmed the cockles of Warwick's heart.

On his part Edward IV knew he had made a serious blunder and given Warwick good reason to feel aggrieved. During the winter of 1464-1465 he sought to repair the breach by granting additional favors to important members of Warwick's faction. Shortly after the archbishopric of York became vacant, Edward translated Warwick's brother George from Exeter diocese to that much greater ecclesiastical office. About the same time Edward conveyed the ancient barony of Mountjoy to Warwick's friend and protégé, Sir Walter Blount, who had been Lord Treasurer since 1462. But those attempts to make amends were too little and too late. Warwick himself failed to profit in a direct way, and many of his supporters were equally offended by the King's blunders.

That Edward failed to conciliate his cousin was also owing to his efforts to assist the Woodvilles, who were eager to receive financial resources commensurate with their new social rank. Because Edward was determined to strengthen the royal revenues and had already disposed of most of the manors obtained as a consequence of the 131 attainders decreed by his first Parliament in 1461, he had few if any estates with which to endow his many brothers- and sisters-in-law. As a result they received almost no estates from him during the 1460s. However, he felt no qualms about arranging fashionable marriages between them and the heirs to great fortunes. As early as September 1464 Elizabeth's sister Margaret married the heir apparent of the wealthy Earl of Arundel, while in January of 1465 the Queen's twenty-year-old brother John married Lady Catherine Mowbray, the fabulously rich dowager Duchess of Norfolk, a woman in her late sixties although she was widely believed to be at least a decade older. By that juncture Lady Catherine had buried three husbands, and a modern historian has described her rather ungallantly as "a ghastly predatory old hag" who was content "to dump her somewhat faded charms and immense fortune into the bed of the King's brother-in-law." [1] Such a strange union strengthened the popular belief that the Woodvilles were an avaricious band intent on feathering their own nest in whatever ways possible. Warwick was probably amused by the public reaction to that unusual marriage, which one chronicler termed "a diabolical match." But Warwick undoubtedly felt a measure of annoyance too because Lady Catherine Mowbray was his aunt, having been born a Neville.

Unfortunately for Yorkist unity, Warwick made a foolish display of his wounded feelings in May of 1465, when Elizabeth Woodville was finally crowned as Edward IV's consort. One of the decade's great social events, that ceremony in the Abbey was attended by almost all of England's peers, the most notable exception being Warwick himself. His failure to put in an appearance was an obvious snub at the King's in-laws, who never forgave it.

Edward himself reacted to the snub in ways that infuriated Warwick even more. Within a short time Edward required Warwick's protégé, Lord Mountjoy, to surrender the great office of Lord Treasurer, which the King granted to the ever-obliging Lord Rivers with a yearly fee of £1,330 (ordinarily the Treasurer received a stipend of only £365 a year). Because Elizabeth Woodville had recently given birth to a healthy daughter, the Princess Elizabeth of York, Edward promoted his genial father-in-law to a considerably higher rank in the peerage by creating him Earl Rivers while conferring the lesser title of Lord Scales on his eldest son, Anthony. Moreover, in 1466 Edward arranged for his sister-in-law Mary Woodville to marry the son and heir apparent of Lord Herbert. On the eve of that lavish wedding at Windsor Castle, Edward raised William Herbert the Younger to the peerage as Lord Dunster.

The grant of that title made it apparent to Warwick that he would never receive the Dunster estates he still coveted so much. From that moment Warwick not only felt deep anger toward the King but also a burning hatred of Lord Herbert, whom he was bent on destroying whenever a good chance presented itself. Finally, in April of 1467 Edward IV decided to remove Warwick's brother George from the great office of Lord Chancellor. On 1 May 1467, Edward himself rode to The Moor, George Neville's palace at Charing Cross, and ordered him to hand over the Great Seal. To succeed the Archbishop in that crucial post, Edward appointed one of the most notorious Bishops of the age, Robert Stillington of Bath and Wells, a complete stranger to the people of his diocese, whom he rarely visited being the most notorious absentee of the period.

While making all those changes, Edward continued to arrange fashionable marriages for his wife's younger sisters. In 1466 Anne Woodville became the wife of William Viscount Bourchier, heir-apparent to the earldom of Kent; while Eleanor Woodville was betrothed to Anthony Grey, son and heir of a wealthy Kentish landowner. More significant than either of those unions was the marriage of Catherine Woodville to the young Duke of Buckingham, a teenager with a princely income of £5,000 a year. Because of his great wealth and direct descent from Edward III, Buckingham was an extremely pompous young man who felt demeaned by his marriage to one of the lowly Woodvilles. Clearly the marriage had been forced on him, and in later years he never cooperated with his in-laws, whom he treated with open contempt. Indeed, he opposed them at every turn with tragic consequences to himself and his retainers, as we shall see in the next chapter.[2]

If Buckingham objected to his marriage to Catherine Woodville, Warwick resented it and the other Woodville marriages of the 1460s just as much. As already noted, Warwick had two daughters who were slated to divide his great estate one day. He naturally wanted them to marry well, and for a time he hoped they would become the wives of Edward's younger brothers, George of Clarence and Richard of Gloucester. But Edward rejected that idea out of hand, so Warwick had to look elsewhere for husbands for his daughters. Yet before he could arrange suitable matches for them, the King invaded the marriage market and secured the most eligible bachelors for his sisters-in-law. Thus the Woodville marriages of the 1460s reduced Warwick's chances of finding appropriate husbands for his daughters, which caused him to be more critical of his cousin than ever.[3] Yet the marriage that offended Warwick most of all was the union of the King's sister Margaret of York to Duke Charles the Bold of Burgundy in July of 1468.

Still determined to reopen the Hundred Years War one day, Edward wanted to reestablish the Anglo-Burgundian alliance of 1419-1435, which had enabled Henry V to impose the Treaty of Troyes on France in 1420. By that treaty, probably medieval England's greatest diplomatic triumph, Henry V had won the hand of Charles VI's daughter Katherine of Valois and been recognized as heir-apparent to the French throne.[4] While the Anglo-Burgundian alliance remained in effect, the English government enjoyed its greatest power over French affairs, and in 1431 the young Henry VI was actually crowned King of France during a great ceremony in Paris. Although England lost all its French possessions except Calais by 1453 owing to the skillful leadership of Charles VII and his generals, Edward IV knew that he was unlikely to enjoy comparable victories unless the Anglo-Burgundian alliance of an earlier era was reestablished.

Despite Warwick's demand for friendly relations with France as a way of undercutting the Lancastrians in exile, Edward appointed Lord Scales and Lord Hastings to go to the court of Duke Philip the Good of Burgundy and conclude a marriage treaty.[5] Those two envoys arrived at Bruges in the spring of 1467, but Philip died before an agreement could be negotiated. However, his successor, Charles the Bold (1467-1477), shared his father's desire for a new alliance with England, which might be a useful counterweight against French efforts to end Burgundian autonomy. In addition, because of the growing health of the English revenues, which Edward IV was in the process of rebuilding, Charles might be able to wring a large dowry from Westminster in return for the marriage agreement the English ruler wanted so much.

Because both parties wished the negotiations to succeed, a marriage treaty was concluded on 16 February 1468. By that treaty Margaret of York was to be married to Charles the Bold on 4 May of that year, provided the first quarter of her enormous dowry of 200,000 gold crowns (£41,666 13s. 4d.) had been handed over. However, because of Edward's inability to raise so much hard cash by the appointed date, the marriage had to be delayed until the summer.

Meanwhile Louis XI had learned of the negotiations between his two greatest enemies, and during the spring of 1468 he sought to thwart them by sending a special embassy to England. The French envoys suggested the conclusion of an Anglo-French agreement that would render the Anglo-Burgundian alliance meaningless. But Edward treated the Frenchmen brusquely and refused to alter his policy in any way. That rebuff caused Louis XI to warn London of the likely outcome if he gave Burgundy meaningful assistance as some future time.

Because Edward persevered in his course, Louis granted money and ships to Jasper Tudor, who returned to North Wales in the summer of 1468. From Harlech Castle, the only important English or Welsh fortress still in Lancastrian hands, Jasper launched several lightning raids against the Welsh Yorkists. However, Edward IV responded quickly and directed Lord Herbert to mobilize an army and contain the troublesome Lancastrians. Within a week Lord Herbert moved north with several thousand crack troops, took control of Harlech Castle on 14 August, and forced Jasper Tudor to sail back to the continent. Those notable achievements prompted Edward to reward Lord Herbert with a higher title on 8 September, when he invested him with Jasper's earldom of Pembroke. That great new distinction awarded his hated rival infuriated Warwick beyond belief.

By that juncture Warwick was determined not only to ruin the new Earl of Pembroke but also to bring an end to his cousin's intolerable rule. For several years Warwick and his friends had been offended by the King's lavish rewards to other men and his adoption of a foreign policy that might provoke a bitter war and drive the English crown over the brink of bankruptcy. In addition a long campaign against France would probably tempt Margaret of Anjou and her son to make another effort to regain control of the kingdom and thereby trigger a new round of the Wars of the Roses. Clearly Edward must be shackled and reduced to the role of a puppet ruler before he plunged the country into another period of violent discord. Of course Warwick's pessimistic outlook and subsequent actions proved to be a self-fulfilling prophecy, producing the very situation he hoped to avoid.

While Warwick was moving toward rebellion during the winter of 1468-1469, Edward was taking new steps to heal their breach before it was too late. In December of 1468 he granted Warwick the wardship of Francis Lord Lovell; and the following February he assigned his cousin several large Percy estates in Cumberland along with the office of chief justice of all royal forests and chases north of the River Trent, which carried an annual stipend of 100 marks. But those overtures had no effect because Warwick was already bent on making Edward a puppet King.

In April of 1469 a rebellion broke out in southern Yorkshire under the leadership of one "Robin of Redesdale," who was probably Sir John Conyers of Hornby, the husband of Warwick's cousin Alice. Sir John had long been one of Warwick's leading adherents, and for at least a decade he had been steward of his great Yorkshire stronghold, Middleham Castle. On raising the standard of revolt "Robin of Redesdale" had support not only from the great Neville affinity but also from Lords

Latimer, Dudley, and Fitzhugh of Ravensworth, all of whom had close ties with Warwick. However, at this early juncture the situation was not critical for Edward IV because Warwick's brother John, who had received the earldom of Northumberland in 1464 as well as many valuable estates from the crown, remained loyal to the King. Indeed, John Neville raised several thousand men and dispersed the rebels within a month.

But almost at once a second rebellion broke out in the East Riding of Yorkshire under one "Robin of Holderness," who was probably the Lancastrian leader Robert Hillyard of Winstead, although this identification cannot be proved. However, it is revealing that Hillyard's house at Winstead was only a few miles from the Percy lordship of Pocklington, and one the rebels' main goals was to secure the removal of John Neville from the earldom of Northumberland, which should be transferred to the rightful heir, Henry Percy, who was still living in Wales as one of the Earl of Pembroke's wards at Raglan Castle. Because the new rebellion sought to deprive John Neville of his cherished earldom and its many estates, he moved north with a large retinue and defeated his opponents before executing a man he believed to be Robin of Holderness.

Because of John Neville's unwavering support, Edward IV felt no danger during the spring of 1469 and left Westminster during the first week of June. Accompanied by his brother Richard of Gloucester, Edward made a leisurely journey into East Anglia and spent a week at Bury St. Edmunds before visiting the shrine of Our Lady of Walsingham. However, while he was travelling through the eastern counties and John Neville was campaigning in Yorkshire, the original insurgents under Robin of Redesdale reassembled and set out for the south, hoping to effect a union with Warwick and his troops several miles north of London. Meanwhile Edward and his retinue had moved on to Norwich, where they learned that a large rebel band had passed through Lincolnshire on its way to the capital, and at that point the King became alarmed. At once he decided to go and confront his enemies, and on 18 June he dispatched letters summoning his greater subjects to join him within several days with whatever troops they could muster. After raising 1,200 men in Norfolk, the King set out for Stamford, whence he sent a message entreating the mayor and burgesses of Coventry to send him immediate aid. Shortly thereafter he passed through Nottingham on his way to Newark, where he learned the rebel army was three times the size of his own. That unhappy news, along with the arrival of less than five hundred reinforcements, caused him to fall back on Nottingham.

Meanwhile, the Earl of Warwick had sailed across the Channel to Calais with his daughter Isabel, his brother George Archbishop of York, his cousin George of Clarence, and John de Vere, the thirteenth Earl of Oxford, who had recently married his sister Margaret. On 11 July, in the presence of a dozen witnesses, Archbishop Neville solemnized the marriage of Isabel Neville to Edward IV's brother George, who was hopeful that Warwick would elevate him to the throne one day, especially if the King failed to father a son by Elizabeth Woodville.[6] The next day the rebel leaders issued a manifesto from Calais in which they denounced Edward IV's evil advisers and condemned the heavy taxation of recent years. They also drew an ominous parallel between Edward IV on the one hand and the three previous monarchs--Edward II, Richard II and Henry VI--who had been overthrown on the other. After announcing their plan to sponsor fundamental reforms, Warwick and his minions urged their many followers in southeastern England to join them at Canterbury on 16 July, armed and ready to take control of Edward IV and his government.

On the morning of 16 July Warwick and his associates sailed back to England and rode into Canterbury about noon that day. They were welcomed by a large crowd of cheering Kentishmen, many of whom accompanied them to the capital two days later. The Lord Mayor and Aldermen of London allowed them to pass through the city on their way into central Hertfordshire, where Robin of Redesdale's forces were still waiting for them to arrive.

Several days before that rendezvous occurred, a major battle occurred in Oxfordshire. Among the magnates Edward IV had summoned to assist him was the loyal William Herbert, now Earl of Pembroke. Pembroke raised 2,000 men and set out to reinforce the King's troops at Nottingham. But as Pembroke marched up from South Wales, the northern rebels wheeled toward the west and blocked his path at Edgecote, where a pitched battle took place on 26 July. Because the opposing forces at Edgecote were almost evenly matched, hundreds of men died on both sides. However, the death toll was especially high in Pembroke's army, although the Earl himself and his brother Richard were taken alive by Warwick's captains. From Edgecote the Herbert brothers were taken under heavy guard to Banbury and thence to Northampton, where on 28 July they were beheaded on Warwick's orders, the Earl having ridden in a short time before. Within another week Warwick's partisans in Somerset captured and executed Earl Rivers and his son John, who had sought a safe hiding place there.

Meanwhile, the King had remained at Nottingham, where he knew nothing of recent events. Shortly after the execution of the Herbert brothers, Edward left that walled city, hoping to join forces with the Welsh contingents he assumed were moving toward his camp. As he travelled through southern Nottinghamshire, he learned of the battle of Edgecote and its unhappy aftermath. Thereupon his troops lost heart and scattered in all directions, leaving Edward isolated. Within a week he was captured at Olney, several miles west of Kenilworth, by men in Archbishop Neville's livery. They took him under heavy guard to Coventry and thence to Warwick Castle, where he remained until 13 August, when they escorted him to Middleham Castle, Yorkshire.

During the next few weeks Warwick and his cohorts were the *de facto* rulers of England. Desperately they sought to establish a viable government, with Warwick assuming the late Earl of Pembroke's most important offices including the stewardships of Cantrefmawr and Cardiganshire and the justiciarship of South Wales. At the same time Warwick appointed a close friend, Sir John Langstrother, to the great office of Lord Treasurer, which had been vacant since Earl Rivers' execution on 12 August. However, the new government had no legitimacy or popular support and was endangered from the start by a Lancastrian rebellion in the far north.

As soon as Edward's imprisonment became widely known, a group of northern Lancastrians gathered and sought to exploit the situation by embarrassing and possibly overthrowing the House of York altogether. By the end of August serious disturbances had erupted at several places along the Scottish border, and on 2 September Warwick felt compelled to cancel a Parliament that was scheduled to open late in the month. Moreover, because hundreds of Yorkists now regarded Warwick with open contempt, he failed to raise enough troops to suppress the northern rebels. After two weeks it was apparent that the Lancastrian uprising could not be contained to the border area unless Edward IV was restored to power. Only his prestige and popularity could save the day for the House of York.

By the middle of September Edward had recovered his freedom and returned to London in triumph. Knowing he must cooperate with the treacherous Warwick for the moment, he made a show of forgiving his cousin's recent actions and concentrated on defeating the Lancastrian rebels near the Scottish border, which was accomplished in short order. By 29 September all the rebel leaders had been captured and taken to York, where after a quick trial they were hanged, drawn, and quartered.

During the next month the King considered how to deal with Warwick and his wayward brother, George, who was now Warwick's son-in-law and most devoted follower. Hoping to clip their wings and destroy their ability to cause him further trouble, Edward looked for new allies to take the place of the Herbert brothers and other followers who had fallen during the recent fighting. During the autumn of 1469 he took steps to increase the power of Sir William Stanley, an important landowner in Cheshire and North Wales, who could probably fill the void left by the Herberts' execution. Even more important, Edward began to groom his brother Richard of Gloucester for an important role.

Born in 1452, Richard of Gloucester had unbounded admiration for Edward IV, whom he had actively supported during the recent crisis. As a consequence Edward decided to appoint him Lord Constable, the ceremonial position Earl Rivers had held for five years. In mid November the King also named his seventeen-year-old brother justiciar of North Wales, and two weeks later he granted him Sudeley Castle and its adjacent manor in Gloucestershire as well as the lucrative offices of chief steward and surveyor of both the earldom of March and the principality of Wales. In mid December Richard additionally became steward of Monmouth, while in January of 1470 he was named to the main offices Warwick had assumed just after Pembroke's execution. These included the stewardships of Cantrefmawr and Cardiganshire and the justiciarship of South Wales.

While increasing Richard's power in all those ways, Edward IV concluded that the Nevilles' power in northern England must be reduced substantially; otherwise Warwick and his followers would probably remain a thorn in his side for years to come. In order to weaken Warwick's faction, Edward decided to restore the rightful Percy heir to the earldom of Northumberland, even if that required the loyal John Neville to relinquish that title and the many estates that went with it. During the autumn of 1469 Edward took the first steps toward recognizing Henry Percy as the rightful Earl of Northumberland, although he did not complete the process until 25 March 1470, the same day John Neville was created Marquess Montagu. By that juncture Edward had granted the dukedom of Bedford (ordinarily reserved for a younger brother of the monarch) to John Neville's oldest son, who had just been betrothed to Edward's eldest daughter, Elizabeth of York. In addition many valuable manors in the southwest that had formerly belonged to the Earl of Devon were transferred to John Neville in order to compensate him for the northern lands he would soon have to hand over to Henry Percy. Altogether John Neville obtained southern estates worth £600 per year, which was £100 less than the value of the estates he was about to surrender. Although he voiced no opposition at the time, John Neville considered this a poor reward for his many valuable services to the crown since 1461. Certainly that development helps explain why he soon turned against Edward IV and threw his support to Warwick.

By January of 1470 Warwick was well aware of his younger brother's dissatisfaction and was looking for ways to exploit it. By that juncture Warwick had also decided to depose Edward IV in favor of George of Clarence. If that were done, the new ruler would be putty in Warwick's hands because George had none of Edward's intelligence or military skill. Although able to cause serious problems for others, George had little potential for statesmanship, and he would probably be content to let his wily father-in-law serve as the power behind the throne.

At any rate, Warwick began to plot Edward's downfall by the first week of February 1470. At that time Warwick and George provoked a serious quarrel between a leading member of the King's entourage, Sir Thomas Burgh, on the one hand and Richard Lord Welles and his brother-in-law, Sir Thomas Dymmoke, on the other. Edward IV sought to mediate that quarrel and ordered Welles and Dymmoke to leave their estates in the midlands and appear before him at Westminster. Although Edward granted them free pardons, Warwick and Duke George played on the fears of Lord Welles' son Robert, who was easily convinced that the monarch was plotting Lord Welles's execution and the imposition of heavy fines on their many tenants in Lincolnshire. Thereupon Sir Robert raised troops and moved south in order to save his father from a nonexistent peril.[7]

Edward responded to Sir Robert's threatening move by calling out troops of his own. On 12 March he faced the rebels in the shortest battle of the period, the encounter generally remembered as the battle of Lose-Cote Field. The battle acquired that name because Sir Robert Welles' men sensed their cause was doomed within fifteen minutes and threw off their liveried coats before scattering in all directions.

Encamped at Coventry on the morning of the battle of Lose-Cote Field, Warwick and George hoped to hear that Edward IV had become mired down and was open to a deadly attack by them and a northern army they expected to arrive on the scene momentarily. But the King's victory and immediate withdrawal to Grantham put an end to that possibility. The next day Edward summoned Warwick and George to appear before him within three days. Still defiant, the insurgents sought to raise additional troops for a campaign against Edward. When their efforts failed they fell back on Rotherham before moving south to Exeter.

Meanwhile Edward had moved from Grantham to Newark, where on 17 March he threatened his enemies with severe punishment if they failed to appear before him soon. Believing they had sought refuge at Chesterfield, Edward appeared before its walls on 20 March. Once he realized his mistake, he wheeled north and spent several days at Pontefract before moving on to York. There he pardoned several of Warwick's subordinates and dispatched letters forbidding his coastal officials in Ireland and Calais to allow them to land. On 26 March the King rode southward again, and five days later he issued a proclamation outlawing Warwick and George and offering a substantial reward for their capture.

Within several days of their arrival at Exeter on 3 April, the two rebels decided to flee abroad. By the 11th they had sailed from Dartmouth; but when their ship reached Calais on the 15th, it was fired upon although Warwick was still the nominal captain of the port. His deputy, Lord Wenlock, supported his request to land but was overruled by Lord Duras, a Gascon in Edward IV's pay and the port's official governor. Warwick's ship remained anchored in nearby waters until 20 April, when a squadron led by Sir John Howard arrived and sought to capture it.[8] Finally, on 28 April the two men and Warwick's daughter Anne landed at Honfleur, near the mouth of the River Seine. There they were welcomed by the Archbishop of Narbonne and the Admiral of France, Louis the Bastard of Bourbon, whom Warwick had met during his French embassy in 1464.

On arriving in France, Warwick requested political asylum for himself and his retinue. Because Louis XI was well aware of the Earl's desire for an Anglo-French *rapprochement* and his opposition to Edward's pro-Burgundian policy, he granted the requested asylum at once. After welcoming the English exiles at Amboise on 8 June, Louis devised a clever plan to destroy Edward IV by means of a reconciliation between Warwick and his old enemy, Margaret of Anjou.

During recent years Margaret and Prince Edward had lived at the château of Koeur-la-Petite in Lorraine. If Warwick and Margaret could be convinced to forget past problems and close ranks against Edward IV, Louis would assist them in restoring the House of Lancaster to the English throne. Once that fortuitous event occurred, Louis believed, a friendly government at Westminster would doubtless remain neutral while he destroyed the power of Charles the Bold and incorporated Burgundy directly into France, the French ruler's most cherished goal.

Although Warwick and Margaret of Anjou hated each other and had no interest in working together, Louis promoted his plan with skill and determination during the summer of 1470. By the first week of July he had won Warwick's tacit approval, the Earl being willing to work with the Devil himself if that was the only way to recover his power in England. Then Louis summoned Margaret and Prince Edward to join him at Amboise, whence all three travelled to Angers for a meeting with Warwick and Margaret's elderly father, René of Anjou. At Angers on 22 July, Margaret and her old nemesis came face to face for the first time in almost a decade. Warwick was unusually deferential to the former Queen, who kept him on his knees for half an hour while berating him in insulting language. Once she had her say, Louis took charge of the discussion and stressed the plan's strengths and chances of success. Besides, should Margaret hold back at this juncture, she would miss a golden opportunity to promote her son's cause, an opportunity that might not reoccur. Once Margaret consulted her chief adviser, Dr. Morton, who seems to have voiced no objection, she expressed guarded interest in the scheme. But Warwick sounded a cautious note because he suspected the Lancastrians might turn on him once they were back in power. To that objection Louis replied that Warwick's daughter Anne was the same age as Prince Edward and there was no reason they should not become man and wife. After their marriage Warwick would be the Lancastrian Pretender's father-in-law, and he would doubtless restrain his mother's thirst for revenge.

Despite serious doubts about a plan that gave Warwick considerable power over the Lancastrians' fate, Margaret failed to marshal convincing arguments against it; and two days later her son was betrothed to Anne Neville at Angers Cathedral, although their wedding did not occur until 13 December. Yet Margaret insisted on one non-negotiable condition as the price of her cooperation. She and her son would not return to England with Warwick and his troops. Only after they overthrew Edward IV and established a viable government would she and Prince Edward set foot on English soil.

On 25 July Warwick's entourage, which now included the Earl of Oxford and Jasper Tudor, left Angers for the Norman coast. At Honfleur and La Hogue, preparations for a voyage across the Channel to England's southern ports began at once. In less than a month a fleet of sixty ships was mobilized, and Louis also supplied Warwick with 2,000 experienced archers.

Meanwhile in London, Edward IV suspected what lay in store for him. To forestall an attack on his realm, he kept sixteen warships on patrol in the Channel; and he strengthened that little fleet with an equal number of warships supplied by his brother-in-law, Charles the Bold. While seeking to keep his enemies pinned down on the continent, Edward was confronted by a serious rebellion in Yorkshire under the leadership of Warwick's brother-in-law, Lord Fitzhugh of Ravensworth.[9] Less than a week later a second rising broke out farther north in Cumberland, where troops took the field under the banner of Richard Salkeld, Warwick's longtime constable of Carlisle Castle.

That Warwick engineered both rebellions from Normandy seems clear enough, if unprovable, and they presented Edward with a Hobson's Choice. If he moved north to reestablish order, he would open the door to a landing by Warwick and his followers on the southern coast. But if he remained on guard in the south, the northern disorders would probably spread until they engulfed the entire region. Confronted by such a difficult choice, Edward had to guess the better option to choose. Because the Anglo-Burgundian fleet was still on patrol on the Channel, he suspected that Warwick's forces would be unable to make a successful crossing from Normandy during the next month. He therefore galloped off to Ripon, where he arrived on 14 August. During the following weeks he fought relentlessly against his northern enemies, hoping to restore peace to the region so he could return to the capital in haste. But while he was still over 250 miles from London, a great storm swept across southern England and the Channel, scattering his protective shield. Before his warships could regroup and resume their guard duty, Warwick and his men embarked from the Norman ports, and on 13 September they dropped anchor at Plymouth and Dartmouth.

The next day the rebel leaders moved inland to Exeter, where they dispatched a circular letter in Henry VI's name. It urged all patriotic Englishmen and their retainers to join in a great movement against the "usurping ruler" Edward IV. Jasper Tudor left at that point to raise an army in Wales, while Warwick, George of Clarence, and the Earl of Oxford marched up the main road toward the midlands. Within several days the Earl of Shrewsbury and Lord Stanley rode in and bolstered their ranks with at least 5,000 men. Other reinforcements arrived during the following week; and by the time the rebel horde reached Coventry, it had grown to 25,000 men.

By the last week of September Edward was well aware of his enemies' whereabouts. After summoning the Marquess Montagu and several other magnates to meet him at Nottingham, Edward set out with 2,000 men, hoping other supporters would join him as he moved south. To his dismay this did not happen, and on reaching Doncaster his confidence was shaken by reports that Montagu had defected to the other side and was about to attack him with 6,000 men. Edward knew he had little chance of defeating Warwick's larger army at Coventry, and there was no section of the realm to which he could withdraw and raise enough troops to ensure victory. His only option was to flee abroad, and during the evening of 30 September he and his brother Richard rode to Bishop's Lynn with an escort of 800 men. Two days later they sailed in three ships for the continent, where they landed the next morning a short distance from the fishing village of Alkmaar.

Welcomed by Jan van Assendelft, the steward of North Holland, they were escorted to a meeting with Louis de Gruthuse, Charles the Bold's governor, who gave them lodging in his own house at The Hague.

On learning of her husband's flight, Elizabeth Woodville took refuge in the Abbey with all her children. A month later the Queen went into labor and gave birth to her first son by the King, whom she immediately named Edward in his father's honor. Meanwhile, on 5 October, Archbishop Neville entered the capital with an army and took control of the Tower, where Henry VI was still a prisoner. The next day Warwick and Clarence, accompanied by Lords Oxford, Shrewsbury and Stanley, made a triumphal entry into the city, where mob violence had broken out. After restoring law and order, all five peers rode to the Tower and conferred with the Archbishop before proceeding to Henry VI's cell and hailing him as England's rightful ruler once again. Then they escorted him through the streets to the Bishop of London's palace, where, to mark his recovery of the throne or formal Readeption of Power, they arranged an elaborate ceremony in the Abbey. That ceremony on 13 October was almost identical to Henry's coronation in 1429, although the anointing with oil was omitted this time. As the old King shuffled down the center aisle of the great church, Warwick carried his train. No one who witnessed the scene could doubt who intended to run the government during the remainder of Henry's life.

By 26 November, when a new Parliament opened, it was apparent that the new regime faced massive problems. Indeed, the government of the Readeption lacked sufficient revenues and was an odd mix of strange bedfellows, an unholy alliance created by the needs of the moment. Warwick, who let no one forget he was the chief architect of the Readeption, was hated by almost all long-time Lancastrians, who withheld much-needed support. In fact, the Dukes of Exeter and Somerset and Viscount Beaumont remained on the continent until January 1471, when they finally returned to England and maintained loose ties at best with the new regime. Their behavior caused many observers to wonder what Warwick's role would be once Margaret of Anjou and the Prince reappeared on the scene. Although the Earls of Shrewsbury and Oxford, Lord Stanley, and Jasper Tudor cooperated with Warwick, old friends like Lords Dinham and Mountjoy refused to assist a man who had demonstrated such crass and unprincipled opportunism. Additionally, the Earl of Northumberland held back out of fear he would lose his title and estates to Warwick's brother, the Marquess Montagu, should the Readeption succeed.[10] At the same time Warwick's government faced relentless hostility from such powerful Yorkist families as the Woodvilles, the Herberts, and the Howards.

The greatest problem of all stemmed from the sudden decline of George of Clarence's prospects. During earlier months Warwick had sought to depose Edward IV in favor of his younger brother. But now, with the restoration of the House of Lancaster, George's chances of ever becoming King vanished at a stroke. Whenever Henry VI died, Prince Edward, who was expected to arrive from France momentarily, was bound to be acclaimed the rightful ruler, which caused George to realize he would never attain the glittering prize he coveted so much. Warwick was not unmindful of his son-in-law's bitter disappointment and granted him the great honour of Tutbury and several valuable sinecures associated with the Duchy of Lancaster. But those rewards were hardly adequate compensation for ceasing to be heir-apparent to the throne, and George was interested in receiving other offers. From his exile at The Hague, Edward IV realized this; and by means of skillful letters to Archbishop Bourchier, Bishop Stillington, and several other followers who were happy to serve as intermediaries, Edward prepared the way for his brother's change of sides during the spring of 1471.

When Edward landed on the Dutch coast on 2 October 1470, his situation seemed hopeless, and only a seer or a madman would have predicted that his grip on the throne would be stronger than ever in seven months. During the autumn of 1470 Edward's prospects remained bleak because Charles the Bold gave him little help and refused to meet with him in person for fear of offending Louis XI. With Warwick's faction in control of English affairs and committed to a policy of close cooperation with France, Louis was finally in a position to take energetic measures against Burgundy without having to worry about a hostile reaction from Westminster. Charles the Bold was therefore reluctant to do anything that would give Louis a pretext for war, even if that meant banning his English brother-in-law from his court.[11]

Despite Charles's friendly gestures, Louis issued a virtual declaration of war on Burgundy on 3 December 1470. In a royal proclamation of that date, Louis announced an impending campaign to recover Amiens, St. Quentin, Montidier, and other towns in the Somme valley that had long been in Burgundian hands. Within another week actual fighting occurred, which caused Charles the Bold to view Edward IV in a different light. The exiled ruler was no longer a liability but a potential ally, especially if he could recover the English throne. Furthermore, some 400 disgruntled Englishmen had joined him at The Hague, thereby increasing his forces to 1,200 men. With a measure of support from Burgundy, Edward and his growing band of followers should be able to return to England and overthrow the beleaguered Warwick government, which would probably lead to a speedy revival of Edward's anti-French policy of the 1460s. On 26 December 1470, Charles sent word to The Hague that he was finally willing to confer with his brother-in-law.

During the first week of January 1471, the two men met on three successive days at Aire, and a week later they also conferred at Saint-Pol, which Edward had been invited to visit as a guest of his wife's uncle, Jacques of Luxembourg. Secretly Charles the Bold gave Edward a present of 50,000 florins (approximately £20,000) with which to prepare a fleet of at least eighteen vessels that would transport him and his troops back to England; and the Burgundian ruler also provided four warships that would participate in the invasion at his own expense.

Once Edward journeyed to the port of Flushing, his chief mobilization point,[12] he obtained help from other quarters as well. By means of a trusted envoy he secured a promise of aid from Francis II of Brittany, who was increasingly fearful of a French assault on his own duchy once Louis succeeded in crushing Burgundian autonomy. Even more important, Edward held out an olive branch to the Hansa, whose trading rights in England he himself had revoked in 1468, thereby triggering an undeclared commercial war. In order to secure the Hansards' help against Warwick, who had strangely neglected to come to terms with the Hansa, Edward made a gesture of reconciliation during January of 1471, which led to direct talks with their representatives. Once he pledged to restore and even extend their trading rights in England after recovering the throne, they provided fourteen ships for his burgeoning fleet, which increased to thirty-six ships in all.

By February of 1471 Warwick was well aware of Edward's naval preparations, which he tried to offset by stationing his own warships in the Channel. But they became bogged down in small skirmishes with the Breton navy because Francis II was now a committed ally of Edward IV. As a consequence Warwick's naval commanders were deflected from their primary objective. At the same time Louis XI kept the French fleet safely in port so it would be ready to transport Margaret of Anjou and Prince Edward across the Channel to southern England at any moment. Because of those two strokes of good fortune, Edward IV's flotilla faced no opposition when it embarked for eastern England on 11 March.

The campaign of 1471 lasted from the middle of March until the end of May and was the longest period of continuous military activity during the Wars of the Roses. Fortunately there is a valuable account of that campaign, generally known as "The Arrivall of Edward IV," which was finished shortly after it ended. Written by an admirer of the

King, who may have been Nicholas Harpsfield, a clerk of the Signet, that detailed narrative was preserved among the papers of the Elizabethan antiquary John Stow and was published in 1838 by the Camden Society. "The Arrivall" reveals in graphic detail how the campaign proceeded and the main reasons for Edward's great victory against almost hopeless odds. Because Warwick and his followers failed to mass their troops, they allowed Edward to retain the initiative and set the pace of the whole campaign. Thus he was able to defeat them individually with smaller forces and to triumph in the end by capitalizing on their mistakes and indecisiveness.

On the afternoon of 12 March Edward IV reached the Norfolk coast but found the Earl of Oxford's grip on the region too tight for his men to make a safe landing. He therefore sailed farther north and went ashore with his troops at Ravenspur in southern Yorkshire. At once he launched a campaign of rapid movement in order to keep his scattered enemies from uniting and defeating him before his supporters in other parts of the realm could mobilize their retainers and ride in. To have any chance of victory, Edward knew that he must avoid an early defeat in the field, which would probably cause his troops to lose heart and melt away. He therefore marched to Beverley and then to York, where he arrived within a week to a chilly reception. Indeed, the mayor and bailiffs refused to let him enter the city with over fifteen men at his back. While in York he felt compelled to tell the citizens that he had returned to England as a loyal subject of Henry VI, his only goal being the recovery of his patrimony as Duke of York.

From York Edward rode south while avoiding an encounter with the Marquess Montagu, who followed along several miles behind with a larger force. Luckily his own ranks began to swell, and as he approached Nottingham on 25 March Sir James Harrington, Sir William Stanley, and Sir William Parr rode in with approximately 1,600 reinforcements. Several days later, as he was nearing Leicester, 3,000 more men raised by Lord Hastings appeared, giving his army another substantial boost. From Leicester Edward rode off to Banbury, where, with assistance from his brother Richard and Lord Hastings, he was reconciled with George of Clarence, who contributed another 4,000 troops to the cause. By that point Edward's army had swollen to almost 10,000 men, and he felt strong enough to declare himself England's rightful ruler once again and condemn his enemies as confirmed traitors.

Meanwhile the Earl of Warwick had taken shelter behind the walls of Coventry, the most strongly fortified town in central England, where he waited for reinforcements to bolster his army of 6,500 men. Probably Warwick was afraid to risk a pitched battle because of Edward's greater numbers and superior military abilities. Whether that was Warwick's actual reason for remaining on the defensive, he refused to venture forth even when Edward challenged him on four successive days to personal combat as a way of ending their venomous rivalry.[13] Ultimately Edward swept around Coventry and entered London without firing a shot on the 12th of April, which happened to be Good Friday. Welcomed enthusiastically by the local population, he took charge of Henry VI and confined Archbishop Neville and several other enemies in the Tower. Then he rode to Westminster, where he was reunited with his wife and gazed for a time on the face of his son Edward, now five months old. After returning to the city he spent the night at Baynard's Castle, the town house of his mother Cecily Neville, the dowager Duchess of York.

By that point Warwick had left Coventry and set out in pursuit of Edward IV with an army that now included Montagu's troops and thousands of other men, perhaps 13,000 in all. Warwick seems to have believed that the citizens of London would refuse to admit Edward's forces, which could thus be pinned against the city walls and destroyed by the Lancastrians' greater numbers and artillery. On 13 April Warwick arrived at the village of Barnet, a short distance from the capital. Late that evening Edward and his troops advanced to meet them, and by dawn on Easter morning one of the most important battles of the Wars of the Roses was underway.

Shortly before 5:00 A.M. Edward launched a fierce attack on Warwick's emplacements at Barnet. Although the King achieved complete tactical surprise, the battle lasted three hours and resulted in heavy casualties on both sides. It was probably the most confused and turbulent encounter of the period, for two reasons. First, it was fought in a heavy fog, causing visibility to be extremely limited; and second, the lines of the two armies did not face one another in neat, parallel fashion, which the result that both commanders were unaware of the actual position of their opponents. After an hour of brutal hand-to-hand combat, Lord Hastings' troops on the Yorkist left were shattered by the Earl of Oxford's regiment on the Lancastrian right. As Hastings' men broke and ran, some 800 of Oxford's troops pursued them for a time. But when they later tried to return to the fray, they were fired upon by their own commander with disastrous results. Although Warwick's army was somewhat larger, the element of surprise, coupled with Oxford's tactical blunder and Edward IV's brilliant leadership, enabled the Yorkists to prevail in the end. Warwick himself was killed during the fighting as was his brother Montagu. The Duke of Exeter was injured so badly that he was left for dead on the field, which made possible his eventual escape to France. As for the Earl of Oxford, he fled north to Scotland before sailing across the Channel to Normandy and engaging in piratical activities until his capture by royal agents in 1474. The Yorkist army suffered almost as many casualties as the Lancastrians but lost none of its main commanders.

In probably the greatest stroke of ill-timing in English history, Margaret of Anjou and her son landed at Weymouth on the very day the battle of Barnet took place. Because the French squadron that had transported them across the Channel doubled back to Normandy at once, Margaret and the Prince were marooned in the southwest, far from their supporters in Wales and northern England. As a result Edward IV was in a good position to defeat them once and for all, which he was determined to do.

Two days later, on learning of the arrival of Margaret and her son, the King directed his followers to meet him at Windsor by the end of the week, ready for another campaign. Shortly afterwards he sent commissions of array into the western counties so he would have enough troops to ensure victory in the event of another pitched battle.

Meanwhile Margaret and the Prince had moved inland from Weymouth to Cerne Abbey, where on 15 April the Earl of Devon and the fourth Duke of Somerset* informed them of Edward IV's great victory at Barnet and the deadly peril that now faced them. Margaret saw at once that their only hope of escape lay in making a forced march toward the north, either to join up with Jasper Tudor's forces in North Wales or to effect a union with Lancastrian stalwarts in Cheshire and Lancashire. No time was lost, and by 28 April the Queen's party had passed through Exeter and Taunton and was well on its way to Gloucester.

On his part, Edward IV was determined to keep Margaret and Prince Edward from eluding him again and returning to the continent, where they might remain a thorn in his side for years to come. By 28 April the King and his troops were at Abingdon, where Edward held a council of war and secured agreement for even faster marches in order to overtake the fleeing Lancastrians. The next day the Yorkists travelled from Abingdon to Cirencester, a distance of more than thirty miles; and from that point they closed in on Margaret's smaller army with exceptional speed. Because Edward suspected his enemies would try to cross the

---

* Henry Beaufort, who had inherited the title in 1463 from his older brother Edmund after his crushing defeat at Hexham and subsequent execution by John Neville.

River Severn at Gloucester, he sent orders for that town to admit no strangers until further notice. Thus, when the Lancastrians arrived there on 2 May, they were unable to gain admission and use the bridge to cross the river before making a beeline for Wales. With a deep sense of foreboding Margaret and her troops marched upstream to Tewkesbury, where the river was shallow enough to be forded on foot. By mid afternoon on 3 May the exhausted Lancastrians had covered thirty-six miles and were too weary to proceed farther. They therefore postponed their crossing until the next day, although they strengthened the base of their strong hillside position with earthenworks before bedding down for the night. In the meantime Edward IV had pushed on through the hills of Wiltshire and, by nightfall on 3 May, his army was approaching Tewkesbury from a more easterly direction. That evening he and his troops encamped only three miles from the Lancastrian position.

Early the next morning another major battle of the Wars of the Roses took place within sight of Tewkesbury Abbey. The Lancastrians were led by the Duke of Somerset, the Earl of Devon, and Lord Wenlock with assistance from Prince Edward, who was now seventeen years old and eager to engage in combat for the first time. On the field below them Edward IV commanded the Yorkist center, while Richard of Gloucester and Lord Hastings were at the helm of the two wings.

A shower of Yorkist arrows preceded a determined charge by Richard of Gloucester's men, who tried to take the hill by storm, but were rebuffed by unexpectedly strong resistance from Somerset and the Lancastrian right. After the Yorkists retreated, Somerset directed several hundred archers to follow him down the hill, taking cover behind trees and bushes as they advanced. Once they reached level ground violent hand-to-hand combat ensued although Somerset's troops had little chance against the greater mass of the Yorkist center. In addition some 200 horsemen the King had stationed in a nearby thicket made a deadly thrust, causing most of Somerset's followers to flee in panic. Seizing that unexpected opportunity Edward IV charged the Lancastrian center, which was under the nominal command of Prince Edward, who was ill prepared for such a critical situation. Within minutes he and his men were overwhelmed by the more experienced Yorkist troops.

Prince Edward was only one of thousands of men who died on the field that day. Other important Lancastrians who perished included the Earl of Devon, John Lord Wenlock, and John Lord Beaufort. As for John Beaufort's older brother, the fourth and last Duke of Somerset of their line, he and Sir Gervase Clifton took refuge in the nearby abbey, from which they were forcibly removed that afternoon on the King's orders. The next morning they appeared in chains before Richard of

Gloucester in his role as Lord Constable of England. After a brief trial they were sentenced to die along with eleven other Lancastrians who had shown through repeated acts of rebellion that they would never submit to a Yorkist government. All thirteen men were beheaded in the marketplace at Tewkesbury on 6 May.

Margaret of Anjou was also captured shortly after the battle, as was her daughter-in-law, Anne Neville, Prince Edward's youthful widow. Brought before the King at Coventry, Margaret was a totally dispirited woman after her son's death, no longer having any real purpose in life. She rode in a gilded chariot during Edward IV's triumphal return to London, which he reentered on 21 May to great rejoicing. Imprisoned in the Tower, she was held there under heavy guard until January 1476, when Louis XI ransomed her for 50,000 crowns (about £10,000). But before she was allowed to embark for the continent, she had to renounce all her dower rights in England and disclaim any further interest in the English throne. Once she did so, she boarded a ship for France, where she died in penniless obscurity in 1482.

Even after Edward IV's impressive victory at Tewkesbury, there were several Lancastrian rebellions that had to be suppressed, including a major uprising in Kent under the Bastard of Fauconberg, a cousin of Edward IV.[14] For that reason it is easy to sympathize with the frustration of the Milanese ambassador in Paris, who, on receiving a dispatch from England, complained to his government:

> I wish the country and the people [of England] were plunged deep in the sea, because of their lack of stability, for I feel like one going to the torture when I write about them, and no one ever hears twice alike about English affairs.[15]

Largely because of all the recent disorder, Edward IV felt the time had come to have Henry VI eliminated. Even if the former monarch was a helpless old man, his continued existence might cause Lancastrian diehards to make another attempt to restore him to the throne. In view of everything that had happened during the last few years, it now seemed a serious mistake to have spared his life after his capture in 1465. As soon as the King reentered London on 21 May 1471, he gave orders for the former monarch to be put to death. The best account of that sad event is in John Warkworth's chronicle.

> And the same nyghte Kynge Edwarde came to Londone, Kynge Herry, beynge [still] ... in persone in the Toure of Londone, was putt to dethe, the xxi day of Maii, on a tywesday nyght, betwyxt xi and xii of the cloke, beynge

> thenne at the Toure [were] the Duke of Gloucesetre, brothere to Kynge Edwarde, and many other[s]; and on the morwe he was chestyde [i.e., put in a coffin] and brought to [St.] Paulys ... that every manne myghte see hyme ... and from thens he was caryed to Chyrchesey abbey in a bote, and buryed there in oure Lady chapelle.[16]

With the murder of Henry VI several weeks after his son's death at Tewkesbury, the direct line of the House of Lancaster became extinct. Thereupon the Lancastrian claim to the throne devolved on Lady Margaret Beaufort, a direct descendant of Edward III (d. 1377) and the future wife of Thomas Lord Stanley, a rich landowner in Lancashire and Cheshire.[17] However, England had never submitted to a female ruler; and during the twelfth century the only surviving child of Henry I, the Empress Matilda, had failed to establish her claim to the throne despite a fourteen-year struggle against her usurping cousin Stephen of Blois. Furthermore, Lady Margaret Beaufort's chances of obtaining the throne were seriously weakened by the fact that she was a tiny person, barely five feet tall, which made her seem a totally unsuitable candidate for the throne. She therefore let her friends and relatives know that she would never press her claim, which she effectively renounced in favor of her only child, Henry Tudor, second Earl of Richmond.

Born in January of 1457, two months after his father's sudden death from plague, Henry Tudor had spent most of his early years at Raglan Castle in the care of his guardian, Sir William Herbert, who became Earl of Pembroke in September of 1468. After Pembroke's death the next spring, Henry Tudor came into the custody of Lady Pembroke's brother, Lord Ferrers of Weobley, who handed him over to Jasper Tudor on his return from France in September 1470. Jasper took his nephew to London, where he was briefly reunited with his mother and introduced to his uncle Henry VI, whose saintly behavior made a lasting impression on the future monarch.[18] Shortly afterward Henry and Jasper Tudor returned to Wales, where they raised an army, but not rapidly enough to assist the other Lancastrians at Tewkesbury. Within several weeks of the Yorkist triumph there, Edward IV sent Sir Roger Vaughan and a small force to arrest the two Welshmen at Chepstow Castle because of the threat they posed to his throne. But when Vaughan tried to capture them, Jasper and his men surrounded his regiment before capturing and executing him.[19]

Jasper and his fourteen-year-old nephew spent the next few months quietly at Pembroke Castle. But in late August Edward IV directed the new Earl of Pembroke, William Herbert the Younger, and his uncle

Lord Ferrers to make another effort to defeat them and their retainers. When a large Yorkist force advanced toward them, Jasper and Henry escaped from Pembroke Castle to the nearby port of Tenby, where they received timely help from the mayor, Thomas White, and his son John. Rich merchants, the Whites provided a ship that took Henry and his uncle to the continent. Hoping to make the coast of France, where Louis XI would probably grant them political asylum, they were blown off course by a storm that caused them to land at Le Conquêt, a fishing port at the tip of the Breton peninsula. From Le Conquêt they journeyed to Nântes, where they were welcomed by Duke Francis II, a clever but unscrupulous man. Because the two Englishmen might be useful pawns in his tense relationship with the French crown, Duke Francis kept them at his court for the next twelve years, moving them periodically from Vannes, the Breton capital, to Elven Castle and the Château de l'Hermine, the Duke's summer residence in the nearby countryside. During the years 1471-1483 Henry grew to manhood in Brittany, developed a clear preference for French manners and customs, and is said to have become "a pleasant and elegant person."[20]

The flight of Henry and his uncle Jasper to the continent alarmed Edward IV, who periodically sought to secure their extradition to England for trial and probable execution. But not knowing what the future might bring, Francis II always found a pretext to reject Edward's request and continued to shelter the Lancastrian Pretender and his devoted uncle.

Because the political situation in England finally entered a tranquil phase during the winter of 1471-1472, all Lancastrian plotting having ceased for the moment, it was increasingly apparent that the House of York was gaining widespread acceptance as the rightful dynasty.[21] By the same token, the Lancastrians' chances of recovering the throne grew perceptibly weaker with each passing year; and if events had continued on that course for a generation or so, Henry Tudor would never have emerged as a viable candidate for the throne. However, the Wars of the Roses broke out anew in 1483 owing to a dramatic turn of events that no one could have foreseen at the time. The fourth and last round of England's longest political crisis will be the subject of the last chapter in this four-part series.

For Further Reading

P. W. Hammond, *The Battles of Barnet and Tewkesbury.* Gloucester, 1990. A general study of the crisis of 1469-1471 and not just an account of its two climactic battles. Well illustrated.

Charles B. Ross, *Edward IV*. Berkeley and Los Angeles, 1974. See especially "Part II: The First Reign, 1461-1471," Chapters 3-7 (pages 41-177). An excellent account.

Paul Murray Kendall, *Warwick the Kingmaker.* New York, 1957. Events from Warwick's perspective.

John Bruce, ed., "The Arrivall of Edward IV." Camden Society, lst series, vol. 1 (1838). An invaluable account of the campaign of 1471 by an unknown participant, possibly Nicholas Harpsfield, a clerk of the Signet. Generally sympathetic to Edward IV, in whose army the writer probably served.

J. A. F. Thomson, "'The Arrivall of Edward IV'--the Development of the Text." *Speculum*, vol. 46 (197l).

C. F. Richmond, "Fauconberg's Kentish Rising of May 1471." *English Historical Review,* vol. 85 (1970). A good account of a troublesome rebellion that occurred after the battle of Tewkesbury.

A. J. Pollard, "Lord Fitzhugh's Rising in 1470." *Bulletin of the Institute of Historical Research*, vol. 52 (1979). Explains the problems Edward IV faced before his flight abroad in late September of 1470.

Richard Vaughan, *Charles the Bold: The Last Valois Duke of Burgundy*. London, 1973. Useful for Edward IV's exile on the continent in 1470-1471 and the support he eventually received from his brother-in-law.

M. A. Hicks, "Edward IV, the Duke of Somerset and Lancastrian Loyalism in the North." *Northern History*, vol. 20 (1984). An important article about the turbulent years 1461-1464.

M. A. Hicks, "The Neville Earldom of Salisbury, 1429-1471."*Wiltshire Archaeological Magazine*, vol. 73 (1980). Criticizes the greediness of both Warwick and his father, the Earl of Salisbury.
Alison Allan, "Royal Propaganda and the Proclamations of Edward IV." *Bulletin of the Institute of Historical Research*, vol. 69 (1986).

John Warkworth, *A Chronicle of the First Thirteen Years of the Reign of King Edward IV*, ed. James O. Halliwell-Phillipps. Camden Society, 1st series, vol. 10 (1839).

James Gairdner, ed., *Three Fifteenth-Century Chronicles.* Camden Society, new series, vol. 28 (1880).

James Gairdner, ed., *The Historical Collections of a Citizen of London in the Fifteenth Century.* Camden Society, new series, vol. 17 (1876).

Ralph Flenley, ed. *Six Town Chronicles of England.* Oxford, 1911.

Charles L. Kingsford, ed. *Chronicles of London.* Oxford, 1905.

A. H. Thomas and I. D. Thornley, eds., *The Great Chronicle of London.* London, 1938.

Edward Hall, *Hall's Chronicle; containing the History of England, during the Reign of Henry the Fourth, and the Succeeding Monarchs to the End of the Reign of Henry the Eighth*, ed. Sir Henry Ellis. London, 1809.

Norman Davis, ed., *Paston Letters.* Oxford, 1958.

James Gairdner, ed., *The Paston Letters,* 4 vols. Westminster, 1901.

Richard Barber, ed., *The Pastons: A Family in the Wars of the Roses.* London, 1981.

Henry S. Bennett, *The Pastons and Their England*, 2nd ed. Cambridge, 1932. An old but still useful work.

Carole Rawcliffe, *The Staffords, Earls of Stafford and Dukes of Buckingham 1394-1521.* Cambridge, 1978. A useful study of a very important family.

J. A. F. Thomson, "The Courtenay Family in the Yorkist Period." *Bulletin of the Institute of Historical Research*, vol. 54 (1979).

Michael K. Jones, "Sir William Stanley of Holt: politics and family allegiance in the late fifteenth century." *Welsh History Review*, vol. 14 (1988).

J. R. Lander, "Marriage and Politics in the Fifteenth Century: the Nevilles and the Wydevilles," in *Crown and Nobility 1450-1509.* Montreal, 1976.

M. A. Hicks, "The Changing Role of the Wydevilles in Yorkist Politics to 1483," in Charles Ross, ed., *Patronage: Pedigree and Power in Later Medieval England.* Gloucester, 1979.

M. A. Hicks, *False, Fleeting, Perjur'd Clarence: George, Duke of Clarence.* Gloucester, 1980. A sound biography of Edward IV's brother.

Geoffrey Hindley, *England in the Age of Caxton.* New York, 1979. Useful for students and general readers.

Paul Murray Kendall, *The Yorkist Age: Daily Life during the Wars of the Roses.* New York, 1962. Written with the author's usual verve.

D. A. L. Morgan, "The King's Affinity in the Polity of Yorkist England." *Transactions of the Royal Historical Society*, 5th series, vol. 23 (1973).

D. A. L. Morgan, "The House of Policy: the political role of the late Plantagenet household, 1422-1485," in David Starkey, ed., *The English Court from the Wars of the Roses to the Civil War.* London, 1987.

B. P. Wolffe, "The Management of English Royal Estates under the Yorkist Kings." *English Historical Review,* vol. 71 (1956).

Ian Rowney, "Resources and Retaining in Yorkist England: William, Lord Hastings and the Honour of Tutbury," in A. J. Pollard, ed., *Property and Politics in Later Medieval England.* Gloucester, 1984.

William H. Dunham, Jr., *Lord Hastings' Indentured Retainers 1461-1483.* New Haven, 1955. More important than the title suggests.

Cora L. Scofield, "An Engagement of Service to Warwick the Kingmaker." *English Historical Review,* vol. 29 (1914).

For other works on the Wars of the Roses, see the suggested readings between the text and the notes of the two previous chapters and the final chapter in this series.

Notes for *The Wars of the Roses, III*

[1] J. R. Lander, in *Kings and Nobles in the Later Middle Ages*, eds. R. A. Griffiths and James Sherborne (New York, 1986), p. 34. Perhaps it should be noted that rich widows needed husbands with political influence to protect their estates from the machinations of greedy neighbors. Thus Catherine Mowbray's willingness to marry John Woodville, a royal brother-in-law, was not quite as odd as it appears at first sight.

[2] At this point it should be noted that, because Catherine Woodville brought him no dowry at all, Buckingham probably preferred to marry one of Warwick's daughters, Isabel or Anne. However, if Buckingham had married either of them and gained eventual control of half of Warwick's valuable estates, his revenues would have increased to more than £7,000 a year, which would have made him an "over-mighty subject" and a potential threat to the crown. Thus Edward's decision for Buckingham to marry a poor girl like Catherine Woodville made political sense at the time.

[3] Perhaps Edward IV should have arranged for one of Warwick's daughters to marry William Herbert the Younger as a way of healing the breach between Warwick and Lord Herbert. Such a marriage might have appeased Warwick, whose descendants would eventually enjoy the lordship of Dunster even if he never did. Because the Herberts' wealth was considerably less than that of the Duke of Buckingham, there would have been no danger of creating an over-mighty subject through such a marriage.

[4] This was the same Katherine of Valois who, after Henry V's death in 1422, married Owen Tudor, the father of her two illustrious sons--Edmund Earl of Richmond and Jasper Earl of Pembroke. Thus Katherine of Valois was the grandmother of Edmund's son, Henry of Richmond, who was born two decades after his grandmother's death and in 1485 won the throne as King Henry VII.

[5] William Lord Hastings, who had known Edward IV as a boy, inherited a small estate in the midlands from his father, Sir Leonard Hastings (d. 1455). Sheriff of Leicestershire and Warwickshire in 1455-1456, Sir William was a "household man" of Richard of York until the latter granted his son, the future Edward IV, a separate military command during the autumn of 1460. Hastings rendered Edward valuable military help at Mortimer's Cross and Towton in February and March of 1461, and thereafter his rise was assured. Within a year of Edward's coronation on 28 June 1461, Hastings received a number of important offices, including Lord Chamberlain and Receiver-General for the Duchy of Cornwall, as well as dozens of valuable manors confiscated from such Lancastrian peers as the Earl of Wiltshire and Lords Beaumont and Roos. In 1462 Edward IV made Hastings a Baron of the realm

as well as a Knight of the Garter. A genial man, Hastings was Edward IV's closest friend, and he even managed to get along with Warwick, whose sister Catherine he married during the winter of 1461-1462.

[6] After her marriage to the King in 1464, Elizabeth Woodville gave birth to three daughters in quick succession--Elizabeth (1466), Mary (1467), and Cecily (1469). But no son was born to the royal couple until the autumn of 1470.

[7] Sir Robert Welles' attempt to save his father led Edward IV to have the older Welles executed. Warwick maintained that Edward had planned to have Lord Welles executed all along, but there is no evidence to support that claim.

[8] A wealthy landowner in East Anglia, Howard had fought on the Yorkist side at Towton, where the King knighted him shortly after the battle. In another few weeks Howard was appointed constable of Norwich, Colchester, and Harwich Castles, and during the following November he became sheriff of both Norfolk and Suffolk. In 1462 he received a grant of seven manors, and between 1466 and 1474 he served as treasurer of the royal household. Because of his loyal service during the crisis of 1469-1471, Edward IV made him a Baron.

[9] After Lord Fitzhugh's marriage to his sister Elizabeth in 1465, Warwick granted him the manor of Worton in Wensleydale, and the next year he appointed Lord Fitzhugh to serve as deputy warden of the west march toward Scotland at a yearly salary of 1,000 marks.

[10] Perhaps Warwick's greatest mistake at that point was to remove the newly-restored Earl of Northumberland from the wardenship of the east march, a post he assigned to his brother, Lord Montagu. While that change solidified Montagu's support of the Readeption, it also suggested that Northumberland and the great Percy affinity would welcome Edward IV's return to power.

[11] During the autumn of 1470 Duke Charles provided less than £42 a month for the maintenance of Edward and his retinue.

[12] Edward's fleet was also assembled at such ports as Middleburg, Vlissingen, and Arnemuiden.

[13] Edward issued his first challenge to Warwick on Saturday, 29 March, the same day he declared himself England's rightful ruler once again. Edward repeated that challenge on the next three days; but Warwick refused to accept it, preferring to wait for the arrival of additional troops.

[14] The Bastard of Fauconberg was an illegitimate son of Edward IV's uncle, William Lord Fauconberg, who had died in 1463, two years after becoming Earl of Kent.

[15] This dispatch is dated 5 May 1471, or the day after the battle of Tewkesbury, which was too soon for someone in Paris to have learned about the outcome of that encounter. See A. B. Hinds, ed., *Calendar of State Papers Milan*, I (London, 1912), p. 194.

[16] John Warkworth, *A Chronicle of the First Thirteen Years of the Reign of King Edward the Fourth*, ed. James O. Hailliwell (London: Camden Society, vol 10, 1839), p. 21.

[17] Lady Margaret's third husband, Sir Henry Stafford, an uncle of the young Duke of Buckingham, died on 4 October 1471; and eight months later she took as her fourth and last husband Thomas Lord Stanley, the steward of Edward IV's household. During that era women of property like Lady Margaret needed influential husbands to help defend their economic interests, as already noted in regard to the dowager Duchess of Norfolk.

[18] After his capture of the throne in 1485, Henry VII petitioned Rome for the Lancastrian ruler's canonization, but the Pope rejected his request on the grounds that Henry VI's mental faculties had been too weak for him to qualify as a true saint.

[19] Vaughan's execution was essentially an act of personal vengeance on Jasper Tudor's part. A decade earlier, shortly after the battle of Mortimer's Cross in February 1461, Vaughan had been responsible for the execution of Jasper Tudor's father Owen .

[20] The opinion of Jean Molinet, a Burgundian chronicler who wrote during the early sixteenth century. See R. A Griffiths and R. S. Thomas, *The Making of the Tudor Dynasty* (New York, 1985), p. 86.

[21] It was at that point that a long-time Lancastrian like John Morton, who had been one of Margaret of Anjou's leading advisers since 1456, made his peace with Edward IV. Delighted and deeply relieved, Edward appointed Morton Master of the Rolls before securing his election to the bishopric of Ely in August of 1478, although his consecration did not take place until early in 1479. During the 1470s another long-time Lancastrian, the great lawyer and judge Sir John Fortescue, developed deep admiration for Edward IV and paid him a generous tribute, as we shall see in the next chapter.

The Wars of the Roses, IV*

After all the violence and turmoil of 1469-1471, England was largely quiet until Edward IV died in 1483. During those years the King was in such a strong political and financial position he was able to engage in foreign adventures, including an attack on France in 1475 and a war against Scotland in 1481-1482. Neither of those conflicts resulted in great military victories, comparable to Henry V's triumphs between 1415 and 1422, although they led to the acquisition of a yearly pension of £5,000 from France and the recovery of Berwick Castle, which the Scots had held for twenty years.

Because Edward increased the crown's total revenues to £80,000 a year by 1478, thereby balancing the royal budget for the first time in decades, he was able during his last few years to launch a number of extensive building projects at Eltham, Windsor, Nottingham, and various other places. Even more significant, he continued his earlier policy, begun during the 1460s, of revitalizing the judicial system, which had languished during the previous century because of aristocratic interference. To that end he travelled around the countryside with the judges of the royal courts at Westminster from time to time.[1] Whenever he attended a local court, his commanding presence lent dignity to the judges' work, thereby lessening the likelihood of jury tampering. In addition Edward was the first monarch since the thirteenth century to participate in the deliberations of the Court of King's Bench; and in 1480 he established a new court, the Court of Requests, which soon became known as "the poor man's Chancery" because its moderate fees gave people of limited income access to the judicial system for the first time.

Largely because of his concern for justice, England became a more stable and peaceful country during the decade after his recovery of the throne in 1471. His efforts to pacify the realm were applauded by all but the most zealous Lancastrians. One of his greatest admirers was Sir John Fortescue, one of the leading lawyers of the age and Chief Justice of the King's Bench for many years before 1461. Although a fervent Lancastrian who had lived in exile with Margaret of Anjou and Prince Edward during the 1460s, Fortescue maintain a short time before his death in 1479 that Edward IV had accomplished

---

* The notes for this chapter begin on p. 256.

> . . . more for us than ever did [any] king of England .... We shall now more enjoy our own goods, and live under [more certain] justice, which we have not done of long time, God knoweth.[2]

Although Englishmen and foreigners alike considered Edward IV one of Europe's most successful monarchs, just below the surface of political life tensions remained strong and threatened to erupt in violence at any moment. Only the King's dynamic personality kept those tensions in check; and shortly after his death in 1483 a bitter struggle for the throne began, which triggered a brief resumption of the Wars of the Roses after a twelve-year hiatus. Before we consider the final round of the conflict, during which the Lancastrians recovered the throne again, this time permanently, we must take a look at the tensions that erupted within a month of Edward's death at the relatively youthful age of forty-one.

In a nutshell, England's stability was endangered by the aggressive actions of the King's younger brothers, Richard of Gloucester and George of Clarence, and by the grasping schemes of the Woodvilles. On one level those difficulties might be viewed as purely personal matters within the House of York. But on another and more basic level, they were intractable problems owing to the great importance of the people involved. Edward's failure to resolve them meant that the Yorkist court was badly divided against its enemies and an explosive situation existed at the time he died.

Richard of Gloucester governed the northern counties as his brother's viceroy between 1471 and 1483. From his headquarters at Middleham Castle, Richard dominated the area as a virtual sub-King and sought to increase his wealth and power in whatever ways he could. His actions were often unscrupulous even by the standards of that era; and he seldom hesitated to seize valuable lands from those who were unable to defend them. These included the dowager Countess of Oxford, whom he threatened with deadly force in 1472 unless she surrendered all her estates to him, an act that caused her such enormous distress that it hastened her death the next year. They also included his mother-in-law, the dowager Countess of Warwick, whom he held under restraint for many years while enjoying the rents from her dower lands.[3]

During the early 1470s Richard's aggressive actions antagonized both the powerful Stanley connection in Lancashire and Cheshire and the great Percy affinity of Yorkshire and Northumberland. Indeed, competition between Richard and the Percies became so intense that Edward IV felt compelled to intervene and prevent renewed violence in the northeast. By a skillful agreement Edward himself brokered in 1474, the counties of that region were partitioned into two zones of influence, the larger controlled by Richard and his retainers and the smaller by Northumberland and his affinity. Moreover, the two men promised to cooperate on all matters of importance, and both agreed not to employ men who were known to be indentured retainers of the other.[4]

Concluded none too soon, the agreement of 1474 signified that the Percies' position in northern England would be respected, and thus it was a significant step in the direction of peace throughout the region. But Richard eventually violated a key provision of that agreement and co-opted men into his service who were known Percy retainers. That development undermined the whole basis of the recent co-operation, and by the early 1480s a new and potentially dangerous source of friction existed in that part of the realm.

In regard to the King's in-laws, Edward IV knew that the Woodvilles' grasping actions had provoked envy and discord during the 1460s, so he held them at arm's length and granted only minor rewards to them during the years 1471-1478. Although his brother-in-law Anthony, second Earl Rivers, served as Prince Edward's governor with a stipend of £200 per year, the King refused to appoint him to his father's great office of Lord Treasurer. In July 1471 Edward even deprived him of the post of Captain of Calais, which he granted to his loyal supporter and boon companion, William Lord Hastings.

The Woodvilles' only important gains during those years came in 1475, shortly before the Queen's oldest son, Thomas Grey, married Cecily, the thirteen-year-old stepdaughter of Lord Hastings. During that year Thomas was elevated to the peerage as Marquess of Dorset and received several valuable estates. But aside from that the Woodvilles obtained almost no lands or distinctions from Edward between 1471 and 1478.[5]

Edward's most difficult problems during those years stemmed from the self-serving actions of his brother George of Clarence. An arrogant and unaccommodating man, George never showed any restraint in his quest for additional wealth. Already the richest landowner in southwestern England, he quarrelled incessantly with Richard of Gloucester about the estates left by their late father-in-law, Warwick the Kingmaker. Ultimately Edward IV intervened and ruled that Richard and his wife Anne should receive half of all those valuable properties. But hoping to retain George's good will, Edward compensated him with extensive lands in Essex and nearby counties. In addition the King arranged for Clarence to receive the ceremonial office of Great Chamberlain of England, which Richard reluctantly surrendered to him. But nothing Edward could do was enough to satisfy George, whose jealousy of Richard bordered on the pathological. During succeeding years, whenever the King allowed Richard to increase his wealth and power in northern England, George demanded a comparable gain for himself, whether he deserved it or not. As a consequence, Edward was soon at loggerheads with his troublesome brother.

In April of 1477, shortly after George's wife Isabel died in childbirth, the Duke behaved in a more intolerable way than ever. He directed several of his servants to travel down to Somerset and kidnap one of the late Duchess's servants, Ankarette Twynyho, a distant cousin of the Woodvilles, which had offended the Duke. Falsely accused of poisoning the Duchess, Mrs. Twynyho was tried before a kangaroo court at Warwick Castle on 15 April. The coerced jurors returned the judgment demanded of them and Mrs. Twynyho was executed that same day. Two local men, John Thurseby and Roger Tocotes, were also accused of complicity in the death of the Duchess and her stillborn son. Like Mrs. Twynyho, Thurseby was convicted by a coerced jury and paid the supreme penalty, although Tocotes escaped and was never seen again.

Because Edward IV was determined to free the courts from aristocratic interference, he had no choice but to take strong action against his own brother. Within six weeks George was arrested and committed to the Tower for tampering with the judicial system for his own private ends. Had he shown any remorse and thrown himself on Edward's mercy, he might have escaped with a relatively light sentence. But he blustered and spread ugly rumors that Elizabeth Woodville was not Edward's legal wife.[6] In addition Clarence sent letters to Louis XI of France, whose help he solicited almost openly, and he also talked recklessly about another marriage for himself, either with Charles the Bold's daughter Mary or with the Princess Margaret of Scotland, James III's sister.

By the autumn of 1477 Edward IV had lost all patience with his troublesome brother; and because the Woodvilles resented George's arrogance toward them, they decided to destroy him once and for all. In short order Elizabeth Woodville convinced Edward IV that the Duke was still dissatisfied with his lot in life and predicted he would make an effort to seize the throne for himself should Edward die in the near future. Such an attempt would naturally come at the expense of their own sons, Prince Edward and Prince Richard, who had been born in

1470 and 1473, respectively.

Although George's modern biographer, M. A. Hicks, acknowledges that the Duke was largely responsible for his own misfortunes, he accuses the Woodvilles of arranging his downfall. Indeed, Mr. Hicks contends that, "In 1478, directed by the Woodvilles, all the King's relatives and servants combined to destroy their common enemy, Clarence. His destruction was the fruit of the Woodville marriages of the 1460s, for at least four of the bridegrooms were actively involved."[7] The least involved of those bridegrooms, at least at the start, was the Duke of Buckingham, who had been forced to marry Catherine Woodville against his will in 1465. On his part, Edward IV resented Buckingham's arrogance toward the Woodvilles and seldom employed him on official business, which caused the latter to spend long periods sulking on his Welsh estates. However, during the autumn of 1477 the King summoned him to the capital on public business for the first and only time.

In December of 1477 Edward and his Councillors considered the best way to deal with George. It was decided that a Parliament should assemble on 19 January 1478; and shortly after its opening session Edward IV himself introduced an attainder bill designed to condemn George to death as a confirmed troublemaker. When the Duke was allowed to speak in his own defense, he showed no remorse for his actions. In addition he sought to buttress his case by calling as a friendly witness John Goddard, a priest who had openly defended Henry VI's claim to the throne in September of 1470. After Goddard's speech no other M. P. said a word on Clarence's behalf. As a consequence the attainder bill sailed through both Houses with large majorities.

In early February Buckingham was appointed Lord High Steward and given the unpleasant duty of pronouncing George's death sentence. Because he languished in the Tower for eleven more days, it appears that Edward still hoped that his troublesome brother would grovel and beg for mercy, which he stubbornly refused to do. Whether George was actually drowned in a butt of Malmsey wine by Richard of Gloucester, as tradition has long held, seems doubtful, but that hoary question is still a matter of debate in some circles.[8]

After George's execution Edward IV enjoyed greater security and contentment than at any time since the early 1460s. He devoted himself to his pleasures and spent long hours in the company of his mistress, Jane Shore. Perhaps out of guilt or a wish to silence the Woodvilles' insistent pleas for greater wealth, he was much more generous to his in-laws, who profited far more from George's elimination than any other political faction. Indeed, during the next few years the Woodvilles made steady gains and emerged as the most important faction at court, which caused them to be more hated than ever.

Within a short time of George's execution, the Queen's oldest son, the Marquess of Dorset, obtained the wardship of the Duke's only surviving son, Edward Earl of Warwick.[9] In addition the Marquess received temporary possession of George's estates in Wiltshire, Hampshire, and Gloucestershire. At the same time Edward IV consented to some lucrative arrangements for the Queen's second son, Sir Richard Grey. In short order that fortunate young man received dozens of valuable estates confiscated from Henry Holland, Duke of Exeter, who had lived in exile on the continent since 1471. During those same years the Queen pressed her husband to find a bishopric for her brother Lionel, who in 1481 received the see of Salisbury, worth approximately £2,000 a year at that juncture.

The Queen did even more to ensure a comfortable future for her youngest son, Prince Richard. On 15 January 1478 that five-year-old child was married to Anne Mowbray, sole heir of the fourth and last of the Mowbray Dukes of Norfolk. On her father's death in 1476, the four-year-old Anne had inherited more than a hundred manors in Sussex, East Anglia, Yorkshire, and the northern midlands, as well as scattered properties in Ireland, Wales, and Calais. Shortly after Anne and Prince Richard became man and wife in 1478, Parliament approved an agreement that violated long-established legal practices. In essence, if Anne died before her husband without giving birth to a child by him, all her lands were to remain with him rather than revert in the normal way to her closest male relatives. In addition, the agreement specified that Prince Richard should receive all the hereditary titles of her late father, including Duke of Norfolk and Earl of Nottingham.

That agreement was scrupulously honored in November of 1481, when Anne Mowbray died at Greenwich several days before her ninth birthday. By that point the King had taken steps to appease one of Anne's cousins, William Lord Berkeley, who would otherwise have inherited over seventy of her estates. In fact, Edward had secured Lord Berkeley's consent to the agreement of 1478 by allowing him to cancel bonds worth £37,000, which he owed the Exchequer and the Earl of Shrewsbury. As a consequence Lord Berkeley was neutralized and never challenged the arrangements made on Prince Richard's behalf. But comparable steps were never taken to appease Anne's other cousin, John Lord Howard, who had served Edward IV loyally and well during earlier years. Lord Howard, whose mother had been a Mowbray, would ordinarily have inherited at least thirty-five manors in East Anglia on his cousin's death, but Elizabeth Woodville was determined that Prince Richard should retain all those lands. Accordingly, Edward IV summoned another Parliament in January of 1483 and secured a measure vesting the entire Mowbray inheritance in the Prince and the heirs of his body. Should he die before fathering any children, those extremely valuable estates would revert to the crown itself.

After the passage of that measure Lord Howard felt deep resentment against the royal couple, who had violated his legal rights without any compensation at all. Unfortunately for Edward and his Queen, Lord Howard was not the sort of man who would respect such an arrangement if he could find a promising way to challenge it. During the summer of 1483 he finally obtained his share of the Mowbray inheritance by throwing his support to Richard of Gloucester, with whom he had occasionally cooperated since 1472, when they united to divide the estates of the dowager Countess of Oxford.[10]

Richard of Gloucester shared Lord Howard's dislike of the Woodvilles, despite his momentary support of them in 1477-1478 at the time of Clarence's downfall.[11] As is well known, Gloucester was a genuinely pious man who founded at least ten chantries during his lifetime. In addition he made frequent visits to important shrines and, according to one of his leading biographers, was in many regards a "rudimentary Puritan."[12] As a consequence he detested the worldliness and sexual escapades that were characteristic of most of the Woodville men. Indeed, the Marquess of Dorset's well-publicized affairs seem to have offended Richard even more than the Woodvilles' relentless quest for wealth. For that reason Richard appeared at court almost as rarely as the Duke of Buckingham. A humorless and taciturn man, Richard lived a solitary life in the north, where he bought more and more estates while disposing of most of his southern properties. He was in residence at his great stronghold in Yorkshire, Middleham Castle, when Edward IV fell seriously ill during the latter part of March 1483.

Only forty-one at the onset of his fatal illness, Edward had become extremely fat and weighed almost three hundred pounds. He seems to have suffered from heart and respiratory problems, although a French chronicler, Thomas Basin, believed his illness began shortly after he gorged himself on a Lenten meal of fruits and vegetables. However, an Italian cleric in England, Dominic Mancini, maintained in his valuable account of the year 1483 that Edward "allowed the damp cold to strike his vitals, when one day he was taken in a small boat with those whom he had bidden go fishing, and matched their sport too eagerly."[13] Whatever the cause of Edward's illness, it grew steadily worse and soon passed into influenza or pneumonia. He may have suffered a stroke as well, although his mind remained clear until the day he died.

During his final hours Edward considered the problems his older son, Prince Edward, would face. The Prince was only twelve and a half at the time, while his brother, Prince Richard, was less than ten. Thus the new King would need a Protector or regent for several years, until he was old enough to take the government into his own hands. Apparently the dying ruler understood this and added a codicil to the will he had drawn up in 1475, just before sailing to the continent to attack France. A copy of that codicil has never been found; but evidence that Edward amended his will in this way is available in the most valuable of all sources for those years, the account known as the Second Continuation of the Crowland Chronicle.[14]

Kept by the monks of a large abbey in central England, the Crowland Chronicle had lapsed several generations before, although it was later extended by two relatively brief "Continuations." The Second Continuation covers the years 1470-1486 and is especially valuable for our purposes. In the words of its modern editors, it was written by an anonymous individual, "a singularly well informed and involved contemporary, of considerable intellectual ability."[15] In recent years several men have been suggested as the probable author of the Second Continuation, including John Morton, Bishop of Ely from 1479 until 1486, when he became Archbishop of Canterbury. But Morton never resided in Lincoln diocese, in which Crowland Abbey was situated and whose internal affairs are often mentioned in the Second Continuation; so a much more likely candidate is John Russell, Bishop of Lincoln and Richard III's Lord Chancellor. Because Bishop Russell was in London during the critical period the Second Continuation describes in detail, there is good reason to consider him its author.[16]

Regardless of the authorship of the Second Continuation, that invaluable source maintains that Edward IV added two codicils to his will shortly before his death. Yet the Second Continuation does not actually say that either of those codicils appointed Richard of Gloucester to be his nephew's Protector or regent. Rather it stresses the friction that existed in 1483 between the Woodvilles on the one hand and William Lord Hastings on the other. Indeed, Lord Hastings is said to have been so suspicious of the Queen Mother's intentions that he threatened to sail across the Channel to Calais if a large Woodville force escorted Edward V from Ludlow to London, a force that would leave Hastings almost defenseless. When the Chamberlain took that stand, Elizabeth Woodville instructed her brother Anthony, the new King's governor since 1471, to limit his escort from Ludlow to 2,000 men,[17] which relieved Hastings' fears because he could usually mobilize 3,000 troops in a crisis.

Despite that victory Lord Hastings did not relax his guard altogether in April of 1483. While ostensibly cooperating with the Woodvilles during the first weeks of the new reign, he turned to the Dukes of Gloucester and Buckingham as a possible counterweight to them. One wishes the author of the Second Continuation had been more specific on this point because he observed only that Hastings "had the greatest trust" in the two Dukes and assumed that they would bring as many troops to the capital as Earl Rivers would have in his army.[18] Undoubtedly Hastings had far less faith in the impulsive and inexperienced Buckingham than in Gloucester, who was both steadfast and well versed in governmental matters. Despite the turmoil of his earliest years in the north, Richard had settled down since 1474 and become more responsible, although his rivalry with the Percies had flared up again in 1480, of which Hastings was probably unaware, however. Furthermore, Richard and Hastings had been comrades-in-arms during Edward IV's great campaign in the spring of 1471 and on several other occasions as well. A partnership between the two of them, especially if the Council recognized Richard as Lord Protector, would enable them to provide firm and stable government for several years and thereby limit the Woodvilles' intrigues and mischief making.

But while Hastings favored Richard's nomination to be Lord Protector, the Woodville faction strongly opposed it. Since 1478, when Richard cooperated with them in securing George of Clarence's destruction, the Woodvilles had seen their relationship with him deteriorate steadily. By 1483 Richard seems to have regretted his part in his brother's downfall and apparently blamed the Woodvilles for orchestrating the plot against him. Whether such a theory is true or not, Richard was openly critical of the Woodvilles' quest for material gain, which was actually no greater than most other magnates' of the era; and Richard also deplored the licentious behavior of the Marquess of Dorset, whose notorious love affairs offended Gloucester's stern and somewhat hypocritical moral precepts.[19]

Elizabeth Woodville and her kindred were well aware of Richard's attitude toward them; and they also suspected that if the Council recognized him as Lord Protector, he would form a partnership with Hastings, whom they had hated for many years. During the early 1460s Hastings had exacted a high price when he helped Elizabeth defend her dower rights from the machinations of greedy neighbors; and in more recent years he had encouraged Edward IV's liaison with Jane Shore, the leading courtesan of the age. In fact, the Queen held Hastings responsible for her husband's well-known affairs, which she considered an intentional slap at herself. As a consequence she loathed the prospect of Hastings remaining at the center of power during her son's minority, especially if she and her kindred were hustled through the back gate to a dreary exile in the countryside. Whatever the case, Elizabeth Woodville and her son Dorset, her chief confidant and adviser, were sorely troubled when they reflected on what lay in store for them. Now that Edward IV was dead and Edward V about to fall under the domination of the two men they disliked most, their season of wealth and power was about to end--unless they could find a way to keep the Council from recognizing Richard as Lord Protector.

It is generally believed that one of the two codicils Edward IV added to his will shortly before he died had nominated Richard for that position, for two reasons. First, Richard's appointment would have seemed perfectly logical to the dying King, who had always received loyal and, in the main, capable service from his youngest brother; and second, neither of those codicils was found after Edward's death, which suggests that they were destroyed almost as soon as they were found. And no one was better placed to dispose of them than the Queen Mother and her eldest son. Whether they actually committed that illegal act can never be anything more than a matter of conjecture, although it is clear that Elizabeth and Dorset realized they could keep anyone, even the Duke of Gloucester, from serving as Lord Protector by having the new ruler crowned quickly. For there was no precedent for such an important official after a new monarch's official coronation in the Abbey. The crowning and anointing with oil cloaked a new King, even if still a boy, with a sacrosanct aura and implied that he was capable of ruling by himself, even if that was manifestly impossible.[20] At any rate, it seems likely that the Woodvilles were responsible for the disappearance of the two codicils Edward IV is believed to have added to his will just before his death, although it is less certain what those codicils specified. However, there can be no doubt that the Woodvilles were responsible for the Council decision that Edward V should be crowned in the Abbey on Sunday morning, the 4th of May.

Because Lord Hastings had no political allies in London at the moment, he felt compelled to agree to Edward V's speedy coronation. But he or one of his trusted agents seems to have sent a messenger to Yorkshire entreating Richard to move south and postpone the coronation for an indefinite period. If the Duke failed to do so, Woodville domination of the new government would be assured; and in that event Richard, Buckingham, Hastings, and any other opponents of the Woodville faction would probably be banished from court for the remainder of their lives.

Once Richard learned of those developments in London, he took vigorous steps to prevent the coronation on 4 May. He first sent a messenger to solicit the cooperation of Buckingham, who was then in residence at Brecknock Castle, Wales. Buckingham had always hated his Woodville in-laws; and because he was known to covet a greater role in government, he was likely to be an enthusiastic participant in any anti-Woodville plot. Furthermore, Buckingham was both naive and inexperienced, so he would probably be putty in Richard's hands, at least in comparison to Hastings who, at fifty-three, was old enough to be Richard's father. Hastings had been at the center of power since 1461, and he would doubtless give Richard advice from time to time because of the latter's long residence in the north. Thus if Richard depended primarily on Hastings, theirs would be a partnership of equals. But if Richard depended chiefly on Buckingham, it would be a different sort of partnership, with Gloucester having the final say on all important policies and appointments.

At any rate an alliance between the two Dukes developed quickly; and in late April they met with their armed forces at Northampton, where they hoped to intercept the royal party as it travelled from Ludlow to the capital. As it happened the King and his guards had already passed through Northampton and reached Stony Stratford, fifteen miles closer to London. Thus Richard's plan to seize his nephew and block his coronation on 4 May seemed to have failed. But at Stony Stratford, Lord Rivers heard about Richard's arrival at Northampton and decided to ride back and confer with him as a way of promoting more harmonious relations in the future.[21] Leaving his nephew at the inn where he was already settled for the night, Rivers and several attendants returned to Northampton, where they received a warm welcome from the two Dukes. Eating and heavy drinking continued until midnight, when Rivers and his men withdrew to their rooms, assuming all was well. But the next morning they were arrested on vague charges. Dispatched under heavy guard to various castles in Yorkshire, they were illegally detained for almost two months before being tried and executed at Pontefract on 25 June.

Meanwhile, Richard and Buckingham had galloped from Northampton to Stony Stratford, where on 30 April they took control of Edward V. To the King's persistent questions about the whereabouts of his uncle and Sir Richard Grey, the new ruler's half-brother, the two Dukes gave evasive and unsatisfactory answers. But Edward's protests counted for nothing now because he was a prisoner in everything but name.

For several days the royal party waited at Northampton so the two Dukes could claim Edward had been unable to reach London in time for his coronation on 4 May. At Westminster Elizabeth Woodville and her faction realized at once that their attempted coup had failed and that Richard's contempt for them was probably even greater than before. They therefore took sanctuary in the Abbey, where Elizabeth was accompanied by her five daughters and two of her four sons, Dorset and Prince Richard. However, Elizabeth's brother Lionel, the Bishop of Salisbury, was apparently in his diocese, from which he later escaped to the continent; while another of the Queen's brothers, Sir Edward Woodville, took control of the royal navy and all the money stored in the Tower before leading the fleet out into the Channel. Thus, even though the Woodville faction suffered a major setback, it was still intact and might recover enough strength to play an important role in the future.

On the afternoon of 4 May the two Dukes finally escorted Edward V into the capital and lodged him in the royal apartments at the Tower. Several days later the Council met and recognized Richard as Lord Protector, although the Councillors insisted that Edward's coronation should occur on Tuesday the 24th of June. Within a week the Council met again and, at the urging of the two Archbishops and Bishop Morton of Ely, rescheduled the coronation for Sunday the 22nd of June.

Those decisions can only have annoyed Richard, who knew that his season of power would end in less than two months unless he secured the coronation's indefinite postponement. To that purpose he created a political machine by appointing trusted associates to key positions. Sir John Wood became Lord Treasurer; Bishop Russell was named to succeed Archbishop Rotherham as Lord Chancellor; Sir Richard Empson was appointed Chancellor of the Duchy of Lancaster; and William Catesby became one of the two tellers of the Exchequer. But the Council was still dominated by several experienced prelates, including Morton and the two Archbishops, who had been devoted servants of Edward IV. They were determined to protect the interests of the late monarch's sons, and Richard found it difficult if not impossible to control their actions during succeeding weeks.

Unfortunately for historians, the month between 10 May and 10 June 1483 is among the murkiest in English history. Despite the Second Continuation of the Crowland Chronicle and the equally valuable account left by Dominic Mancini, the surviving evidence is too patchy to permit definitive answers to the most important questions, namely when and why Richard of Gloucester decided to usurp the throne. Certainly he had reached that decision by 10 June, when he summoned military support from the north, although he may have made it several days before. But his motive for overthrowing Edward V is still hotly debated because neither of the two main theories, which stress Lord Hastings' pivotal role, is strongly supported by the surviving evidence.

The first theory holds that at some point before 10 June, Lord Hastings turned against Richard, with tragic results to himself. As already noted, Hastings feared the Woodvilles so much that he had been eager to cooperate with Richard against them, provided the latter consulted him on all important matters. But the Protector soon made it clear that he planned to rely on Buckingham, Catesby, Empson, and several other advisers and thus had no real use for Hastings, who should retire to his estates in Leicestershire and live out his days there. But Hastings was unwilling to be put out to pasture quite so soon, nor was he prepared to leave the sons of his old friend and benefactor, Edward IV, to their fate. So by the first week of June he had decided to salvage his career by changing sides and establishing an alliance with the Woodvilles. Should that alliance manage to force the Protector to hold Edward V's coronation on 22 June as the Council had recently decreed, Hastings would doubtless recover his influence at court, whereas Richard and Buckingham would again face the prospect of a bleak future, this time for good. Such a plan might have worked had it not been discovered by one of the Protector's closest associates, William Catesby, who coveted Hastings' wealth and position in the midlands for himself.

The second theory holds that Lord Hastings was not involved in a conspiracy to stop the Protector in his tracks; indeed, when Richard suddenly ordered Hastings' execution, the latter was as amazed and aghast as anyone. According to this theory, Richard's clerical opponents on the Council were proving difficult to manage because of their insistence that the rights of Edward IV's sons must be scrupulously honored. But if that were done and precedent followed, Edward V would be declared of age in less than three years, as Henry VI had been in 1436 on reaching his fifteenth birthday; and at that point Richard's power would come to an irreversible end. At that juncture the Woodvilles would reappear on the political stage, more furious at him than ever; and with a still malleable teenager on the throne, he would have little chance of surviving. Thus, Richard had to postpone the coronation and the declaration of Edward V's majority for at least a decade, which Morton and the two Archbishops would doubtless oppose. As a consequence Richard needed to break the clerical opposition on the Council, which would be no easy task. To a deeply religious man like Richard, the thought of beheading a Bishop or an Archbishop was almost unthinkable--but why not make an example of a fussy and somewhat officious layman like Lord Hastings? Hastings was strongly opposed to any violation of Edward V's rights, and his sudden elimination might unnerve his clerical allies and force them into reluctant compliance. Furthermore, Richard's most capable follower, Catesby, a lawyer and minor landowner, hoped to assume Hastings' commanding position in central England, and there can be little doubt that Catesby goaded Richard into taking swift action against the man he hoped to replace.

Perhaps there are elements of truth in both theories; but whatever the case, Richard seems to have made his decision to usurp the throne and destroy Hastings by 10 June. On that day he sent a trusted messenger, Sir Richard Ratcliffe, to York, where the Protector still enjoyed widespread support. Ratcliffe took a letter entreating the mayor and burgesses of York to send troops to London at once to assist the Protector "against the Queen, her bloody adherents and affinity, which ... intend to murder and utterly destroy us and our cousin the Duke of Buckingham and [all] the royal blood of the realm."[22] By couching his request in those terms, Richard was confident it would receive a positive response. Furthermore if one of Hastings' agents happened to intercept the letter, he would fail to comprehend the real meaning of those words.

Even before any northern troops reached London, Richard carried out his coup. On Friday the 13th of June, a sub-committee of the Council met at the Tower to discuss the preparations for Edward V's coronation, now only nine days off. After a brief opening session and a short recess, Richard reentered the Council chamber and hurled bitter accusations at Hastings. When Hastings sought to defend himself, the Protector cried out, "Treason! Treason!," a prearranged signal for his élite guards to enter the room and arrest Hastings. But as they did so, a violent struggle took place, during which Morton and Archbishop Rotherham were both wounded and taken into custody. As for Lord Hastings, he was escorted down to the Tower green and told to confess his sins to a waiting priest. Within minutes he was beheaded before a crowd of amazed onlookers.

The execution of Lord Hastings, Richard's first despotic act, seems to have had the desired effect on his opponents. That such a powerful man, one of England's leading figures for two decades, could be executed without a trial of any sort was frightening in the extreme, and the public was temporarily dissuaded from acts and even statements that might offend the Protector. As for Richard, he was heartened by the public reaction and saw no reason to halt his march toward the throne.

Knowing it would be dangerous to allow the younger Prince to remain at liberty, Richard sent a regiment to retrieve him from the Abbey on Monday, the 16th June. That regiment's spokesman was the elderly Archbishop of Canterbury, Thomas Bourchier, a saintly man who seems to have had little understanding of the political issues involved; but its actual leader was Lord Howard, who was determined to wrest the Mowbray lands in East Anglia from the Prince's grip. When the Archbishop appeared before Elizabeth Woodville, he maintained that her youngest son should be handed over because Edward V needed companionship at the Tower and it looked strange for one brother to remain in sanctuary, as if he feared mistreatment at the hands of the other. The Queen Mother was suspicious of such arguments and struggled to retain her youngest son, knowing great harm might befall him if she did as requested. But the Abbey was surrounded by Lord Howard's men, and they threatened to break down the door and take the boy by force if she insisted on shielding him. In the end the distraught woman entrusted him to the Archbishop's care after he swore no harm would come to him at the Tower.

Once Richard of Gloucester had both nephews in his power, he was in a position to claim the throne for himself, although he needed a theoretical justification for doing so. Unless the English people believed him to be their rightful King, Richard would always be considered a usurper and his grip on the throne would be weak. This was evident to the most cynical and ambitious prelate of the age, Bishop Stillington of Bath and Wells, who had briefly served as Lord Chancellor during the late 1460s and hoped to hold that office again. Stillington sensed how the political winds were blowing; and in an effort to ingratiate himself with the Protector, he suggested that his two nephews were illegitimate and thus without any right to the throne. Stillington based his argument on the unprovable claim, advanced some years before by George of Clarence,[23] that shortly before marrying Elizabeth Woodville, Edward IV had been precontracted to Lady Eleanor Butler. If Edward IV had in fact been precontracted to a woman other than his eventual wife and all the formalities short of marriage had been observed, as Bishop Stillington insisted they had been, then Edward's union with Elizabeth Woodville should be considered bigamous and all their offspring illegitimate, according to contemporary practice. But there were two serious problems connected with the Bishop's theory. First, it was unprovable because there was no trace of such a precontract and neither of the principals, who were both dead by that juncture, had ever alluded to it, either verbally or in writing. And second, even if the theory had been provable, Richard of Gloucester would not have been the next claimant to the throne because there was another male who came ahead of him in the royal succession. This was George of Clarence's only surviving son, Edward Earl of Warwick, whom Richard had sent off to Middleham Castle under heavy guard in late April.[24] Thus Stillington's theory had to be rejected on purely practical grounds.

Because of the great problem posed by the young Earl of Warwick's existence, Richard decided to dispute the legitimacy of his own two brothers, Edward IV and George of Clarence. Because they had both been fair-haired and extremely tall, almost 6' 4" in their stocking feet, Richard could easily maintain that they had borne no physical resemblance at all to himself or their alleged father, Richard of York (d. 1460). Like Richard of York, Richard of Gloucester was dark and swarthy and of roughly average height (i.e., 5' 9") for a nobleman of that era.* By implication, therefore, Richard of Gloucester should be considered a true son of Richard of York whereas Edward IV and George of Clarence should not be. But that theory implied that the mother of all three brothers, Lady Cecily Neville, had slept with an unnamed lover, whose identity has never been discovered or even suggested by a writer of that or a later time. However, if that unnamed lover had been the actual father of Edward IV and George of Clarence, their children had no claim whatsoever to the throne, which meant of course that Richard of Gloucester was the legal ruler by indefeasible hereditary right. Still alive in 1483, Lady Cecily was infuriated by her youngest son's slanderous charge and never forgave him for making it.

Despite the obvious weakness of his argument, Richard had nothing better to offer and directed a popular preacher, Ralph Shaa, to publicize it in whatever ways he could. On Sunday the 22nd of June, the day Edward V should have been crowned, Father Shaa preached an open-air sermon to a large crowd at Paul's Cross near the northeastern corner of St. Paul's Cathedral, the most important pulpit in the entire kingdom. As his text Father Shaa chose the biblical verse, "Bastard slips shall never take deep root," and he also resorted to several other arguments to prove that Edward IV's offspring "were not the rightful inheritors unto the Crown, and that King Edward was not the legitimate son of the Duke of York as the Lord Protector was."[25] That sermon provoked angry boos and catcalls, however, and Faher Shaa never recovered his reputation for honesty and integrity. According to the Great Chronicle

---

* Other than this, almost nothing is known about Richard's physical appearance. Thus there is no evidence for Shakespeare's portrayal of him as a hunchback, which was a form of dramatic license intended to help audiences recognize a thoroughly corrupt and depraved man immediately.

of London, he soon became so remorseful for his sermon that he entered a period of decline and died within several months.[26]

Three days later a carefully chosen group of Richard's followers met at the Guildhall and declared themselves a true Parliament. Buckingham dominated the proceedings and urged the members to recognize Richard as the country's rightful monarch. After a brief discussion they unanimously agreed and drew up a petition entreating Richard to take the throne at once. It was presented to him at Baynard's Castle later that day by a large delegation headed by Buckingham and the Lord Mayor, Sir Edward Shaa, the unfortunate friar's brother. After initially declaring himself unworthy of such an exalted position, Richard acceded to the request, and then, in Mancini's memorable words, "the whole business was transacted, the oaths of allegiance given, and other indispensable acts duly performed."[27] The next day Richard rode to Westminster Hall and occupied the monarch's seat in the Court of King's Bench, which made it clear to the general public that a new reign had begun.

During the next week Richard III dispensed generous rewards to those who had helped him usurp the throne. Buckingham was appointed Lord Constable and Great Chamberlain of England, and he was also promised the lands of his ancestor, Humphrey de Bohun, Earl of Hereford and Northampton, which were worth almost £700 a year. Francis Lord Lovell was appointed Chamberlain of the King's household, while William Catesby, who had spied on Lord Hastings, obtained several of his most important offices, including Chancellor and Chamberlain of the Exchequer. But the most valuable rewards of all went to Lord Howard, who had dislodged the younger Prince from the Abbey on 16 June. Twelve days later Lord Howard was appointed Lord Admiral and created Duke of Norfolk, the most important title the Prince had received in 1478. In addition Lord Howard was granted all the Mowbray estates in East Anglia.

Recently a distinguished scholar, C. F. Richmond, has suggested that Prince Richard and Edward V were both dead by the time Lord Howard was created Duke of Norfolk on 28 June. In fact, Mr. Richmond maintains that both boys were probably killed on Sunday the 22nd of June, the day Edward V's coronation should have occurred and Father Shaa delivered his sermon denying their legitimacy and right to the throne.[28]

At first glance Mr. Richmond's theory seems convincing because Richard III and his followers realized it was in their self-interest to eliminate Edward IV's sons quickly in order to forestall future plots to free and elevate one of them to the throne. But if the boys were murdered on 22 June, it was a deed carried out in such secrecy that reports of their demise did not begin to circulate until two months later. Indeed, after Richard III's coronation on 6 July and his departure two weeks later on a long progress to the West Country and Yorkshire, there was an attempt by Edward IV's former household servants to free his sons from the Tower. Obviously those men believed the boys were still alive at the end of July; otherwise they would not have risked their lives on their behalf. And it is difficult to believe that able and experienced servants of the late King were so ignorant of events in London, still a city of fewer than 50,000 people, that they were completely unaware of the boys' elimination more than a month earlier, if such was actually the case.

The traditional view, first expressed in Sir Thomas More's unfinished account of Richard III's reign, holds that the Princes were killed in mid August of 1483. According to More's book, which dates from 1513, Richard III and his attendants had reached Warwick by the middle of August; and for some reason (doubtless the attempt by Edward IV's household servants to free the boys), Richard sent verbal directions for the constable of the Tower, Sir Robert Brackenbury, to have them killed at once. But the upright Brackenbury refused to comply; so Richard summoned a loyal follower, James Tyrell, a Suffolk gentleman who had just received a sinecure at the Exchequer, and directed him to see to the deed. Thereupon Tyrell galloped down to London, where he gained entrance to the Tower and enlisted the services of Miles Forest, one of the Princes' jailers, who was aided by Tyrell's own horse keeper, John Dighton, "a big strong knave." About midnight one evening, when everyone else in the Tower was asleep, Forest and Dighton entered the Princes' bedchamber and

> ... suddenly lapped them among the bedclothes--so bewrapped and entangled them, that within a while ... they gave up to God their innocent souls into the joys of heaven.*

---

* In 1674, during a renovation of the White Tower, two skeletons were unearthed at the foot of the staircase where More said the Princes' bodies had been buried. Those skeletons were interred in a burial urn in Westminster Abbey, where they remained undisturbed until the 1930s, when they were taken out and examined by a noted pediatrician and a dentist who specialized in the care of children's teeth. After a careful examination those two scientists concluded that the skeletons were those of boys about the ages of twelve and nine-and-a-half, which corresponds to the Princes' ages when they were probably killed in August 1483. The scientists also observed that

Once the Princes were murdered in that way, their bodies were buried at the foot of the staircase in the White Tower and Tyrell galloped back to Warwick, where Richard "gave him great thanks and, as some say, there made him a knight."[29]

The detailed nature of More's account, which gives the names of several individuals involved, conveys the ring of truth.[30] Moreover, More's book does not conflict or disagree with the account of those weeks written by Dominic Mancini, who left London shortly after Richard III's coronation.[31] Once he returned to the continent, Mancini committed his recollections to paper at the suggestion of his patron, Archbishop Cato of Vienne, the current Chancellor of France. In January of 1484 Archbishop Cato accused Richard of arranging the murder of his nephews in a speech before the Estates-General at Tours.

Thus well-informed men in France as well as in England itself held Richard responsible for the deed; and there was also a general belief that Edward IV's sons did not live out the summer of 1483.[32] Had that belief been wrong, it seems certain that Richard would have produced them on his return to London in October. By parading them through the streets of the capital he could have silenced ugly rumors that undercut his own reputation and power. But he made no effort to do so, and there are indications that he actually encouraged the belief his nephews were dead, hoping his subjects would conclude there was no practical alternative to him as their rightful ruler. Certainly he never launched an investigation into the Princes' fate in order to clear himself of all responsibility for their disappearance. As a consequence, it is difficult to avoid the conclusion that he bears much of the blame for what happened, even if More's account of the reign is flawed in some respects, particularly the windy speeches he put into the mouths of his main characters.[33]

Regardless of the precise date of the Princes' death and the extent of Richard III's responsibility for that cruel deed, reports of their demise began to spread in late August of 1483. One of Edward IV's former officials probably visited their cell at the Tower and found it empty, causing him to become suspicious. Whatever the case, London was seething with angry rumors by mid September. Even in that brutal age the murder of two young boys, sons of a monarch who had been deeply esteemed if not revered, could not be condoned. Medieval monarchs were expected to obey the law and dispense justice to all their subjects

---

the larger skull showed signs of a cranial fracture, which suggests that the older and stronger boy put up a struggle before being struck on the head with a blunt object, while the smaller skull showed no such fracture.

in accordance with Christian precepts. If Richard III was guilty as assumed, he was a villainous ruler who had forfeited the loyalty and allegiance of his people by his own crimes and misdeeds.

Thus a new mood fraught with possibilities emerged in London that autumn. One of the first persons to sense the possibilities was Lady Margaret Beaufort, the chief heiress of the House of Lancaster. Arguably the most important woman of the age, Lady Margaret had played a minor part in the coronation on 6 July, carrying Queen Anne's train down the main aisle of Westminster Abbey. Thereafter she remained in the capital while her fourth husband, Thomas Lord Stanley, with whom she had only a platonic relationship, returned to his estates in Lancashire.

A clever person with sharp political instincts, Lady Margaret understood that Richard III was now so unpopular he might be overthrown. At first she had no intention of seeking the throne for her son Henry Tudor, Earl of Richmond, who had lived in exile in Brittany since 1471. Rather her principal objective was to negotiate her son's return to England so he could hold high political office, provided a man other than Richard III was on the throne. For Richard would never allow an important Lancastrian like Henry Tudor to return from abroad and remain at liberty, let alone hold a powerful position. But if Richard could be replaced with a man of friendlier outlook, someone who felt gratitude to Lady Margaret and her son for their support at a critical moment, then her goal might be realized in short order. To that end Lady Margaret decided to promote the cause of Henry Stafford, Duke of Buckingham.

Buckingham was known to be dissatisfied because he had not received the great Bohun inheritance Richard III had promised him in late June. In fact, shortly after the coronation Richard had made it clear that Buckingham would never receive those estates until Parliament approved the transaction, which left the issue in considerable doubt. Moreover, the King was no longer swayed by the Duke's opinions, to the latter's great annoyance. Because Richard often conferred with sharper and more capable men such as Catesby, Empson, and Ratcliffe, Buckingham sensed that he would wield no more influence during Richard's reign than he had under Edward IV. Indeed, he had been shunted to the sidelines just as Lord Hastings had been, and he made no effort to cloak his dissatisfaction.

Of course, Lady Margaret had close ties with Buckingham's family, the great House of Stafford. Her third husband had been Sir Henry Stafford, Buckingham's uncle, to whom she had been married from

1459 until his death in 1471. Although Lady Margaret married Lord Stanley the next year, she remained in close touch with the Staffords and eventually became the guardian of Buckingham's only son, who lived in her household for more than a decade.

Lady Margaret was doubtless aware of Buckingham's ambitious nature and great pride as a direct descendant of Edward III. Although the Duke is said to have been a well educated person and "of nature marvelously well-spoken," he lacked sound political instincts and might be putty in the hands of others who hoped to use him for their own ends. Of course Lady Margaret was not completely sure he would turn against Richard, whom he had actively supported at first. She therefore decided to approach him through a trusted intermediary, John Morton, Bishop of Ely since 1479 but a zealous Lancastrian before he entered Edward IV's service in 1471 as Master of the Rolls.

As already noted, Morton was wounded during the Council meeting on 13 June 1483, when Richard hurled bitter accusations against Lord Hastings before having him summarily executed on the Tower green. Arrested at the same time, Morton was held in the Tower until being assigned to Buckingham's custody at Brecknock Castle, Wales. Sometime in early or mid September 1483, Lady Margaret sent her chaplain, Dr. Christopher Urswick, to Brecknock Castle to talk with Morton, who could probably be persuaded to hold confidential talks with the Duke. In that way Buckingham could be informed of the new mood in the capital and the possibility of overthrowing Richard III and placing a more law-abiding man on the throne.[34]

It is generally assumed that Buckingham agreed in late September of 1483 to back Henry Tudor's claim to the throne with armed force. That assumption rests mainly on the fact that Richard III's only Parliament was told in January of 1484 that the Duke had sent a confidential letter to Henry Tudor in Brittany several months before. In that letter of 24 September, Buckingham supposedly recognized Henry Tudor's superior claim to the throne and urged him to assert it with military force in the near future. But a copy of that letter has never been found, and the later assertion to Parliament appears to have been political propaganda designed to achieve two goals simultaneously: (1) the posthumous attainder of Buckingham, who, after being captured by the sheriff of Shropshire, was taken in chains to Salisbury and executed on 2 November; and (2) the outright condemnation of Henry Tudor as a confirmed traitor.

In any event, Buckingham seems to have felt he was striking a blow for his own cause when he raised the standard of revolt on 18 October; and it is noteworthy that no decree asserting Henry Tudor's claim to the throne was published until shortly after Buckingham's execution. Furthermore, once Buckingham's death became widely known, support for his uprising vanished like fog on a warm spring morning, which would not have happened had the rebels thought their main goal was to elevate Henry Tudor to the throne. At the very moment a decree asserting Henry Tudor's claim to the throne was published, he was ready to go ashore in western England, although the rebellion's speedy collapse caused his ships to double back to Brittany.

Although the Buckingham rebellion seemed to have been a complete failure owing to a great storm that swept over Wales and southern England, causing rivers to burst their banks and halt the Duke's advance at a critical moment, it actually had several significant results. First, it demonstrated the deep hatred most southerners felt for Richard; and in that way it gave strong encouragement to those who might plot against him in the future. Second, during the aftermath of the uprising, several hundred men who had taken up arms against Richard fled across the Channel to Brittany for safety's sake. Many of those men had been important members of their communities in the vicinity of London or the West Country and, in a number of cases, the holders of important positions under Edward IV. To fill the vacancies that suddenly existed, Richard had little option but to appoint men he already knew and trusted--his northern followers, who were inevitably assailed as greedy carpetbaggers when they arrived to take up their new positions in the south. By the autumn of 1484 at least two-thirds of the sheriffs in southern England were northerners; and in the central administration a critical position like King's Solicitor was held by Thomas Lynom, an aggressive and hated Yorkshireman.[35] Thus, dissatisfaction with Richard's rule increased all the more during the wake of the uprising, and the King found it impossible to claim that his chief goal was to continue his late brother's policies.

Third and last, most of the men who fled to the continent after the collapse of the Buckingham rebellion offered their services to Henry Tudor in Brittany. Consequently, the Pretender emerged during the following weeks as a viable alternative to Richard III. By early December Henry had acquired a force of 400-500 enthusiastic followers who were eager to return to England under his banner. Furthermore, Buckingham's execution had removed an ambitious man with a claim to the throne at least as strong as Henry Tudor's; and to make matters even worse for Richard III, the new spokesman of the forces ranged against him was a more capable and intelligent man than Buckingham had been.

Although not well educated in a formal sense, Henry Tudor was a person of sound judgment and common sense. After twelve years in exile he was aware of the need to be wary of overtures and offers of future help made by men he barely knew; and with but one exception he never gave his trust to an individual who later proved disloyal.[36] Clever, confident, and courageous, he was not a skillful military commander, although his uncle Jasper could provide the military experience he himself lacked. Furthermore, Henry was soon joined by a general of even greater ability than Jasper Tudor--John de Vere, thirteenth Earl of Oxford. During the 1460s and early 1470s Oxford had been an important Lancastrian commander, until his capture by Edward IV's agents on the Cornish coast in 1474. After a brief period of captivity in England, he was sent across the Channel and imprisoned in Hammes Castle, one of the main fortresses in Calais' elaborate defensive system. In December of 1483 Oxford escaped from Hammes Castle and rode to Henry's camp in Brittany, where he put his vast military experience at the the Pretender's disposal.

As Henry's forces grew in strength, making a successful attack on Richard III more likely, a nagging question arose in his followers' minds. If Henry and his troops managed to overthrow the Yorkist monarch, what was to prevent their triumph from being just another episode in the long rivalry between Lancaster and York? For a time Henry might lead a successful Lancastrian government; but then, under the cover of darkness, the Yorkists could be expected to rebuild their strength, hoping to topple Henry and recover the throne for themselves within several years. Thus unless additional steps were taken, the long struggle within the royal family might continue indefinitely, which was hardly a comforting thought to anyone.

To resolve that fear Henry made a well-publicized declaration on Christmas Day 1483. After attending mass at Rennes Cathedral, he addressed his followers and a large group of curious Frenchmen at the western door of the great church. In a ringing voice he promised that, once he captured the throne that was rightfully his, he would marry Elizabeth of York, the oldest of Edward IV's daughters by Elizabeth Woodville. Because Elizabeth's brothers were widely believed to be dead, she was now a leading candidate for the English throne. But if she and Henry, the Lancastrian Pretender to the same throne, became man and wife, the blood of both Lancaster and York would flow in the veins of their children; and in that way the two warring factions would be permanently reconciled. In effect England would gain a reunited royal family, greatly strengthening the chances of a lasting peace.

Within months Henry's promise to marry Elizabeth of York became widely known throughout England and Wales and had the desired effect. Public opinion shifted decisively in his direction because of his obvious wish to halt the violence of recent years.[37]

Of course, Richard III was alarmed by Henry's promise to marry Elizabeth of York, which undercut his own position. Shortly after his wife Anne Neville died on 16 March 1485, the King announced that he himself would marry Elizabeth as a way of forestalling Henry's plan. But because Elizabeth was his own niece, Richard's union with her was strictly forbidden by canon law. In addition Richard himself had cast doubts on her legitimacy by maintaining that her parents had never been married in the eyes of the Church. Thus, a union between the two of them would probably be interpreted as a frantic ploy by a deeply frightened man.

Furthermore, if Richard actually married his own niece, the rehabilitation of the Woodville faction would probably follow within a few years, which meant that Richard's northern supporters would lose most their lands and offices in the south, a bitter pill for them to swallow. Consequently, several of the King's leading advisers, including Catesby and Ratcliffe, begged him to reconsider. Indeed, they predicted that if he married his niece, even his most devoted northern followers would accuse him of arranging his wife's death "in order to enter an incestuous relationship, and ... he must deny any such scheme."[38]

Because of the strong opposition of his own followers and a prediction by twelve eminent theologians that the Pope would never recognize such a marriage, Richard declared that he had no intention of marrying Elizabeth. He issued that unique disclaimer during a speech in the Great Hall of the Knights of St. John of Jerusalem on 30 March 1485. On that occasion he swore he had never had an interest in his niece and bore no responsibility at all for his wife's death. Eight days later he sent letters to York and several other towns in which he again denied any wrongdoing in regard to Queen Anne's death. That he felt compelled to make such embarrassing disclaimers is ample proof of his subjects' deep reservations about his character and integrity by that juncture.[39]

During the spring of 1485, while Richard was making frantic efforts to salvage his crumbling position, Henry Tudor was in a stronger position than ever owing to another miscalculation on Richard's part. Less than a year before Richard had hoped to secure the Pretender's extradition to England, where he could be executed for high treason. But as long as Henry's protector, Francis II of Brittany, retained control of his own government, there was little likelihood that Richard would achieve his goal. However, during the summer of 1484, Francis II fell ill and the Breton Council came under the domination of its greedy Treasurer, Pierre Landois. Landois was soon contacted by English agents; and in return for a substantial bribe, he agreed to assist in the apprehension of Henry, who would be returned to London forthwith. But in the nick of time, only an hour before Landois' troops set out to arrest him, the Pretender was informed of the plot. He and several personal attendants put on disguises and rode across the border into France, where they quickly gained asylum from Charles VIII (1483-1498) and his older sister and official regent, Anne of Beaujeu. Ultimately the other English exiles followed Henry across the border to Paris and obtained promises of support from the French crown, which was deeply worried about Richard III's foreign-policy intentions.

For more than a decade Richard had been known to be bitterly anti-French. During the mid 1470s he had been a strong supporter of Edward IV's plan to attack France; but when Edward came to terms with Louis XI at Picquigny in 1475, Richard had denounced that peace settlement and urged his brother to keep on fighting until he won a victory comparable to Agincourt. Nine years later Richard still dreamed of reopening the Hundred Years War and winning military glory for himself as Henry V had done; and if he ever felt secure in his own realm, he was likely to make such an attempt.[40] As a consequence, the French hoped to find a way to neutralize the serious threat posed by his rule. To that end Charles VIII and his sister Anne decided to assist Henry Tudor, who had lived in Brittany for thirteen years and was known to have a clear preference for French manners and fashions. Should Henry manage to overthrow Richard with French assistance, the new monarch would doubtless be grateful to the French crown, causing the danger of an English attack to recede. Accordingly in November of 1484 the French Council of State voted to provide Henry with 3,000 *livres tournois* to help him equip a large invasion force. Six months later the French crown granted him an additional 40,000 *livres* and sent a regiment of 1,500 infantrymen to bolster his ranks.

Even with those French troops Henry's army of approximately 2,000 men had little chance of defeating Richard III. Fortunately for the Lancastrian cause, Henry was able to secure help from two other quarters. First, he appealed to James III of Scotland, who was still smarting from the loss of Berwick Castle in 1482 after a long siege directed by Richard of Gloucester himself. Whoever controlled Berwick dominated the eastern sector of the Anglo-Scottish border, and the castle's loss was a serious blow to James III's prestige. (Ultimately it led to his death during the battle of Sauchieburn in 1488.) Because of his magnates' growing dissatisfaction, James III desperately wanted to recover Berwick Castle, which seemed a slight possibility at best while Richard III remained on the English throne. James therefore concluded that his best hope lay in assisting the Pretender, who might be so grateful for Scottish help that he would voluntarily return the castle at some future point. Although that hope proved illusory, James responded to Henry's appeal for help; and while the Pretender was still in France, a regiment of 1,000 Scottish archers arrived at his camp under the command of the experienced Bernard Stewart, Seigneur d'Aubigny.

While still in France Henry also secured pledges of support from the leading Welsh chieftains of the period, including John Morgan, Walter Herbert, Richard Griffiths, and especially Rhys ap Thomas. Indeed, the powerful Rhys promised that he and his fellow chieftains would provide at least 4,000 soldiers if Henry launched his attack on Richard III from Wales.

The Welsh were willing to risk their lives in Henry's cause because they had long hoped to secure the repeal of several oppressive measures passed against them during Henry IV's time. By those laws of 1401 and 1403, the Welsh were forbidden to intermarry with the English or to acquire, either through gift, purchase, or inheritance, estates anywhere in England. In addition they were excluded from all political and administrative offices in England and from the most important positions in their own country. Although those statutes were enforced sporadically if at all, they were deeply resented by the Welsh people and would remain a serious irritant until Parliament and the English crown repealed them. Owing to the Welsh hatred of those laws, a prophecy had arisen that a great Welshman would appear one day and conquer England, after which he would end the oppression of the past. Because the Tudors were a prominent Welsh family that had supported the Glendower Rebellion against Henry IV, the Pretender seemed to be the deliverer the Welsh had expected for years. Indeed, he fit their prophecy to a "T" and offered them a chance to strike a blow for political and social equality with the English.

By the last days of July 1485 Henry and his multinational army of slightly over 3,000 men was ready to set sail from Harfleur at the mouth of the Seine. They embarked on 1 August and, propelled by a "soft south wind," their ships reached Milford Haven six days later. After establishing a beachhead on the coast of St. Anne's Head, they moved inland and took control of Dale Castle, which offered little if any resistance. The following day they proceeded to Haverfordwest, where they waited for Welsh reinforcements to appear. To Henry's dismay, the expected help was slow to materialize. In fact, the Welsh chieftains insisted on receiving definite assurances for the future before bolstering his ranks. Rhys ap Thomas, for example, had been Richard III's chief lieutenant in Wales since Buckingham's execution in 1483, and he was determined to hold the same position under Henry. As a consequence, the Pretender felt compelled to announce that Rhys would retain viceregal authority in the principality after his cause triumphed; and several days later the Welshman arrived at Henry's camp with more than a thousand followers. During the next two days most of the other Welsh chieftains followed suit, and as a consequence the Pretender's army increased to 7,000 men by the time it crossed the English border and advanced toward Shrewsbury on 15 August.

Meanwhile Richard III had taken steps to beat back the invasion. As early as December 1484 he had directed his followers to be ready for military action at a moment's notice. For the next six months he assumed that his enemies would land at one of the ports on the southern coast, which led him to instruct Lord Lovell to keep a strong fleet in readiness at Southampton. Yet he did not ignore the possibility of a landing in Wales and had a system of signalling lamps set up in the hills of Pembrokeshire. In mid June Richard himself took up residence at Nottingham Castle, the most centrally-located fortress in the country, from which he could strike in any direction against an invading force. He was still at Nottingham on 9 August, when he received word that the long-dreaded campaign was finally underway.

Because the Pretender had landed in Wales with only 3,000 men, Richard considered the invasion a minor threat at first. In fact, Richard seems to have felt that Henry and his troops would be bottled up in South Wales by Rhys ap Thomas or in North Wales by the Stanleys. Consequently he took no steps to mobilize an army of his own until 11 August, when he sent out letters directing his principal followers to assemble their forces and meet him at Leicester within a week. But he soon learned that Rhys ap Thomas and the other Welsh chieftains had joined Henry with 4,000 men; and by the time the rebel army crossed the border into western England on the 15th, he was seriously alarmed, knowing there was no way to avoid a pitched battle somewhere between Shrewsbury and London. On 19 August Richard finally set out from Nottingham with his army. Within two days he passed through Leicester and reached the summit of Ambien Hill, a short distance from the village of Market Bosworth.

Richard's army consisted of approximately 11,000 men that day. Many of his troops had been supplied by the Duke of Norfolk and his capable son, the Earl of Surrey. Also among Richard's backers were Francis Lord Lovell, Sir Richard Ratcliffe, Sir William Catesby, Sir Robert Brackenbury, and Sir James Tyrell. In addition, John de la Pole, the young and inexperienced Earl of Lincoln, was a lesser commander in the King's army. Lincoln was Richard's favorite nephew and intended heir should the monarch die on the field.[41]

A less dependable backer of the King was Henry Percy, Earl of Northumberland. Between 1471 and 1474, as noted earlier, the two men had quarrelled over lands and political power in northern England. Although their rivalry had died down between 1474 and 1479, owing to Edward IV's timely intervention, it flared up again during the early 1480s, when Richard retained men who were known to belong to the Earl's affinity. In 1482 Northumberland rendered no support to Richard's invasion of southern Scotland and siege of Berwick Castle. However, he seems to have presided over the trial and execution of Lord Rivers and Sir Richard Grey at Pontefract on 25 June 1483; and he was the acknowledged leader of 3,000 troops who mustered at Pontefract in mid August of 1485 before joining Richard on the summit of Ambien Hill a week later. Still, Richard was so suspicious of the Earl's loyalty that he stationed his men safely at the rear, making it almost impossible for them to defect to Henry's side once fighting began. Unfortunately for Richard's cause, that gave Northumberland and his followers a good pretext to remain inactive and withhold much-needed support.

Even more doubtful was the loyalty of Thomas Lord Stanley and his brother Sir William. Because Lord Stanley's second wife, Lady Margaret Beaufort, was the Pretender's mother, the Stanleys had no reason to fear a Lancastrian restoration, especially if they assisted Henry at a critical moment. But because of the Stanleys' refusal to support the Buckingham rebellion of 1483 out of deep hatred of the Duke, Richard III had assumed he could win their whole-hearted support in time. As a consequence he heaped lands and offices on them after 1483, hoping to make them a pillar of his rule. For example, Lord Stanley received estates confiscated from Buckingham's heir with a clear annual value of £700, and he also succeeded Buckingham as Constable of England and one of the thirteen Knights of the Garter. Shortly afterward Lord Stanley recovered his old office of Lord Steward of the royal household, worth £100 a year, which he had held during Edward IV's last years. Finally Stanley and his eldest son, George Lord Strange, were appointed to serve on Richard III's Council. As for Lord Stanley's brother Sir William, he was appointed constable of Caernarvon Castle as well as Chief Justice of North Wales; and he additionally received lands worth approximately £600 a year.[42]

Despite the many rewards they received from Richard, the Stanleys were not altogether satisfied with his rule. In particular Lord Stanley seems to have coveted the stewardship of all Duchy of Lancaster estates north of the Trent, which Henry VII granted him shortly after Bosworth.[43] The relationship between Richard and the Stanleys was also strained by some dubious arrangements that the King made in regard to Lady Margaret Beaufort's chattels and estates. After learning of Lady Margaret's role in fomenting the Buckingham rebellion of 1483, Richard allowed Sir Robert Brackenbury to seize most of her movable goods.[44] Yet when Richard's only Parliament met in January of 1484, the King sought to appease Lord Stanley by exempting his wife from the attainder bill that confiscated the estates of 131 conspirators. In fact, Richard allowed Lord Stanley to receive the rents of approximately £1,000 a year from his wife's dower lands for the remainder of her days. But whenever she died all her estates were to revert to the crown, which meant that Lord Stanley's enhanced prosperity might last only a decade or two longer.

By the summer of 1485 Richard III knew that the Stanleys might rally to the Pretender's cause, and for that reason he repeatedly directed his slippery Steward to return to court from Lancashire. But Lord Stanley always found a pretext to remain in the countryside. Ultimately Richard grew tired of his excuses, and in early August he arrested his son, Lord Strange, and threatened to have him executed if his father took a single suspicious step. That the Stanleys' relationship with Richard had declined to such a low ebb caused them to look hopefully in Henry's direction. For if Richard prevailed and remained on the throne without their support, they were unlikely to enjoy royal favor again in the foreseeable future. Indeed, Richard would probably find reasons to strip them of all their offices and banish them from his court forever. Even if they aided Richard against Henry Tudor at the last minute and helped him win a narrow victory, the King would probably remain wary of them for years to come.

However, the Stanleys realized the danger of committing themselves to Henry's cause too soon. If they did so, Richard would probably have Lord Strange executed at once. Thus, when Henry met with Sir William Stanley at Stafford on 17 August, the Pretender failed to secure a firm promise of support from him. At Atherstone the next day, Henry met with both Stanleys, who remained as noncommittal as ever. When Henry pressed them to merge their 3,000 retainers with his own army, they refused, which must have caused nagging doubts in his mind, given their reputation for opportunism and the distinct possibility they might cast their lot with Richard at the last minute. However, that same day Henry's prospects improved markedly when Sir John Savage rode into his camp with "a choice band" of 400 men. Thus if the Stanleys came over to him on the day of the battle, the Pretender would have almost as many men as Richard. Of course, if the Stanleys lined up with the the King as fighting began, he would have a numerical advantage of 14,000 men against approximately 7,500.

The only encounter between Richard's army and the Pretender's troops occurred on 22 August 1485. Known as the battle of Bosworth Field, it seems to have lasted about two hours, and most of the surviving sources hold that it took place in the mid morning. However, an Italian scholar, Polydore Vergil of Urbino, who arrived in England in 1501 as a papal tax collector, maintained in his famous history of England that the rebels attacked from a southwesterly direction during the early afternoon, which seems unlikely. Regardless of when the battle began, it was probably preceded by a rebel bombardment of the King's position on the slopes of Ambien Hill. Henry's troops seems to have sequestered several large guns from Tamworth Castle and other decaying fortresses within thirty miles of Bosworth. Whether Richard's supporters possessed artillery has never been determined, although they probably did. However, it seems unlikely that they had 300 serpentines and heavy bombards, as a recent account of the period alleges.[45] Even if a heavy bombardment preceded the first infantry charge, the outcome of the battle was determined by hand-to-hand combat with the main weapons used by English soldiers for centuries--swords and lances, bows and arrows, poleaxes and similar weapons of war.

During the greater part of the battle only the opposing vanguards took an active part. Richard's vanguard was led by the Duke of Norfolk, who was vigorously challenged by the rebel vanguard during a bold charge led by the Earl of Oxford. Both sides suffered heavy casualties that morning. The royalists lost more of their leaders than the rebels, who seem to have fought with greater determination owing to a deeper commitment to their cause. Among Richard III's commanders, Norfolk, Catesby, Ratcliffe, and Brackenbury were all killed during the first hour, while the Earl of Surrey was wounded so badly he begged to be put out of his misery. Yet the Yorkist faction was not completely shattered because the Earl of Lincoln escaped to safety as did Francis Lord Lovell. On the other side, neither of Henry's principal commanders, Jasper Tudor and the Earl of Oxford, died or even suffered serious wounds, although several of Henry's élite guards were killed by

Richard III himself as he was trying to reach and kill the Pretender.

By the day before the battle Richard had concluded that he needed to capture or kill the Pretender in order to end his threat to the throne. In a rousing speech to his troops, Richard branded Henry a "Welsh milksop" before announcing, "as for me, I assure you ... I will triumph by victory or suffer death for immortal fame."[46] Because of Richard's grim view, he fought furiously once his vanguard failed to smash the opposing line and put an end to Henry's life. With a small band of followers, the King rode down one side of the hill, thereby avoiding the violent combat in the centre, and approached the spot where Henry was sitting on his horse in the midst of his élite guards, some twenty or thirty men in all. Capitalizing on the element of surprise, Richard and his troops closed in, and Richard himself unhorsed Sir John Cheyney, "a man of great force and strength," and ended the days of Sir William Brandon, Henry's standard bearer. Henry was less than twenty yards from the spot where Brandon fell, and Richard probably assumed that victory was at hand. But to his great misfortune, the Stanleys were watching the action from the sidelines, waiting for a good moment to intervene, preferably on Henry's side; and once Richard became separated from the body of his army, they realized they could destroy him without serious risk to themselves. They hurled themselves into the fray, and within minutes the King was brought down fighting manfully to the end. In the famous words of the Crowland Chronicler, "King Richard received many mortal wounds and, like a spirited and most courageous Prince, fell in battle on the field and not in flight."[47]

Once they realized their leader was dead, most of the Yorkists threw down their arms and surrendered, while others fled the field on foot or grabbed a horse and galloped away to safety. The golden circlet Richard had attached to his helmet that morning was soon found, possibly in a thornbush as legend has always held, and its finder took it at once to Lord Stanley, who carried it to the place where Henry was still sitting on his horse. Lord Stanley urged his stepson to dismount and kneel, and thereupon Henry was crowned King of England and Wales, to the cheers of his exuberant troops. Although Henry's official coronation in the Abbey did not take place until 30 October, a new reign began on the field that day. A Lancastrian restoration against long odds had occurred, although Yorkist diehards who survived the battle sought to rebuild their strength in the hope of achieving a completely different outcome within several years.

Henry had no doubts about what his most zealous enemies had in mind for him, and as a consequence he was unusually conciliatory toward moderate and cooperative Yorkists. After hundreds of them rode in and voluntarily swore allegiance to him, he granted them a general pardon in mid September and named them to important positions in his government. Indeed, within six months of Bosworth he appointed scores of Edward IV's former servants to major offices, knowing it would be risky to hold them at arm's length, which would probably alienate them and strengthen the conspiratorial element.[48]

Finally, on 18 January 1486, Henry honored his promise of Christmas Day 1483 to marry Elizabeth of York. Fortunately, Elizabeth soon became pregnant and was delivered of a healthy son the following September. Other children followed in quick succession, and in that way the blood of Lancaster and York mingled in the veins of their children. That fact, along with Henry's obvious desire to provide fair and stable government for all his subjects regardless of past allegiances, caused the great majority of the English people to rally around his throne. Even the aristocracy was pleased with its new ruler, his keen intelligence and sound judgment as well as his occasional deviousness; and in short order most men of wealth and power ceased to plot as they had done so heedlessly since 1450. The greater stability and respect for law that Edward IV had sought to promote finally blanketed the countryside, despite the attempt to murder Henry at York in 1486 and the minor plot to assassinate him at Worcester several months later.[49] But because Henry never relaxed his guard, those and other plots had little chance of success; and although his later enemies gained a measure of support from European rulers who deplored his refusal take their side in expensive conflicts, they were completely ignored by the English people. Thus the battle of Bosworth Field marked the true end of the Wars of the Roses, the longest series of interlocking crises in English history. It is true that Henry had to defend his throne during a battle at Stoke, in the northern midlands, in June of 1487. But that encounter against a poorly armed force only half the size of his own was a pale imitation of the decisive encounter that occurred near Market Bosworth less than two years before. On that day the long conflict between Lancaster and York came to an end in the same sort of setting it had begun a generation earlier.

For Further Reading

Charles B. Ross, *Edward IV*. Berkeley and Los Angeles, 1974. See especially "Part III: The Second Reign, 1471-1483," chapters 8-12.

Charles B. Ross, *Richard III.* Berkeley and Los Angeles, 1981. The best life of Richard III yet to appear. Scholarly and analytical although a bit too sympathetic to its subject.

Paul Murray Kendall, *Richard the Third.* New York, 1956. A work of great literary merit that reads more like a novel than history, which was the author's intention. Sees events too much from Richard's perspective, however.

Sir Clements Markham, *Richard III: His Life & Character.* London, 1906. A whitewash from start to finish.

James Gairdner, *The History of the Life and Reign of Richard the Third.* Cambridge, 1898. The first critical study of Richard, by a distinguished Victorian scholar. Too hostile but still worth reading.

Desmond Seward, *Richard III: England's Black Legend.* London, 1983. In the tradition of Gairdner. Eminently readable.

Rosemary Horrox, *Richard III: A Study of Service.* New York, 1989. Shows how Richard gained power before losing it.

Rosemary Horrox, ed., *Richard III and the North.* Hull, 1986. Five important essays by Horrox and other leading scholars.

M. A. Hicks, "Richard III as Duke of Gloucester: A Study in Character." York, Borthwick Paper No. 70, 1986. An important reexamination of Richard's career between 1471 and 1483. Casts Richard in an unsympathetic light.

M. A. Hicks, "The Last Days of Elizabeth, Countess of Oxford." *English Historical Review,* vol. 103 (1988). Shows Richard's treacherous dealings with a rich but helpless widow in the early 1470s.

A. R. Myers, "The Character of Richard III." *History Today*, vol. 4 (1954). An excellent brief study by a master historian. Especially suitable for students and general readers.

A. R. Myers, "Richard III and Historical Tradition." *History,* vol. 53 (1968). An extremely useful short study.

Mortimer Levine. "Richard III--Usurper or Lawful King?" *Speculum,* vol. 34 (1959). A usurper.

Alison Hanham, *Richard III and His Early Historians*. Oxford, 1975. Analyses the writings about Richard between 1485 and 1535.

Taylor Littleton and Robert R. Rea, eds., *To Prove A Villain: The Case of King Richard III*. New York, 1964. Excerpts from the works of men who have written about Richard III, including the Crowland Chronicler, Polydore Vergil, and Sir Thomas More.

P. W. Hammond, *Richard III: Loyalty, Lordship and Law*. London, 1986. Eight important essays by eight different scholars.

A. J. Pollard, *Richard III and the Princes in the Tower*. Stroud, Gloucestershire, 1991. An important study that assesses the known evidence about Richard's life and reign and contends that we may never know what caused him to usurp the throne.

Dominic Mancini, *The Usurpation of Richard the Third*, trans. by C. A. J. Armstrong, 2nd ed. Oxford, 1969. An unusually valuable eyewitness account of the events of 1483.

Nicholas Pronay, and John Cox, eds. *The Crowland Chronicle Continuations, 1459-1486*. London, 1986. Another extremely important eyewitness account of Richard's usurpation and subsequent reign, probably written in the spring of 1486 by John Russell, Bishop of Lincoln and Richard III's Lord Chancellor.

Sir Thomas More, *The History of King Richard III*, ed. Paul Murray Kendall. New York, 1965. Flawed but still an important source.

Sir Henry Ellis, ed. *Three Books of Polydore Vergil's English History, comprising the Reigns of Henry VI, Edward IV, and Richard III*. Camden Society, 1st series, vol. 29 (1844).

Denys Hay, ed. *The Anglica Historia of Polydore Vergil*. Camden Society, new series, vol. 74 (1950).

James Gairdner, ed. *Letters and Papers Illustrative of the Reigns of Richard III and Henry VII*, 2 vols. Rolls Series, 1861-1863.

Alison Hanham, ed. *The Cely Letters, 1472-1488*. Early English Text

Society, No. 173 (1975).

H. E. Malden, ed. *The Cely Papers*. Camden Society, 3rd series, vol. 1 (1900).

A. J. Pollard, "The Tyranny of Richard III." *Journal of Medieval History*, vol. 3 (1977). A valuable article that shows how Richard's dependence on northerners after Buckingham's rebellion alienated the people of the south.

J. S. Roskell, "William Catesby, Councillor to Richard III." *Bulletin of the John Rylands Library* (1959-1960). An important article about a key figure during the murky events leading up to Lord Hastings' execution and Richard III's usurpation of the throne.

Alison Hanham, "Richard III, Lord Hastings and the Historians." *English Historical Review,* vol. 87 (1972). Argues that Lord Hastings was executed not on 13 June 1483, as long believed, but a week later, thereby sparking a bitter scholarly debate.

B. P. Wolffe, "When and Why did Hastings lose his Head?" *English Historical Review*, vol. 89 (1974). A rejoinder to Hanham.

J. A. F. Thomson, "Richard III and Lord Hastings--a Problematical Case Reviewed." *Bulletin of the Institute of Historical Research*, vol. 48 (1975). Another rejoinder to Hanham.

Alison Hanham, "Hastings Redivius." *English Historical Review*, vol. 90 (1975). Hanham's defense of her original argument.

Charles T. Wood, "The Deposition of Edward V." *Traditio,* vol. 31 (1975). Argues that while Richard III was crowned on 6 July 1483, he did not truly become King until recognized as such by Parliament in January of 1484.

J. W. McKenna, "The Myth of Parliamentary Sovereignty in Late-Medieval England." *English Historical Review,* vol. 94 (1979). A vigorous refutation of the argument in the previous article.

C. F. Richmond, "The Death of Edward V." *Northern History,* vol. 25 (1989). A brief article that argues that Edward V and his brother were probably murdered on 22 June 1483 and certainly by 28 June, when

Lord Howard was created Duke of Norfolk. An intriguing but unconvincing argument because of the later plot by Edward IV's household officials to free the two Princes.

L. E. Tanner and W. Wright, "Recent Investigations regarding the Fate of the Princes in the Tower." *Archaeologia* (1935). Reports the findings of the two scientists who examined the skeletons discovered in the White Tower in 1674 at the very spot where Sir Thomas More said the Princes' bodies had been buried.

D. E. Rhodes, "The Princes in the Tower and Their Doctor." *English Historical Review*, vol. 77 (1962).

J. A. F. Thomson, "Bishop Lionel Woodville and Richard III." *Bulletin of the Institute of Historical Research*, vol. 69 (1986). A short article that casts new light on Bishop Woodville's actions.

E. W. Ives, "Andrew Dymmock and the Papers of Antony, Earl Rivers, 1482-3." *Bulletin of the Institute of the Institute of Historical Research*, vol. 41 (1968).

Elizabeth Jenkins, *The Princes in the Tower*. New York, 1978. A general study of the period 1461-1485 by a popular historian. Marred by excessive hostility toward the Woodvilles, whose acquisitiveness was only marginally greater than that of most families of the period.

Ralph A. Griffiths and R. S. Thomas, *The Making of the Tudor Dynasty*. Gloucester, 1985. A careful study focusing on the Tudors' rise to power by two gifted scholars. Well illustrated, with many insights.

Linda Simon, *Of Virtue Rare: Margaret Beaufort, Matriarch of the House of Tudor*. Boston, 1982. A brief study intended for students and general readers.

Michael K. Jones and Malcolm G. Underwood. *The King's Mother: Lady Margaret Beaufort, Countess of Richmond and Derby*. Cambridge, 1992. A detailed work based on extensive research. Intended for other scholars.

I. Arthurson and N. Kingwell, "The Proclamation of Henry Tudor as King of England, 3 November 1483." *Bulletin of the Institute of Historical Research*, vol. 63 (1990).

Albert Makinson, "The Road to Bosworth Field, August 1485." *History Today*, vol. 13 (1963). A good brief study.

Peter J. Foss, "The Battle of Bosworth: Towards A Reassessment." *Midland History*, vol. 13 (1988). A reexamination of all the known sources relating to the battle in light of a detailed topographical knowledge of the site. Intended primarily for specialists.

C. R. Richmond, "The Battle of Bosworth." *History Today*, vol. 35 (1985). A brief but useful study.

Alfred H. Burne, "The Battle of Bosworth," in *The Battlefields of England*, 2nd ed. London, 1951. Dated but still useful.

Michael Bennett, *The Battle of Bosworth.* Gloucester, 1985. A much broader work than the title suggests.

S. B. Chrimes, *Henry VII.* Berkeley and Los Angeles, 1972. A scholarly study of the life and reign of the first Tudor monarch. Stresses government and administration and makes little effort to probe Henry's personality. Useful nonetheless for Henry's early life and the campaign of 1485.

Eric N. Simons, *Henry VII: The First Tudor King.* London, 1968. A popular study.

Michael V. C. Alexander, *The First of the Tudors: A Study of Henry VII and His Reign.* Totowa, N. J., 1980. Stresses the earlier years of the reign and argues that until 1500, Henry should not be pictured as the miserly ruler he became during his final years.

Gladys Temperley, *Henry VII.* London, 1917. Old but still useful.

R. L. Storey, *The Reign of Henry VII.* London, 1968. Sound but rather dull.

For other works on the Wars of the Roses, see the suggested readings between the text and the notes of each of the three previous chapters.

Notes for *The Wars of the Roses, IV*

[1] Edward is known to have accompanied the judges on their circuits in 1462, 1464, 1467, 1469, 1473, 1475, and 1476. He may have accompanied them in other years as well.

[2] Quoted in Seward, *The Wars of the Roses,* pp. 226-227.

[3] In 1472 Richard married Anne Neville, the younger daughter of Warwick the Kingmaker and the younger sister of George of Clarence's wife Isabel. Duke George tried to block that marriage because he wanted the enormous Warwick inheritance entirely for himself, which enraged his younger brother, who never forgave the slight. As for his elderly mother-in-law, Richard kept her in custody because he was determined to enjoy the revenues of her dower lands. For Richard's mistreatment of her and the dowager Countess of Oxford, see M.A. Hicks, "The Last Days of Elizabeth, Countess of Oxford," *English Historical Review*, vol. 103 (1988).

[4] As a way of helping his younger brother save face, Edward IV convinced Northumberland to become one of Richard's indentured retainers. But that provision of the 1474 agreement was symbolic in nature only.

[5] Perhaps it should be noted that in 1474, Edward granted Anthony Woodville the reversion to nine manors confiscated from John Lord Roos in 1461. Anthony was to receive those estates as soon as Lord Roos' widow, Margery, died; but because she was still alive in 1482 and Anthony himself was executed on 25 June of the following year, he enjoyed little if any benefit from that grant.

[6] According to Clarence, Edward IV had been contracted to another woman, Lady Eleanor Butler, before he married Elizabeth Woodville in 1464. Although baseless, that charge would be revived in 1483, ten weeks after Edward IV's death, when his two sons were smeared by it. That matter will be discussed at greater length later in this chapter.

[7] M. A. Hicks, "The Changing Nature of the Wydevilles in Yorkist Politics to 1483," in Charles Ross, ed., *Patronage: Pedigree and Power in Later Medieval England* (Gloucester, 1979), p. 80.

[8] See for example the comments of M. A. Hicks in *False, Fleeting, Perjur'd Clarence* (Gloucester, 1980), pp. 200-204, and of Charles Ross in *Richard III* (Berkeley and Los Angeles, 1981), pp. 32, 34.

[9] Dorset paid £2,000 for that wardship, however.

[10] Because the dowager Countess of Oxford had been born a Howard, she was

Lord Howard's paternal aunt. Lord Howard coveted a portion of his aunt's many lands and worked closely with Richard of Gloucester in the early 1470s, thereby establishing a political alliance that would be strengthened during their joint campaign against Scotland in 1482. Ultimately it would bear evil fruit during the troubled years 1483-1485.

[11] During the late 1470s Richard sought to curry favor with Elizabeth Woodville by granting financial support to Queens' College, Cambridge, of which Elizabeth became the patron in 1475. But that brief period of cooperation failed to produce a lasting friendship between Gloucester and the Woodvilles.

[12] Paul Murray Kendall, *Richard the Third* (New York, 1956), p. 353.

[13] Dominic Mancini, *The Usurpation of Richard III,* trans. by C. A. J. Armstrong, 2nd ed. (Oxford, 1969), p. 59.

[14] Nicholas Pronay and John Cox, eds., *The Crowland Chronicle Continuations: 1459-1486* (London, 1986), pp. 153, 155.

[15] *Ibid,* p. 34.

[16] Because it was situated in Lincoln diocese, Crowland Abbey was subject to Bishop Russell's triennial visitation. If in fact Russell was the Second Continuation's author, it is entirely understandable why his account of the year 1470-1486 was eventually deposited in the muniments room of a monastery within his diocese that had long prided itself on its chronicle.

[17] Pronay and Cox, eds., *The Crowland Chronicle Continuations,* p. 155.

[18] *Ibid.*

[19] Richard had several mistresses in the north and fathered a number of illegitimate children by them.

[20] Richard II had been crowned in 1477 at the age of ten, while Henry VI was crowned in 1429 at the age of eight. A Lord Protector was never appointed for either of those monarchs.

[21] Rivers is unlikely to have known about the codicils that Edward IV had added to his will. Thus he probably thought Richard had travelled south simply to do homage to the new King. As a consequence, he should not be criticized unduly for riding back to Northampton, which caused the Queen Mother's power-play to fail and soon cost Rivers and many other men their lives.

[22] James O. Halliwell-Phillips, ed., *Letters of the Kings of England* (London, 1848), I: 250-1.

[23] See above, footnote 6.

[24] After Clarence's execution in February 1478, his sole surviving son, Edward Earl of Warwick, became a ward of the Marquess of Dorset, who took sanctuary in the Abbey at the end of April 1483. About that time Richard of Gloucester's agents escorted Warwick to Middleham Castle, where he remained a prisoner until September of 1485, when Richard's supplanter, Henry VII, had him transferred to the Tower of London.

[25] Sir Thomas More, *The History of Richard III,* ed. Paul Murray Kendall (New York, 1965), p. 86.

[26] A. H. Thomas and I. D. Thornley, eds., *The Great Chronicle of London* (London, 1938), pp. 231-232.

[27] Mancini, *The Usurpation of Richard III,* p. 97.

[28] C. F. Richmond, "The Death of Edward V," *Northern History,* vol. 25 (1989), pp. 278-280.

[29] More, *The History of Richard III*, pp. 103-106. The only major problem with More's theory is that Brackenbury remained loyal to Richard and died while fighting in his army at Bosworth Field in 1485. It seems unlikely that Brackenbury would have remained loyal to Richard if given such an unsavory order by the King, or would have retained his post at the Tower had he disobeyed such an important command. However, it is possible that Brackenbury abased himself later, claiming he had not known the King's messenger and was hesitant to hesitate to carry out such an important verbal command when it might not be valid.

[30] Of course More, who lived from 1478 until 1535, could have been influenced by Tyrell's execution for treason in 1502 at the hands of Henry VII. Shortly before his death Tyrell signed a confession that he had directed the murder of Edward IV's two sons, a confession he might have signed under duress because of his close association with William de la Pole, Earl of Suffolk, a Yorkist claimant to the throne and a serious problem to Henry VII for many years. However, this point cannot be proved, and it is generally assumed that More based his account of Richard III's reign on the oral tradition that developed soon after Richard's death in 1485.

[31] Mancini left England for the continent about the end of July. On his de-

parture he believed the Princes were already dead or would be so soon.

[32] In his *Kalendar* for the year 1483, the recorder of Bristol, Robert Ricart, wrote: "In this year the two sons of King Edward were put to silence in the Tower of London." See *The Maire of Bristowe Is Kalendar*, ed. L. Toulmin Smith (Camden Society, new series, V, 1872), p. 46. Dominic Mancini, as already noted, held the same view, and so too did a Spanish observer, Mosen Diego de Valera, who was unusually well informed about English affairs. See Goodman and MacKay, "A Castilian Report on English Affairs, 1486," *English Historical Review*, vol. 88 (1973), pp. 91-99.

[33] As is well known, More modelled his writings on ancient Roman models, as most other Renaissance writers did. More was especially influenced by the Roman historian Tacitus, who had composed long speeches for his main characters. Of course it might be argued that Richard was not directly involved in his nephews' murder, which was carried out by a zealous follower on his own initiative without the King's knowledge or approval. But in that event, Richard would probably have launched an inquiry into what happened, knowing its results would not have implicated him in any way. Furthermore, if Richard had wanted to keep a zealous follower from murdering his nephews during his absence in the north, he should have tripled or quadrupled the jailers around their cell at the Tower, which he did not do. Indeed, he allowed them to be guarded by only four men, who seem to have stood individual watches of six hours each, which made it an easy matter for an assassin to bribe one of those men. For good comments about the accuracy of More's account of what happened, see A. F. Pollard, "The Making of More's *Richard III*, " in *Historical Essays in Honour of James Tait*, J. G. Edwards (Manchester, 1933). See also the comments of R. S. Sylvester in *The Complete Works of St. Thomas More* (New Haven, 1976), II, lxv.

[34] Lady Margaret used another agent, her Welsh physician Dr. Lewis Caerleon, to inform the dowager Queen in sanctuary at the Abbey of the developing conspiracy and to obtain a pledge of Woodville support. Some historians maintain that the two women agreed to promote a future marriage between Henry Tudor and Elizabeth of York, but there is little evidence to support that contention.

[35] For the names of northerners who were now given important local offices in the south, see A. J. Pollard, "The Tyranny of Richard III," *Journal of Medieval History*, vol. 3 (1977), pp. 159-190. See also Keith Dockray in P. W. Hammond, ed., *Richard III: Loyalty, Lordship and Law* (London, 1986), pp. 47-49.

[36] The one exception was Sir William Stanley, whom Henry VII executed in

1495 for hedging his bets once again by maintaining close ties with a Yorkist imposter, Perkin Warbeck.

[37] As already noted, Elizabeth of York (1466-1503), had taken sanctuary in the Abbey with her mother, four sisters, and brother Prince Richard during the spring of 1483. She and the other female members of her family remained there until 1 March 1484, when the King enticed them out of sanctuary, which was a major embarrassment to him, by guaranteeing their personal safety and promising them sufficient financial support. Thereafter he paraded them around his court as if to say he could not have been responsible for the elimination of his two nephews.

[38] J. S. Roskell, "William Catesby, Councillor to Richard III," *Bulletin of the John Rylands Library*, XLI (1959-1960), p. 169. See also A. J. Pollard, *Richard III and the Princes in the Tower* (Stroud, Gloucestershire, 1991), p. 167, and Rosemary Horrox, ed., *Richard III and the North* (Hull, 1986), pp. 5-6.

[39] Apparently Richard's efforts to convince his subjects that he had not been responsible for his wife's death failed. On 24 June 1485 he appeared at the London Guildhall and repeated the declaration he had made at Clerkenwell eleven weeks earlier.

[40] Perhaps it should be noted that on 23 December 1482, Louis XI had signed the Treaty of Arras with the Archduke Maximilian, by which France received the counties of Burgundy and Artois in full sovereignty while Maximilian's daughter Mary was betrothed to the Dauphin. Shortly after that Louis renounced the Treaty of Picquigny and cancelled his yearly pension of £5,000 to England, which gave Richard III a convenient pretext for war whenever he felt secure enough on the throne to leave England.

[41] Richard's only legitimate son, Edward of Middleham, had died on 9 April 1484, and his many illegitimate children, including his favorite son, John of Pontefract, had no right to the throne. Thus Richard had to designate someone else as his intended heir. His choice fell on his favorite nephew John Earl of Lincoln, the oldest son of his sister Elizabeth, who was the Duke of Suffolk's wife.

[42] Horrox, *Richard III: A Study in Service* (New York, 1989), p. 321. According to Michael Jones, Sir William Stanley received Buckingham's valuable manor of Thornbury, in Gloucestershire, in November of 1483. On 10 December 1484, however, he returned that manor to the crown and received in return the lordships of Bromfield and Yale in North Wales, which were worth over £700 a year. See Michael K. Jones, "Sir William Stanley of Holt: politics and family allegiance in the late fifteenth century." *Welsh*

History Review, vol. 14 (1988), p. 10.

[43] Horrox, *Richard III: A Study in Service,* p. 322.

[44] Malcolm G. Underwood, "Politics and Piety in the Household of Lady Margaret Beaufort." *Journal of Ecclesiastical History,* vol. 38 (1987) p. 43.

[45] Seward, *The Wars of the Roses,* p. 306.

[46] Halliwell-Phillipps, ed., *Letters of the Kings of England,* I: 163-164.

[47] *Ibid,* p. 183. Much the same view was held by Polydore Vergil, who wrote a famous history of England at the suggestion of and with some assistance from Henry Tudor. See Denys Hay, ed., *The Anglica Historia of Polydore Vergil* (Camden Society, new series, vol. 74, 1950), p. 89.

[48] Shortly after Bosworth Henry reappointed all twelve judges of the common law courts. As his first Lord Treasurer, he appointed Archbishop Rotherham of York and as his first Lord Chancellor Bishop Alcock of Worcester. As his initial Chamberlain he named his stepfather Thomas Lord Stanley, whom he also created Earl of Derby; and as his clerk of the navy he made good use of Thomas Roger, who had served both Yorkist Kings diligently and effectively. Because of these and numerous other examples that could be cited, it is fair to say that Henry VII created, in modern American terminology, a "bipartisan administration" during his first six months on the throne as a way of healing the bitter feud between Lancaster and York.

[49] For the continuation of Yorkist plotting in 1486 and 1487, see Michael Bennett, *Lambert Simnel and the Battle of Stoke* (New York, 1987). See also C. H. Williams, "The Rebellion of Humphrey Stafford in 1486." *English Historical Review,* vol. 33 (1918). Those matters are also treated in my book, *The First of the Tudors: A Study of Henry VII and his Reign* (Totowa, N.J., 1980), pp. 49-58.

Index